Research Reports ESPRIT

T0250859

Project 688 / 5288 · AMICE · Vol. 1

Edited in cooperation with
the Commission of the European Communities

ESPRIT Consortium AMICE (Eds.)

CIMOSA:
Open System Architecture for CIM

2nd, revised and extended edition

 Springer-Verlag

Berlin Heidelberg New York
London Paris Tokyo
Hong Kong Barcelona
Budapest

Editors

ESPRIT Consortium AMICE
2 Bd. de la Woluwe
B-1150 Brussels, Belgium

ESPRIT Project 5288 (AMICE II / M) builds on the results from ESPRIT Projects 688 (AMICE) and 2422 (AMICE II / P) within the domain 5, Computer Integrated Manufacturing and Engineering (CIME), of ESPRIT, the European Specific Programme for Research and Development in Information Technology supported by the European Communities.

The aim of these projects is to design, develop and validate an Open System Architecture for CIM (CIMOSA) and to define a set of concepts and rules to facilitate building and operating future CIM systems. Migration paths are provided for the evolution of already installed CIM subsystems.

Important aspects of project work have been the contribution to European and international standardisation activities and the liaisons with other ESPRIT projects or other related development efforts on manufacturing enterprise architectures and their validation.

Dissemination of results and public demonstration of CIMOSA capabilities are major objectives of the ESPRIT Consortium AMICE. These objectives will continue to be realised in the ESPRIT Project 7110 (AMICE III / P) which will apply CIMOSA in manufacturing industry oriented enterprise modelling as well as model based enterprise operation control and monitoring.

The 21 members of the ESPRIT Consortium AMICE consist of CIM users, CIM vendors, software houses and research organisations from 9 European countries.

CR Subject Classification (1991): J.6, K.6

ISBN 3-540-56256-7 Springer-Verlag Berlin Heidelberg New York
ISBN 0-387-56256-7 Springer-Verlag New York Berlin Heidelberg

ISBN 3-540-52058-9 1 Auflage Springer-Verlag Berlin Heidelberg New York
ISBN 0-387-52058-9 1st edition Springer-Verlag New York Berlin Heidelberg

Publication No EUR 15044 EN of the
Commission of the European Communities,
Scientific and Technical Communication Unit,
Directorate-General Telecommunications, Information Industries and Innovation,
Luxembourg

Typesetting Camera ready by authors
45/3140 – 543210 – Printed on acid-free paper

Preface

Enterprise operation efficiency is seriously constrained by the inability to provide the right information, in the right place, at the right time. In spite of significant advances in technology it is still difficult to access information used or produced by different applications due to the hardware and software incompatibilities of manufacturing and information processing equipment. But it is this information and operational knowledge which makes up most of the business value of the enterprise and which enables it to compete in the marketplace. Therefore, sufficient and timely information access is a prerequisite for its efficient use in the operation of enterprises.

It is the aim of the ESPRIT project AMICE to make this knowledge base available enterprise-wide. During several ESPRIT contracts the project has developed and validated CIMOSA: Open System Architecture for CIM. The CIMOSA concepts provide operation structuring based on cooperating processes. Enterprise operations are represented in terms of functionality and dynamic behaviour (control flow). Information needed and produced, as well as resources and organisational aspects relevant in the course of the operation are modelled in the process model. However, the different aspects may be viewed separately for additional structuring and detailing during the enterprise engineering process.

CIMOSA supports the complete life cycle of the operational system from capturing of requirements to operation and model maintenance. An Integrating Infrastructure aimed at model execution copes with the heterogeneities of manufacturing and information technology. It provides a set of generic services to be made available system-wide connecting the model with the real-world system components.

This book significantly extends the specification on CIMOSA in several ways. In Part 2 of the book constructs for modelling of resources and organisational aspects are presented as well as an extended Integrating Infrastructure Framework. The latter takes into account latest developments in OSI, ODP and other relevant standards. Application of CIMOSA is represented by a User Guide for requirements modelling. Using examples from project-internal case studies, the use of the templates developed for the CIMOSA modelling constructs is demonstrated (Part 3). Specific subjects, such as enterprise integration of heritage and legacy systems, and formal representation of constructs, are addressed in several technical reports of the AMICE project in Part 4 of the book.

The editors

ESPRIT Consortium AMICE
2 Bld la Woluwe,
B - 1150 Brussels, Belgium

Phone: +32 2 770 09 43
Fax: +32 2 772 45 17

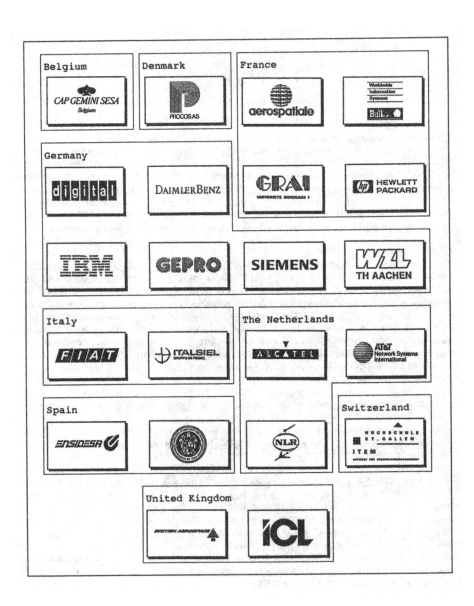

Table of Contents

Introduction

On Enterprise Integration

Enterprises more than ever are facing severe competition in the global marketplace. Efficient operation and innovative management of change are essential for future survival. Heterogeneous manufacturing and information systems are of serious concern in improving the current enterprise operation. In addition, trying to meet competition and to exploit new opportunities enterprise operations have to continuously evolve, thereby creating new heterogeneities and adding to the problems of the past. To manage efficiently the evolution in enterprise operation is the major challenge for the manufacturing industry.

Manufacturing enterprises today try to cope with these challenges by introducing new concepts like 'Just in Time', 'Lean Production', etc. But knowledge about and access to information is the prerequisite for both management of change and improving enterprise operation. CIM (Computer Integrated Manufacturing) does not provide magic solutions for improving the business operation. In spite of its significant advancements over the past, Information Technology is still hampered by hardware and software incompatibilities. The many software packages which run on the IT systems - MRP, CAD, CAP, CAQ - are usually implemented piecemeal rather than in an integrated fashion. The rise of the PC means that many departments have installed software to meet only their local needs. On the shop floor advancements in manufacturing technology has compounded the complexity with the introduction of machine controllers , AGV's, NC machines, automatic warehouses, often from different vendors and mostly not compatible for information interchange. Day-to-day operation of the enterprise encompasses many different organisational units and many systems are all contributing to achieving the business goals and objectives. It is necessary to understand the complexity of the enterprise, or part of it, before one can safely improve its operation.

The information held in all these isolated systems is a substantial capital investment in enterprise knowledge and a significant asset as well. Enterprises who exploit this knowledge fully for decision support, operation control and monitoring can gain serious advantages over their competitors. However, to take benefit of this knowledge requires the user to understand which information is available to him and how it is related to the business as a whole. The business relations have to be provided in terms of functions which require and create information, resources needed to carry out the function and organisational units which own and are responsible for the different parts of the operation. The relations between all relevant organisations and assets involved in the business have to be known and understood. Organisations involved in product development, manufacturing and distribution as well as those concerned with finance, marketing, personnel and purchasing. Organisations which employ resources as different as people, machines on the manufacturing floor and computers hosting the enterprise information.

To obtain this overview on information needed and provided explicit models of the enterprise operation are required. Such models will provide not only the information about the enterprise information itself, but about its usefulness as well. Only if information user, provider and owner are identified can meaningful management of change and enterprise wide use of the operational knowledge be achieved. If such models can be provided with a sufficient level of detail and can be kept up-to-date as well model based operation control and monitoring will be the ultimate use of enterprise models. It is the aim of CIMOSA to enable enterprise modelling for efficient exploitation of the enterprise knowledge.

On CIMOSA (Open System Architecture for CIM)

An architecture structures and helps in understanding the operation. In today's environments it would be very helpful if models of different enterprise were consistent to also support business processes involving several enterprises of vendors and customers.

We define an architecture as a means to structure and design enterprise operations or parts thereof. The architecture has to be generic enough to enable intra and inter enterprise operation as well but which recognises the particular enterprise solutions providing its competitive edge over competitors. The architecture has to provide common elements which enable operation engineering and design through modelling and simulation. Model simulation which will be used for validation and verification of the model itself as well as its use in enterprise management.

CIMOSA provides an architecture enabling descriptive rather than prescriptive modelling of enterprise operation. Modelling which allows to capture the operation needs for information as well as the information produced during the operation itself. Support for system design and implementation derived from business requirements is provided as well. CIMOSA generic building blocks and modelling macros support model engineering by the business user rather than the IT professional. In addition, different views on the model (function, information, resource, organisation) enable the user to structure and detail specific enterprise aspects without being confused by the complexity of the model as a whole.

CIMOSA provides a consistent enterprise modelling methodology and an integrating infrastructure for model engineering and execution support. CIMOSA is based on a process oriented modelling approach describing all enterprise activities in a common way. Such activities include manufacturing processes on the shop floor, as well as management and administrative processes.

CIMOSA modelling covers the life cycle phases of the operational system from business requirements definition to system implementation description, operation and model maintenance even enabling model based operation control and monitoring. For model engineering and operation support the AMICE project has developed an Integrating Infrastructure. This infrastructure provides a set of generic services aimed at CIMOSA model execution but coping with the heterogeneity of manufacturing and information technology.

On the AMICE Project

The ESPRIT Consortium AMICE has carried out several ESPRIT contracts since 1986. The partner in the Consortium (see below) represent major manufacturing companies, leading IT vendors and key establishments across Europe. On CEC request, the Consortium was widly based to grant the project results industrial awareness and acceptance and gain the support of European and international standardisation.

The AMICE project has developed the CIMOSA concepts and provided a basic set of generic building blocks aimed at enterprise modelling and model based operation control and monitoring. This includes the CIMOSA Integrating Infrastructure as well as work on requirements for CIMOSA modelling tools. CIMOSA has been validated in various case studies in consortium member companies in the Aerospace, Automotive and IT industry. In addition, other ESPRIT projects (CIMPRES, CODE, VOICE) have validated CIMOSA as part of their own workplans.

The project work has lead to inputs into standardisation on modelling and integrating infrastructure. The latter takes into account current work on standards like OSI (Open System Interconnection), ODP (Open Distributed Processing), etc. Preliminary European standardisation has been achieved for the Modelling Framework (ENV 40003) which has become the base for the international standardisation in ISO TC 184/TC5/WG1. Recent efforts in EC/US cooperation on Enterprise Integration have recognised CIMOSA as a major contribution to EI.

CIMOSA is a pre-normative development effort aimed at guiding and supporting users and vendors in enterprise integration as well as in the development of compliant products which will ease enterprise integration. It will be usable in an evolutionary mode starting with enterprise model engineering and decision support and moving gradually into new modes of enterprise operation and management. To further verify CIMOSA goals and objectives the project concentrates on feasibility implementations of CIMOSA models and the Integrating Infrastructure which prepare the project for a future implementation of an industrial pilot.

More detailed descriptions and specifications on modelling and the Integrating Infrastructure are provided in part 2 of the book itself with a further level of detail given in the Formal Reference Base of the AMICE project which is referenced in the book and which can be obtained directly from the ESPRIT Consortium AMICE.

Participating Organisations

As partners in the ESPRIT Consortium AMICE 28 organisations from nine European countries contributed to the results presented in this revised version of CIMOSA. Under the current contract the following 22 companies are co-operating in the AMICE project EP 5288.

Aerospatiale (F), Alcatel (NL), AT&T-NSI (NL), British Aerospace (UK), Bull (F), CAP Gemini SESA (B), Daimler Benz (D), Digital (D), ENSIDESA (E), FIAT (I), GRAI, (F), GEPRO (D), Hewlett Packard (F), IBM (D), ICL (UK), ITALSIEL (I), ITEM (CH), NLR (NL), PROCOS (DK), Siemens (D), University of Valladolid (E), WZL (D).

The work was carried out in Workpackages staffed by people assigned from the participating organisations. The project results have been reviewed and accepted by the Consortium members.

List of Project Participants

Company	Name	
AEG Aktiengesellschaft	M	Klittich
Germany	W	Seifert
AEROSPATIALE	J	Audy
France	R	Gaches
ALCATEL	G	Dureau
Belgium	A	Leffi
	J	Schoemaker

4

List of Project Participants (continued)

Company	Name	
AT&T Network Systems The Netherlands	W J D	Lobbezzo Vliestra Zoetekouw
BRITISH AEROSPACE Plc United Kingdom	G R M	Beadle Fleming Stenhouse
BULL France	N F J L C T B H R M	Brownlow De Belenet Gimza Guillier Keul Lelion Posingies Rüsch Sourd
CAP GEMINI SESA Belgium	D P P P P J P R N C B A C H A B C	Beeckman Collins Daoust de Lichtervelde De Swert Dorlhac Ducoffre Koch Lewis Mandy Meehan Scheller Schlueter Steiner T'Jampens Vanclair
CAP SESA INDUSTRIE France	A L T	Charue Dronne
CoCo Systems Ltd United Kingdom	S	Hamer-Moss
Daimler Benz AG Germany	D O M	Haban Keles Klittich
Digital Equipment GmbH Germany	M A U A U J D	Actis-Dato Bauer Brunet Cote Flatau Gemsjäger Wüstefeld

List of Project Participants (continued)

Company		Name
DORNIER Luftfahrt GmbH	A	Harter
Germany	O	Hasenfuss
	J	Nagel
ENSIDESA	M	Morante
Spain	F	Requejo Monso
	L	Sancho Méndez
ESPRIT Consortium AMICE	K	Kosanke
Belgium		
FIAT S.p.A.	L	Barengo
Italy	V	Calamani
	E	Ceroni
	M	Mollo
	F	Naccari
	C	Shuster
GEC Electrical Projects Ltd	J	Fowle
United Kingdom	A	Mistry
	P	Smith
	P	Wright
GEPRO mbH	T	Klevers
Germany	H	Mehring
GRAI Laboratoire	D	Chen
France	G	Doumeingts
HEWLETT PACKARD	D	Boisson
France	E	Lutherer
	J P	Mainguy
	D	Pothier
	B	Querenet
	V	Vigne
	P	Viollet
IBM Deutschland GmbH	H	Ebinger
Germany	B	Endres
	H	Jorysz
	R	Panse
	G	Preiss
	K	Rittmann
	E	Stotko
	M	Zelm
INRIA-LORRAINE	F	Vernadat
France		
INTERNATIONAL COMPUTERS Ltd	B	Rowley
United Kingdom	P J	Russell

List of Project Participants (continued)

Company		Name
ITALSIEL	M	Arman
Italy	P	Benini
	F	Boero
	M	Bonfadini
	B	Scialpi
ITEM	A	Bienert
Switzerland	W	Dreyer
	V	Hrdliczka
	S	Messina
	S	Nittel
	A	Ploetz
	G	Schuh
	M	Suter
	A	Walti
	H	Zimmermann
National Aerospace Laboratory		
The Netherlands	U	Aktu
	W	Loeve
	R	Van Den Dam
	P	Van Mourik
Nederlandse Philips Bedrijven B.V.	G	Kaashoek
The Netherlands	R	Kommeren
	K	Metzger
	J	Van Den Hanenberg
PROCOS A/S	P	Andersson
Denmark	H	Andreasen
	P	Blom Petersen
	C	Gry
	P E	Holmdahl
	J	Jorgensen
	L	Nielsen
	T	Norup-Pedersen
	M	Shahbazi
SEIAF spa	M	Busatti
Italy	F	Cavagnaro
SEMA GROUP Plc	K	Farman
United Kingdom		

List of Project Participants (continued)

Company		Name
SIEMENS AG	K P	Blume
Germany	L	De Ridder
	N	Haberkorn
	N	Klensch
	H	König
	N	Lutkemeyer
	N	Tran-Binh
	S	Unsinn
	D	Van Rillaer
	M	Wieck
UNIVERSIDAD DE VALLADOLID	I	Dimitriadis
Spain	J	Lopez Coronado
	S	Martinez De La Pera
	J	Perez Turiel
	R	Rodriguez Rubio
	J	Rodriguez Sanchez
VOLKSWAGEN AG	K	Pasemann
Germany	G	Teunis
WZL RWTH AACHEN	B	Dahl
Germany	A	Friedrich
	B	Katzy
	T	Klevers
	G	Müller
	F J	Stepprath
	E	Zahn

On the Book

This book is a completely revised version of the 'Open System Architecture for CIM' published by Springer in 1989. The revision is based on the results of the ESPRIT Project AMICE obtained during the previous ESPRIT contracts (EP's 2422 and 5288).

With the publication of this book we aim to:

- promote CIMOSA and its concepts on enterprise integration, enterprise modelling and model based management and operation control and monitoring support.
- enlarge the community of people and organisations interested in CIMOSA
- inform the Manufacturing and Information Technology community at large on CIMOSA, its use and its benefits.

The book provides an update on the CIMOSA concepts and construct specifications both for enterprise modelling and the Integrated Infrastructure. It provides new information on modelling for resource and organisation modelling as well as a new structure for the Integrating Infrastructure.

The book is structured into 4 parts each one providing specific information on particular aspects of CIMOSA. Part 1 starts with a management overview on CIMOSA and its role, contribution and benefits in enterprise integration. The CIMOSA Modelling Framework, Reference and Particular Architecture and enterprise modelling are described at considerable level of detail in Part 2. CIMOSA Environments and System Life Cycle are explained as well. This part also contains the description of the Integrated Infrastructure, its new structure and specifications. Relations to existing and emerging standards have been taken into account and major standards are referenced in the description. A User Guide on enterprise modelling for the requirements definition modelling level presents the detailed description of the CIMOSA modelling constructs (Part 3). How to use CIMOSA in requirements modelling is demonstrated through the application of CIMOSA templates to examples taken from a project case study. Part 4 of the book presents some specific topics presenting recent advancements in enterprise modelling, integration and model based operation control and monitoring.

We gratefully acknowledge the support received from the officials of the European Community without whom we could not have obtained the results presented in this book. Equally important for the achievements reached in the project are the many excellent contributions made by the project participants. Without their dedication to the work, their spirited motivation and excellent cooperation across so many different European cultures and professional backgrounds the current state of the work would not have been achieved. All of your work is gratefully acknowledged as well.

Brussels, January 1993

on behalf of the ESPRIT Consortium AMICE

Kurt Kosanke   Ed Beadle
Project Director   Chairman - AMICE Executive Committee

Part 1

Management Overview

Part 1 provides a general overview of the approach adopted by the Open Systems Architecture for CIM (CIMOSA) to the challenge of enterprise integration. It indicates the current status of the work on CIMOSA being undertaken by the ESPRIT Consortium AMICE.

1   Enterprise Integration - the Need

Enterprise Integration (EI) is a need arising from the continuous evolution of enterprises to meet challenges and opportunities imposed by external changes. Unless very well managed internal responses will increase operation complexity and lead to inconsistencies and incompatibilities in the enterprise operation.

Our industrial enterprises operate and produce in an environment which becomes more and more global and highly competitive. The dynamics of world wide markets of goods, services, capital and know-how lead to this ever increasing global competition. A competition driven by severe market changes causing significant evolution in enterprise operations (Fig. 1.1). To cope with such changes in market demand, in product and manufacturing technology and not the least, with changes in the financial and social environments, enterprise operations will require more and more flexibility. In addition, most enterprises need active cooperation with large networks of vendors and customers in this global economy[1]. Cooperation which has to be supported by real time information interchange but which may also be subject to very fast changes in nature and contents.

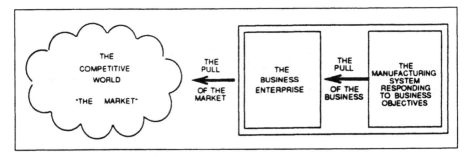

Fig. 1.1: Market 'pull' drives need for management of change and operational flexibility

The introduction of computers as a new technology in information processing is a case in point. Computers have significantly increased information processing speed and thereby enabled processing of huge amounts of data. However, insufficient coordination and lack of standardisation has led to many incompatible solutions (islands of information) hampering the exchange of information between different IT applications. E.g. information produced during the manufacturing process is not directly usable in invoicing, product design information can not easily be used for production planning and NC programming.

Manufacturing companies are facing these challenges by introducing concepts like 'Just in Time', 'Continuous Flow', 'Kanban', 'Lean Production', to name but a few. Computer Integrated Manufacturing (CIM) is viewed as an all embracing solution to the manufacturing industry providing:

- management of change, flexibility of enterprise operations and efficient use of enterprise assets - people, capital investments, and information.

Computer Integrated Manufacturing draws upon many of the traditional areas of manufacturing automation including CAD, CAM, MRP, etc. It is not the sum or

---

[1]   CALS (Computer Aided Acquisition and Logistic Support) is an example of a current solution for this requirement

totality of these components but the linking of them into an interoperating system that will satisfy the enterprise's business strategy and objectives.

In addition CIM and enterprise integration have to be understood as integration processes evolving over time, adapting to new technology and continuously leading to more flexible and more efficient operations especially in manufacturing enterprises. Integrating the enterprise also means that many different disciplines are involved in the design and implementation of a CIM system. Therefore there is a need for a common descriptive language to provide unambiguous communication of enterprise design information between these various disciplines but one which still allows the different disciplines to express themselves in their natural terminology through compatible dialects.

In spite of the many advances in Information Technology (IT), information processing is still hampered by the heterogeneity of both IT hardware and software. In the manufacturing industry heterogeneity extends into the production domain as well with the multiple solutions provided by shop floor equipment manufacturers. Incompatible vendor system and application software make it very difficult to communicate and interoperate between different systems even inside a single enterprise. This heterogeneity makes it virtually impossible to establish other than very basic IT based cooperations across enterprise boundaries. International standards are moves into the right direction[2]. However, a more general approach is needed to make enterprise integration successful over time.

The need for a global industrial information infrastructure enabling inter and intra enterprise cooperation has become paramount for any enterprise operating in a global environment. An infrastructure focussing on operation flexibility and efficiency and enabling consistent information processing by hiding hardware and software heterogeneity. The need has been recognised by many people and numerous efforts have contributed partial solutions to the general state of the art in Enterprise Integration[1][2].

Beside the methodical and technological solutions needed for enterprise integration, there are psychological, social and educational barriers to be overcome in order to get acceptance for a new industrial enterprise paradigm. Awareness for EI needs and benefits as well as IT capabilities and acceptance of the consequences will require enormous efforts in publicity, training and education. The new modelling capabilities for model maintenance and real time management of change require special attention over an extended period of time to enable all potential users to appreciate and exploit the potential benefits.

The ESPRIT project AMICE[3] is developing an Open System Architecture (CIMOSA) for the manufacturing industry. The main goal of CIMOSA is to support process oriented modelling of manufacturing enterprises and to provide execution support for operation of enterprise systems based on those models.

---

[2]   Standards related to CIM:
EDI: Electronic Data Interchange
DOAM: Distributed Office Application Model
MAP: Manufacturing Automation Protocol
ODP: Open Distribution Processing
OSI: Open System Interconnection
STEP: Standard for Exchange of Product Data

[3]   AMICE: European Computer Integrated Manufacturing Architecture (in reverse)

Emphasis in CIMOSA is on modelling support for business users[4] rather than for modelling specialists.

2   Enterprise Integration - the Solution

Enterprise integration has to provide flexibility of enterprise operations and efficient use of enterprise assets. Therefore, a modular approach to integration is the most promising one. An approach which models the operation as a set of cooperating processes exchanging results and request (events) between themselves. Only the exchanged objects need a representation common between partners. This minimal unification of objects, together with an integrating infrastructure hiding heterogeneity, can cope with enterprise integration through exchange of objects.

The CIMOSA approach enables integration of both re-engineered and existing systems.

2.1   Management of Change

Companies are not always organised for fast decision making processes. Departments are still managed according to their own sub-goals rather than to the overall enterprise objectives. Responsibilities are still structured in one dimensional hierarchies which mix responsibilities for enterprise assets with those for enterprise operations. Matrix organisations are still a rather theoretical concept. In addition, the decision making process in many companies is still based on traditional information processing - information gathering with 'paper and pencil', on request and from inconsistent sources. This process is defined in view of a rigid management hierarchy and very prone to severe information losses. The process is very time consuming and often yields only insufficient or even wrong information and decisions. To achieve 'real time' operational flexibility, delegation of responsibility and authority are needed to allow people to make changes as the are required rather than going through a hierarchy of many levels for decision sign-offs. Ease of access and more efficient use of information will enable delegation of more responsibility and authority.

Therefore, active management of change is the most significant future requirement for successful enterprise operation. This means recognising and reacting to external changes as early as possible and defining and implementing internal modifications to their response. Business process re-engineering and simplification as tasks of enterprise engineering are prerequisites for enterprise integration.

Decision support is an essential part of management of change; which implies timely access to right information and disposition of decision making process results to the right places. Decision making requires clear and explicit knowledge about relevant Business processes and their contents (information, resources, responsibilities and authorities), definition of alternative solutions and analysis of their impact on the total enterprise operation. Therefore computer simulation of potential solutions is a requirement on future decision support systems.

CIMOSA provides decision support through its up-to-date models (identification of relevant information, analysis of alternative solutions and propagation of verified decisions) and ease of Business Process re-engineering.

---

[4]   Business Users (or Business Professionals) are all those people with responsibilities for particular Business Processes. Business Users are: technical staff, administrative staff and all levels of management.

2.2   Scope of Enterprise Integration

Industry needs an implementation strategy in which an existing, semi-automated enterprise can steadily progress in discrete steps towards CIM. The manufacturing plant must continue to operate day by day, but incorporate changes in the direction of both automation and integration. Since it is impossible to purchase all the components required for realizing an enterprise environment from a single vendor, standards are required to ensure correct interworking of components from multiple sources.

In addition to its capital investments the enterprise knowledge about its business and technical processes is one of its most valuable assets, often differentiating it from its competitors. The integration of this internal knowledge with the external one arising from other sources (e.g. trade associations, de facto standards, standards) is vital for an enterprise trying to remain competitive and cost effective.

Enterprise operation also consists of internal and external parts. Internal operation of an enterprise is the set of Business Processes needed to market, develop, manufacture, distribute and sell products and administer and manage the operation itself. External operations which are coupled to the internal ones cover relationships with suppliers, customers, financial institutions, government agencies, etc. The main focus of enterprise integration is on internal environments. However, relations to the external environments and their impact on the internal operation have to be made visible as well. Only if these dependencies are known and have become part of the business models can the impact of changes be fully evaluated. However more detailed modelling is required for internal operations than for external ones. Whereas, the control flow of internal Business Processes is needed even for simulation of alternatives, identification of shared information and dependencies is mostly sufficient for modelling the external relations.

Information technology hardware makes it possible even today to install very large networks of computer systems with almost unrestricted performance and processing capabilities. The ability to handle the vast amount of information needed and existing in the manufacturing enterprise and to process the right information, for the right purpose, at the right time and in the right place is still a major problem.

CIMOSA provides means to describe in a consistent way internal and external enterprise operations and their information needs. In addition, it clearly distinguishes between model engineering and model use and defines in its System Life Cycle a formal engineering release for operation.

2.3   Enterprise Engineering and Operation

Enterprise evolution leads to a continuous need for enterprise integration. A need to be fulfilled by new engineering tasks concerned with maintaining and extending enterprise operation efficiency and flexibility. Therefore, enterprise integration has to be conceived as a modular approach structuring and modelling the business into manageable units (processes) which cooperate with each other according to identified needs and sharing information on request. Only with the enterprise modelled as a set of cooperating processes rather than a large monolithic entity can changes be implemented and operation modifications and extensions be made in 'real time'. Only then can sufficient operational and organisational flexibility be achieved.

IT based integration support for Business Model Engineering:

- definition of Business Process flow of control and information needs
- definition and organisation of enterprise assets (resources and information)
- definition and organisation of enterprise responsibilities and authorities
- maintenance of business models (modifications and extensions) by the business user

The set of Business Processes which make up the enterprise operation have to operate and interoperate in a highly efficient and flexible manner. To assure operation flexibility and efficiency easy accessible knowledge of the operation has to be provided through up-to-date business models. Better structuring and modelling of enterprise operation will hide process complexity and thereby improve decision making and business management.

Operation flexibility will be greatly enhanced by direct use of models for operation control and monitoring. Business changes will be implemented and validated in the model and directly released for operation. Improved enterprise logistic control and superior asset management will also contribute to operation flexibility and efficiency.

IT based integration support for Business Model Execution:

- evaluation of impact of change and alternative solutions (model simulation)
- model based operation control and monitoring

2.4 Coexistence with Heritage/Legacy Systems

New system components, re-engineered according to new paradigms in modelling still have to interoperate with the existing parts of the enterprise operation. With an average life time of e.g. 12 years for Mainframe applications[5] there will be many years of such coexistence.

Therefore, any new methodology and technology used in enterprise operation has to provide means for interoperating with the existing world. The most promising approach to achieve interoperability between incompatible systems is the use of information objects shared between different parts of the system. With this approach agreement on common representation is only necessary between partners sharing the same objects. This enables identification of classes of information objects according to their degree of sharing e.g. private, common, public. This is the approach taken also by people working in AI on classes of ontologies.

CIMOSA provides solutions for enterprise integration of re-engineered and heritage systems.

2.5 Business Benefits

Enterprise re-engineering and process simplification are tasks which will coordinate enterprise evolution as well as improving enterprise performance in general. In the IT arena availability and sharing of information between different business areas and common use of computer services will reduce operation cost, but more importantly it will improve operation quality and flexibility. Providing relevant information in real time to the decision makers will enable faster reaction to

---

[5] T. Goranson, paper at ICEIMT

different market changes (markets on goods, services, knowledge, technology and money). It will also base enterprise strategies on real life facts rather than fictions.

CIMOSA will provide benefits for enterprises by:

- improving enterprise operation flexibility and efficiency by re-engineering and simplification of Business Processes.
- supporting management of change by evaluation of alternatives through operation simulation.
- improving operation flexibility and efficiency and reducing operational cost through better business management (people, process, resources, information).
- reducing lead times trough sharing and re-use of relevant information, modelling building blocks and system components.

3   Enterprise Modelling and its Requirements

Enterprise business modelling is a prerequisite for successful enterprise integration[6]. However, enterprise operations have to be well understood and explicitly described and presented to identify inconsistencies and incompatibilities and analyse their consequences. Alternative solutions can than be modelled and evaluated through simulation. Also enterprise modelling has to meet the requirements of a number of different users in their day-to-day operations. Therefore modelling has to be based on business objectives and describe the operation in terms of related functionality and dynamic behaviour (control flow). Enterprise modelling should not be done as a one time all encompassing venture. A modular structure will allow evolutionary model building and model maintenance. However, to assure consistency, all modules have to be parts of, derived from and linked to a common model. These sub-models must meet specific user needs for optimising and structuring certain aspects of the operation without being constraint by a huge model. Levels of abstraction are needed to support strategic, tactical and operational planning and decision making. Again, all levels have to be abstractions from the same underlying model.

Model engineering needs heavy IT support to enable creation of consistent and easily maintainable and extendible models. The user has to be guided through the model engineering process by providing identification of re-usable building blocks already known to the system. Ease of maintenance is needed to adopt models in real time to the changing internal and external environment as well as to enable evaluation of alternatives to the existing situation (As-Is versus To-Be models).

Unlike other approaches CIMOSA allow users to model different parts of the enterprise and to integrate them later. CIMOSA provides a modular approach (Domain Process) for business modelling identifying 3 modelling levels (requirements definition, design specification and implementation description) and four views as part of an open set (function, information, resource, organisation).

4   CIMOSA Approach

CIMOSA provides a framework for guiding CIM users in enterprise system design and implementation, and CIM vendors in system component development. It provides a descriptive, rather than a prescriptive methodology supporting the System Life Cycle. CIMOSA does not provide a standard architecture to be used by

---

6)   ICEIMT (Intern. Conference on EI modelling technology) 1992

the whole manufacturing industry, but rather a Reference Architecture from which Particular Architectures can be derived which will fulfil the needs of particular enterprises.

The Reference Architecture provides constructs for the structured description of business requirements and for CIM system design and implementations. CIMOSA compliant enterprise systems will support organisational and operational flexibility, extensive use of multi-disciplinary enterprise information (knowledge) and graceful system integration. Through the business modelling framework a generic modelling concept is provided which is applicable to enterprises in many industries. A modelling concept which will vastly enhance communication and interoperability via Information Technology within an enterprise, as well as between different enterprises. Model execution in heterogeneous manufacturing and IT environments is supported by the implementation of an integrating infrastructure.

CIMOSA supports new paradigms in enterprise management enabling explicit description of enterprise processes at different levels of abstraction for strategic, tactical and operational decision support. Decision support through extensive simulation of alternatives and evaluation of impacts on all relevant parts of the enterprise. Specific definition of responsibilities and authority will allow for decision deferring in time and reduction of management levels to enable flexible and efficient enterprise operation.

Applying CIMOSA modelling methodology results in complete descriptions of enterprise domains and their contained Business Processes including relationships to external agencies (suppliers, customers, even government regulatory bodies, etc..) This enterprise model is stored on and manipulated by the relevant information technology base of the enterprise. CIMOSA allows modelling of the enterprise to be done incrementally rather than following an overall top-down approach. It structures the enterprise operation into a set of interoperating Domain Processes exchanging results and requests. Different views of the manufacturing enterprise content and structure are required to satisfy the needs of the different users of such an architecture. CIMOSA provides the necessary constructs to enable these multiple views to be created and manipulated by those users who have specialist knowledge of their particular field but are not experts in IT.

4.1   System Life Cycle

Enterprises are very complex undertakings which can be rendered more manageable by structuring their complex operational domain into a set of interoperating modules and its time domain according to a life cycle concept. CIMOSA employs the concept of Domain and Business Processes for modular structuring and System and Product Life Cycle for the time domain. Product Life Cycle is a well known notion used to structure the different phases of a product's life. Within a given manufacturing enterprise many such Product Life Cycles exist - one for each product - which gives rise to a set of overlapping life cycles as shown in Fig. 1.2. In order that the tasks associated with each step of the Product Life Cycle may be executed in a controllable manner enterprises define the procedures to be followed. These normally take the form of company standards, work instructions, process sheets, etc.. Different parts of the organisation may be responsible for different phases. For example Use and Maintain is normally a 'client' rather than a 'supplier' task.

This principle of life cycle can be extended to the enterprise system or parts thereof (Domains). Whilst today's Business Processes are in operation, their successors may be in the process of implementation. Strategic business plans under development today will set the stage for the systems implementations of tomorrow. Thus in an analogous way to products, the enterprise system which creates those products goes through a System Life Cycle of development and use (operate) as shown in Fig. 1.3.

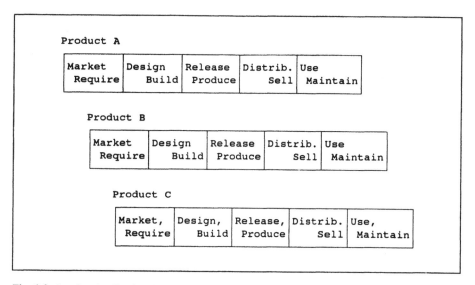

Fig. 1.2: Overlapping Product Life Cycles

Fig. 1.3: System Life Cycle

The tasks of the Enterprise System Life Cycle support both enterprise engineering and enterprise operation. Enterprise engineering tasks are concerned with the definition, description, creation and updating of the procedures and system components which govern and support the tasks of the Product Life Cycle. The operational phase of the System Life Cycle identifies the execution of Product Life Cycles. Thus Product and System Life Cycles are intimately inter-related. This relationship between the Product and System Life Cycles is summarised in Fig. 1.4. Whenever it is required to define a new or revised process supporting some part of a Product Life Cycle it will be necessary to carry out the tasks belonging to one or more phases of the associated System Life Cycle. The operational phase of the System Life Cycle is the execution of the relevant Product Life Cycle phases itself. Thus by assigning enterprise tasks to one or the other of the life cycles it is

18

possible to structure the workings of the enterprise into enterprise engineering and operation and so render more effective the management of change.

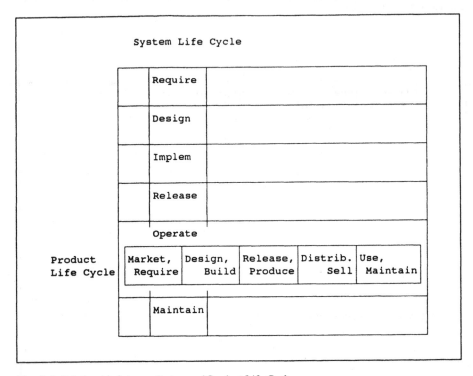

Fig. 1.4: Relationship between System and Product Life Cycle

4.2 Enterprise Integration

From the foregoing it will be recalled that enterprise integration has to be an on-going process rather than a one time effort. Enterprise will evolve over time according to both internal needs and external challenges and opportunities. The level of integration should remain a managerial decision and should be open to change over a period of time. Hence, one could find in some parts of a CIM enterprise, a set of tightly coupled systems and elsewhere, a set of loosely coupled systems according to choices made by this particular enterprise. The need to implement multivendor systems both in terms of hardware and software and easy reconfigurability requires the provision of standard interfaces. To solve the many problems of the industry, integration has to recognise and proceed on more than one operational aspect. The AMICE project identifies, and addresses, three levels of integration covering physical systems, application and business integration (see Fig. 1.5).

Business Integration is concerned with the integration of those functions which manage, control and monitor Business Processes. Functions which provide supervisory control of the operational processes and in turn coordinate the day-to-day execution of activities at the Application level. Modelling of Business Processes and their interrelations and its use for decision and operational support is key to business integration.

Application Integration is concerned with the control and integration of applications (applications in the data processing sense) which means there has to be interoperation between applications and users (human beings as well as machines) and supply and removal of information through inter and intra system communication. Integration at this level means providing a sufficient Information Technology infrastructure to permit the system wide access to all relevant information regardless of where the data reside.

Physical System Integration is concerned with the interconnection of manufacturing automation and data processing facilities (e.g. join CAD to CAM, flexible manufacturing cells, computerised scheduling, etc..) to permit interchange of information between the so called 'islands of automation' (inter system communications). Dictated by the needs of the individual enterprise the interconnection of physical systems was the first integration requirement to be recognized and fulfilled. This need has led to a number of information technology concepts becoming well accepted standards in this area[7].

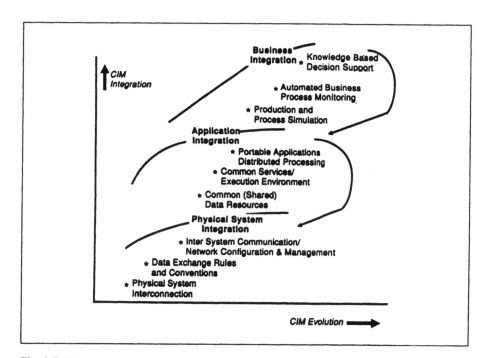

Fig. 1.5: The Levels of Enterprise Integration

Even when business integration has been achieved at one point in time business opportunities, new technologies, modified legislation will make integration a vision

---

7)   For example:
    OSI: Open System Interconnection
    MAP: Manufacturing Automation Protocol (an OSI implementation for the manufacturing floor).

rather than an achievable goal. However, this vision will drive the management of the required changes in the enterprise operation.

5   CIMOSA Overview

To satisfy the above issues of Management of Change, Flexibility and Enterprise Integration CIMOSA provides three inter-related concepts:

(1)   Modelling Framework (Reference Architecture, Particular Architecture, Enterprise Model).
(2)   System Life Cycle and Environments (Engineering and Operation).
(3)   Integrating Infrastructure.

CIMOSA recognises previous efforts in enterprise integration especially in the manufacturing industry and draws from the experienced gained in enterprise modelling and computer systems integration. Some of the efforts which have been of particular importance for the development of enterprise integration are given in reference [1].

5.1   CIMOSA Modelling Framework

The CIMOSA Modelling Framework provides the necessary guidance to enable end users to model the enterprise and its associated CIM system in a coherent way. The CIMOSA modelling approach is based on a Reference Architecture from which Particular Architectures and Enterprise Models can be developed. The structuring and decoupling of user concerns from implementation constraints provided by the framework contributes to enterprise flexibility. The Modelling Framework provides a structure which clarifies the relations between the parts which make up the enterprise operational system (Information Technology and Manufacturing Technology Components) and the methods and software tools which are required to describe, simulate and operate such an industrial system.

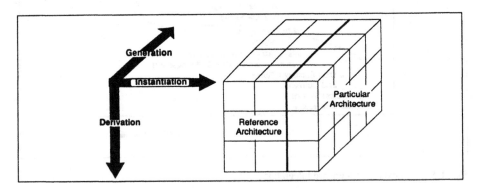

Fig. 1.6: The CIMOSA Modelling Approach

When modelling an enterprise there are many aspects and viewpoints to be examined that cannot be structured in a one dimensional framework. CIMOSA identifies a three-dimensional framework offering the ability to model different aspects and views of an enterprise (see Fig. 1.6):

- the **genericity dimension** is concerned with the degree of particularisation. It goes from generic building blocks to their aggregation into a model of a specific enterprise domain. This dimension differentiates between Reference and Particular Architecture.

- the **modelling dimension** provides the modelling support for the System Life Cycle starting from statements of requirements to a description of the system implementation.

- the **view dimension** is concerned with system behaviour and functionality. This dimension offers the user to work with sub-models representing different aspects of the enterprise (function , information, resource, organisation).

5.1.1 CIMOSA Reference Architecture

Within the Modelling Framework, CIMOSA provides the CIMOSA Reference Architecture. It resembles a catalogue of reusable building blocks which contains generic building blocks and aggregations of generic building blocks (Partial Models) applicable to specific modelling needs.

User oriented Generic Building Blocks are provided for:
Behaviour: Domain & Business Process, Event, Procedural Rules, Objective, Constraint
Function: Enterprise Activity, Functional Operation (input/output for function, control, resource), Objective, Constraint
Information: Enterprise Object, Object View, Information Element
Resources: Capability, Functional Entity, Resource Unit, Resource Cell
Organisation: Responsibility, Authority, Organisational Unit, Organisational Cell/Decision Centers

IT oriented Generic Building Blocks complement user building blocks supporting IT system design and implementation description. Such building blocks are Schemas, Transactions, Configurations and specific Functional Entity types representing the Integrating Infrastructure.

Partial Models are aimed at particular types of enterprise domains or even types of enterprises. Such partial models are created using the set of generic building blocks. Such partial models will be provided by vendors to be used as macros to enhance the model building process and as implementable components for system implementation.

5.1.2 CIMOSA Particular Architecture

The structuring of particular enterprise domains follows the framework of modelling levels and views. In the Process/Activity/Operation approach an enterprise is seen as a collection of inter-related but non-overlapping domains, which are subsets of the enterprise business. Enterprise engineering is concerned with requirements, design and implementation of enterprise operations. Enterprise operations are defined in two distinct levels linked to each other by events:

- a network of event driven cooperating Domain Processes.

- an explicit description of functionality and behaviour of the individual Domain Processes presented as a network of Enterprise Activities/Functional Operation initiated by events and driven by an explicit set of procedural rules.

22

The network of Domain Processes may consist of CIMOSA and non-CIMOSA Domain Processes; Domain Processes with or without an internal CIMOSA structure. This approach provides a potential solution for enterprise integration of heritage systems. Fig.s 1.7 and 1.8 represent the two levels of structuring. Fig. 1.7 shows a set of Domain Processes cooperating on shared objects (results and events). One of those processes is detailed in the following Figure demonstrating the engineering process of decomposition (top-down) leading to a network of Enterprise Activities as well as function aggregation (bottom-up) into Business and Domain Processes. Decomposition can be either into Business Processes representing lower level behaviour or Enterprise Activities representing functionality. For system design Enterprise Activities are further decomposed into Functional Operations which relate functionality to enterprise resources for execution.

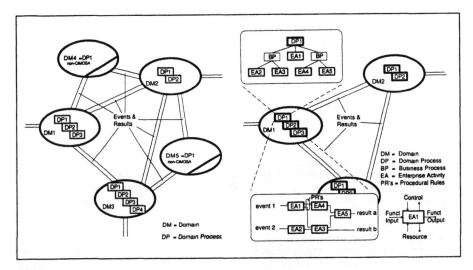

Fig. 1.7: Network of
Domain Processes

Fig. 1.8: Internal
Structure of Domain Processes

5.1.3 CIMOSA Enterprise Model

According to the structure provided for the particular architecture CIMOSA models capture business knowledge globally as networks of Domain Processes and as Enterprise Activities representing detailed local functionality and Business Processes representing intra process behaviour. Identification of all inputs required and outputs produced (information, control, resources and organisational) will be done for the different parts of functionality. Modelling is done through instantiation of generic building blocks or partial models.

Within an enterprise, tasks (Domain Processes) are usually organised into sub-tasks (Business Processes, Enterprise Activities, Functional Operations) which need to be realised to achieve the business objectives. Within each domain (unsolicited) real-world happenings and requests (events) to do something will occur which will trigger Domain Processes. Domain Processes can also have exchange with domains external to the enterprise. To represent tasks and actions performed within an enterprise CIMOSA forces users to think in terms of "processes", "activities" and "operations", where operations define the lowest level of granularity to represent tasks performed within an enterprise. The level of detail to be described in the model is at the users discretion and not dictated by CIMOSA.

Model modifications can be made via Domain Process internal and external behaviour and its functionality. Internal changes will be through modification of internal control flow and/or functionality, changes in external behaviour through modifications of its external relations (interoperation with other Domain Processes).

The CIMOSA modelling approach includes and extends previous functional modelling approaches[7] already in use in industry or being considered by standardisation bodies which essentially only recognize the concept of activity (also called function). The most significant extension is the modelling of the business process behaviour. Through this recognition of the business dynamics model based operation control and monitoring becomes possible.

CIMOSA differentiates between AS-IS and TO-BE modelling. Modelling of an existing implementation will start with bottom up description of the current operation. Abstraction from the AS-IS description and modifying the operation would lead to requirements and design of the TO-BE model and analysis of its intended behaviour. No specific methodology has been prescribed by CIMOSA leaving freedom for iterations as required between decomposition and aggregation as well as between modelling levels.

5.2 CIMOSA System Life Cycle and Environments

Life Cycle	Environment	Model Executed
System	Enterprise Engineering	Engineering Implementation Model
Product	Enterprise Operation	Particular Implementation Description

Fig. 1.9: CIMOSA Life Cycle and Environments

To support its modelling concept, CIMOSA defines an enterprise System Life Cycle and corresponding environments in which the relevant life cycle processes can be executed. These environments contain a dynamic definition (a model) of the life cycle tasks in the form of a set of processes; a set of resources providing the functionality required to carry out those tasks and a set of common services providing system wide support for the execution of processes. This concept decouples the engineering of the enterprise's system(s) from day-to-day enterprise operations.

In order to permit the processes for one task within the Product Life Cycle to be designed/updated without interfering with the execution of current operational tasks CIMOSA provides two mutually independent, but inter-related, environments (see Fig. 1.9).

1) The Enterprise Operational environment in which products are developed, produced, marketed and sold, orders are issued and received, bills are paid and invoices submitted to customers in accordance with the processes defined for the enterprise's Product Life Cycles.

2) The Enterprise Engineering environment in which particular enterprise domains are modelled (including the simulation/evaluation of alternative solutions), built, validated and released for operation in accordance with the processes defined for the enterprise's System Life Cycle (except for the system operation phase).

In both cases life cycle processes are defined by a CIMOSA compliant model. In the case of the Enterprise Operations environment this user created model is unique to the particular enterprise. The model of the Enterprise Engineering environment is constructed by the IT vendor and customised to the users needs. Conformance to the CIMOSA Model Creation processes and the CIMOSA Model Consistency rules ensure that the end result is a CIMOSA compliant model (see also Fig. 1.12).

CIMOSA defines the basic phases of the System Life Cycle in terms which are independent of the modelling methodology employed. CIMOSA does not populate the System Life Cycle with a set of unique processes but leaves it open for tool vendors to define their various proprietary methodologies in a CIMOSA compliant model. Thus alternative models (tool sets) will exist for the System Life Cycle to reflect different modelling methodologies (e.g. waterfall, fast prototyping, concurrent engineering, etc.) for creating CIMOSA conformant enterprise models. For example the creation and execution of a CIMOSA compliant process involves the following basic tasks:

- identify the business domain
- select relevant building block types from a catalogue of CIMOSA building blocks;
- customise the selected types by adding enterprise specific parameters to make instances of the building block types;
- if required install and describe any additional resources;
- release the enterprise model which contains the instances, into the operational system;
- add at execution time technical parameters and logistic variables to a copy of the released instances (create occurrences).

CIMOSA proposes a formal engineering release of the enterprise model at the phase-over from the engineering to the operational environment. Changes to be made to the operational system have to be implemented, validated and documented in the engineering mode rather than in the operational mode. Only then can a sufficient engineering discipline be introduced into the enterprise operation and model consistency can be assured. This release process acts as a 'bridge' between the system and the Product Life Cycle.

It should be noted that emphasis in CIMOSA Enterprise Engineering is on model maintenance (up-date, modification, extension) rather than on model creation. The latter is seen as a one time affair, whereas the former is a continuous task of redefining the model contents. Only if the model reflects the reality of the enterprise operation will model based operation control and monitoring and decision support become a reality.

5.3 CIMOSA Integrating Infrastructure

CIMOSA copes with heterogeneity by providing the CIMOSA Integrating Infrastructure (IIS). This IIS provides a structured set of system wide services thereby avoiding redundancy of function in the enterprise's systems. By making use of these generic services the application systems in the CIMOSA Environments need no longer contain the specifics of the data processing environment. This provides increased portability and flexibility of the application systems and reduces the maintenance tasks considerably.

The IIS supports integration by providing homogeneous access to system components. The services of the CIMOSA Integrating Infrastructure address the problems of Application Integration (as defined in Section 5.3). The IIS supports model execution and engineering through a set of five generic service entities (see Fig. 1.10). It also provides a unifying software platform to achieve integration of heterogeneous hardware and software components.

The CIMOSA Integrating Infrastructure is tuned to the execution of CIMOSA models. Triggering of Domain Processes invokes the Business Entity which will process the request and initiate creation of a Domain Process occurrence and its subsequent processing by other services according to the nature of the event. The services of the Business Entity will schedule resources and execute Functional Operations through the Presentation Entity providing and removing information via the Information Entity. Communication across the entire system and system management are provided by the remaining two entities (Common and System Management Entity).

Entity	Service Provided
Business	execution of enterprise model according to business rules
Presentation	homogeneous access to humans, machines, software applications
Information	high level of consistent information
Common	system wide homogeneous data communication
System Management	management of CIMOSA Environments

Fig. 1.10: Service Entities of the Integrating Infrastructure

The AMICE project defines functionality of the IIS services but its implementation is under the discretion of the IT vendors. The IIS may be implemented according to any standard or proprietary solution which provides the expected functionality. Access to the different services is specified by interfaces or protocols. Therefore, depending on the degree of software integration, the IIS software may be a very small extension or a large software packet added to the vendor system software.

6 Applying CIMOSA

Fig. 1.11 illustrates the use of CIMOSA. The Reference Architecture provides the constructs (Generic Building Blocks) and standardised processes (Partial Models) which are used to create and maintain the particular enterprise model and to implement the IIS. The enterprise model describes the Product Life Cycle processes (Domain Processes) of the particular enterprise and their interrelations. These processes are composed of Enterprise Activities and Functional Operations. Resource are selected from vendor catalogues or from the installed enterprise base.

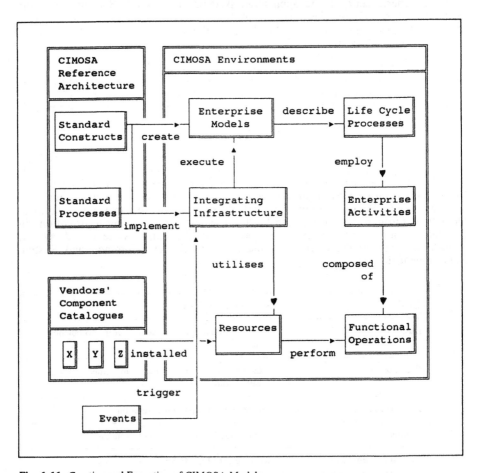

Fig. 1.11: Creation and Execution of CIMOSA Models

Model creation, implementation and maintenance are part of the engineering environment and follow the System Life Cycle concept. Model execution is concerned with the processes of the Product Life Cycle. These processes are performed through utilisation of relevant resources which are identified in the different processes as resource inputs of the Enterprise Activities. Model execution is initiated by events which represent real world happenings like receiving a customer order or identifying a due dates. Any event will start execution of at least one Domain process (see above).

Model based operation control and monitoring requires a consistent and up-to-date model of the operation. Therefore, modelling has to be done by the people responsible for the operation and authorised to modify and adapt the particular part of the model according to negotiated and accepted needs and opportunities. Knowledge about interrelations and impact of change have to be made known to the parties involved in the engineering phase and prior to release to operation. Therefore analysis and evaluation of change is an important part of model creation and maintenance and have to be employed by all people involved in enterprise engineering. Assignments of responsibility and authority in the engineering environment are very important and have to be made with a clear understanding of the consequences involved.

7 Summary of Architecture and Basic Concepts of CIMOSA

Today the manufacturing industry is faced with a rapidly changing business environment. Varying market demands require frequent operational and organisational changes in the individual enterprise. CIMOSA therefore enables the user to describe his enterprise from two distinct standpoints:

- the Business Environment as seen by the business user

- the Physical Environment (the Manufacturing and Information Technology implemented in the enterprise).

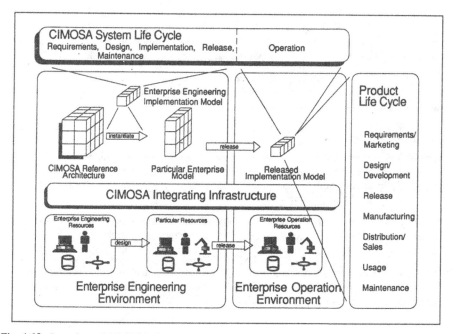

Fig. 1.12: Overview of CIMOSA Concepts

The prime goal of CIM and enterprise integration is to use Information Technology to integrate the enterprise operations. CIMOSA achieves this by linking the Enterprise Activities, Functional Operations and Functional Entities into a dynamic state network, thus integrating activities and resources performing them. This concept is applicable for operational processes designed according to CIMOSA as well as for those operating with the enterprise heritage and legacy systems.

Fig. 1.12 summarises the contents and use of CIMOSA in its two environments and the relations of its three major concepts with one another and the real enterprise world.

- Modelling Framework
- System Life Cycle
- Integrating Infrastructure

CIMOSA provides a Reference Architecture in its modelling framework for the specific description of a particular enterprise. The architectural constructs of CIMOSA guide the CIM business user in the creation and maintenance process to obtain and maintain a consistent system description. These constructs will also guide CIM suppliers to develop, produce and market products which will fit the defined user requirements and comply with the implemented system. The architectural constructs provided for the description can be viewed as the semantic for a manufacturing enterprise description language. This approach constitutes a completely new method for manufacturing system development. The method allows the end user to define, to prototype, to design, to implement and to execute the business according to his needs. The architecture also defines the necessary support environment for development and execution.

CIMOSA facilitates a System Life Cycle which guides the user through model engineering and model execution. Starting with the collection of business requirements in a Requirements Definition Model, through their translation into System Design Model, to the description of the implemented system (System Implementation Model). These phases are followed by a model release for operation and model execution for operation control and monitoring. To derive the system description all specific constraints of the particular enterprise are taken into account in the Design Specification Model. Model maintenance is a very important part of the System Life Cycle as well.

Model engineering and model execution are supported by the CIMOSA Integrating Infrastructure. The Integrating Infrastructure provides a set of generic services which process the released enterprise model and provide access to information, connect to resources and handle exceptions through reference to identified responsibilities and authorities. This infrastructure also hides the heterogeneity of the underlying Manufacturing and Information Technology.

The ESPRIT Consortium AMICE has developed CIMOSA and has validated its concepts in various case studies in its member companies. Validation work has also been done in other ESPRIT projects which will also lead to development of partial models in specific industry areas and particular modelling aspects. The project itself will further verify CIMOSA through industrial pilot implementation. Work on pre-pilots in enterprise modelling and model based operation control and monitoring has been started. Results from this work will become available in 1993.

8 References

[1] General work in enterprise integration described in numerous publications:

- ICAM project 1105: Conceptual Design for Computer Integrated Manufacturing
- CAM-I DPMM: Discrete Parts Manufacturing Model
- NBS AMRF: Automated Manufacturing Research Facility
- ISO TC 184/SC5/WG1 N51: Ottawa Report on Reference Models for Manufacturing Standards
- ESPRIT Pilot Project 34: Design Rules for Computer Integrated Manufacturing Systems
- ANSA: Advanced Networked System Architecture

[2] ICEIMT Proceedings, MIT Press 1992 (Intern. Conference on Enterprise Integration Modelling Technology, Hilton Head/SC, USA, June 1992)

[3] ENV 40003 Computer Integrated Manufacturing / Systems Architecture / Framework for Enterprise Modelling CEN/CENELEC/AMT/WG-ARC N100, 1990

[4] ESPRIT Consortium AMICE: "Open System Architecture for CIM", Springer, 1989

[5] publications by AMICE project members:

- Jorysz, H.R.; Vernadat, F.B.: CIMOSA Part 1: total enterprise modelling and function view. Intern. Journ. of CIM, 1990, Vol.3
- Jorysz, H.R.; Vernadat, F.B.: CIMOSA Part 2: information view. Intern. Journ. of CIM, 1990, Vol.3
- Klittich, M.: CIMOSA Part 3: CIMOSA integrating infrastructure - the operational basis for integrated manufacturing systems, Intern. Journ. of CIM, 1990, Vol.3
- ESPRIT Consortium AMICE: Integrated manufacturing - a challenge for the 1990's. Computing & Control Engineering Journ., 1991, Vol. 2
- Kosanke, K.: The European approach for an Open System Architecture for CIM (CIMOSA) - ESPRIT project 5288 AMICE. Computing & Control Engineering Journ., 1991, Vol. 2
- Russell, P.J.: Modelling with CIMOSA. Computing & Control Engineering Journ., 1991, Vol. 2
- Querenet, B.: The CIMOSA integrating infrastructure. Computing & Control Engineering Journ., 1991, Vol. 2

[6] "CIMOSA AD 1.0 - Architecture Description" private publication by the ESPRIT Consortium AMICE 1991

[7] General work in enterprise modelling described in numerous publications:

- SADT (Ross, IEEE Transactions on Software Engineering, Vol. SE-3; 1979.)
- GRAI (Doumeingts, Computers in Industry 9; 1987)
- IDEF0 (Bravoco, Yadav; Computers in Industry 6; 1985;)

Part 2

CIMOSA Technical Description

Part 2 provides a basic understanding of the Open System Architecture for CIM (CIMOSA) and its application to an enterprise. Enterprise Modelling and the Integrating Infrastructure are both presented together with System Life Cycle and Engineering and Operation Environment concepts[1]. The presentation is based on the current status of the work on CIMOSA being undertaken by the ESPRIT Consortium AMICE.

---

[1]   Throughout this Part of the book reference is made to more detailed specification presented in the Formal Reference Base (FRB Item) of the ESPRIT Project AMICE. Copies of this document can be obtained from the Project Office of the ESPRIT Consortium AMICE in Brussels.

1 General Objectives & Requirements

1.1 AMICE Project Objectives

The general AMICE project objectives are:

- to develop the concept of an Open System Architecture to guide and manage enterprise integration in view of the forthcoming era of perpetual change and evolution in enterprise operation. Such an architecture will embody all relevant enterprise knowledge in a form processable by information technology and usable for real time control of enterprise operation.

- to develop means for integrating enterprise internal operations and connecting with those of external suppliers, customers and other organisations. Integration will be across heterogeneous manufacturing and information technology environments.

- to support migration of existing enterprise systems towards the Open System Architecture environment. Integration will encompass, without major change, existing systems (e.g. special manual operations, stand-alone automated systems, etc.), existing applications (e.g. database applications, bill-of-materials processors, in-house developed software packages, etc.) and new developments.

1.2 Requirements for an Open System Architecture

These objectives lead to the identification of a number of requirements to be satisfied by an Open System Architecture:

- provide an architecture to describe the real world of the manufacturing enterprise;
  This description is to be used to control and monitor the enterprise operation and to plan, design and optimize updates of the real operation environment.

- permit end users to directly control and maintain enterprise systems without needing specialist knowledge of information technology;
  There is a need for user friendly descriptive languages to document End User's Requirements, a System Design supporting those requirements, and the final Implemented System. Such languages need adequate facilities for computer assisted translation between these languages;

- provide an adequate series of concepts to structure an enterprise so easing the management of change by minimising the cross impact of changes;
  The separation of user requirements definition from changes in implementation technology;
  The separation of functionality and behaviour, making it possible to revise behaviour in order to meet changing circumstances without altering the installed functionality;
  The application of the principles of abstraction, modularity and open-endedness to provide an industry wide catalogue of re-usable building blocks;

- provide selective perceptions of an enterprise which emphasise some particular aspects and suppresses others;

- make a clear distinction between the tasks necessary to update/modify the current enterprise systems from the tasks of operating those systems to create goods and services delivered to clients;
- provide an information technology based infrastructure which provides for portability of computer applications, enables system wide information exchange and supports multi-vendors hardware and software components.

1.3 The CIMOSA Approach to Open Systems

The major goal for CIMOSA is to enable enterprises to handle the issues of Management of Change, Flexibility, and Integration as outlined in Part 1 of this Architectural Description. To meet this goal CIMOSA provides three inter-related concepts, the CIMOSA Modelling Framework, CIMOSA Environments and CIMOSA Integrating Infrastructure.

The **CIMOSA Modelling Framework** contains a Reference Architecture and Particular Architectures for the manufacturing industry. Particular Architectures can be derived, from the Reference Architecture, which will fulfil the needs of particular enterprises in structuring and describing their manufacturing operations, and maintaining their CIM system implementation. This Particular Architecture embodies all necessary knowledge about the enterprise in a form which can be directly processed by Information Technology.

A CIM system implementation is to be based on enterprise objectives and requirements which are collected in a *Particular Requirements Definition Model*. These user requirements and system capabilities are then matched and optimised, producing a *Particular Design Specification Model*, which isolates user requirements from system implementation concerns. From this, a *Particular Implementation Description Model* is derived, being a description of an integrated set of Manufacturing and Information Technology components necessary for effective realisation of the enterprise operations.

The **CIMOSA Environments** enable a clear separation to be maintained between those tasks associated with the day-to-day running of the enterprise (Product Life Cycle tasks) and those tasks associated with the update and maintenance of enterprise systems (System Life Cycle tasks). This will prevent enterprise operations from being disrupted by the evaluation of alternative design solutions and render the management of change feasible;

- The **Enterprise Operation** Environment in which day-to-day operations are performed and controlled using the enterprise model;

- The **Enterprise Engineering** Environment in which the models are developed, tested and maintained using building blocks provided by the Reference Architecture and assisted by computer-aided tools (CAEE Tools).

The **CIMOSA Integrating Infrastructure** provides standard interfaces to active components of the enterprise (Functional Entities) in the form of presentation services or wrappers; supports enterprise-wide system, application and business integration of components of the enterprise through operational support for system-wide access to information; and assists in the execution of the enterprise model (Particular Implementation Description Model) to control (or at least monitor) the day-to-day operations of the enterprise.

Such an Open System Architecture is depicted by Fig. 2.1.

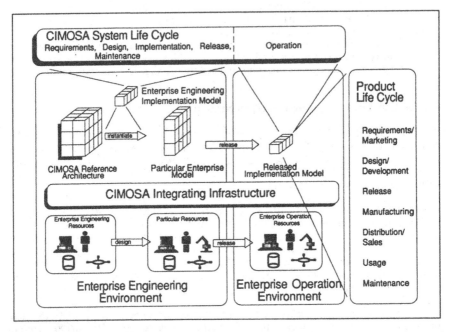

Fig. 2.1: Open System Architecture

1.4 CIM Architectures - State of the Art

Enterprise integration has a long history. Division of Labour could only start from a view of the whole operation identifying its parts and their relations[2]. Even F. W. Taylor's approach to improve enterprise efficiency was driven by a systems view on the manufacturing operation, but taking an extreme deterministic view on operation decomposition. More recent attempts on enterprise integration focussed on linking parts of the operation rather than decomposing and breaking them down further. Starting from the needs of manufacturing enterprises especially in the USA work has been carried out sponsored by government agencies in Computer Integrated Manufacturing (CIM). ICAM, CAM-I, work in NBS are some of the initiatives carried out and IDEF, DPMM and AMRF are some of the results. In Europe ESPRIT has been the major initiate in this area with numerous ESPRIT project focussing on different aspects of enterprise integration from enterprise engineering (EP 34) to business (EP 688 & follow ones), operation (EP 955 & follow-ones, 2277) and system architectures (EP 2267).[3]

---

2   Adam Smith, An Inquiry into the Nature and Cause of the Wealth of Nations, (Modern Library, New York, 1937)

3   EP 34: Design Rules for Computer Integrated Manufacturing Systems
EP 688&ff: European CIM Architecture (AMICE)
EP 955&ff: Communications Network for Manufacturing Applications (CNMA)
EP 2277: CIM for Multi-Supplier Operations (CMSO)
EP 2267: Integrated Systems Architecture (ISA)

Evaluating the state of the art (Section 6.1 Ref [1] to [7]) for contributions to enterprise integration the following criteria have been applied (results of this evaluation are summarised in the table below):

- Scope/Architectural Goals
- Industrial Environment (Industry Type) addressed
- Enterprise Functions covered
- Architectural Models provided
- Methodology and Tools applied

Area	State of the Art	CIMOSA
Scope	architecture/model for particular unique industrial environment	Ref. Architecture to model operation for all industrial environments and guide-lines for CIM product development
Environment	discrete parts manufacturing with emphasis on mechanical parts and aerospace manufacturing	discrete parts manufact. (electrical, mechanical) and CIM vendors (machine tool and IT industry) process industry, service industry
Functions	focus on manufacturing functions, complementary functions taken into account	all functions internal and external to a manufacturing enterprise
Models	hierarchical/top down decomposition of functions and data (control structure and management)	reference catalogue for requirements, design and implementation modelling enterprise modelling top-down, bottom-up, iterative, maintainable (up-date and modification)
Methodology	free form textual description, graphs & flow charts DVM: (Data Vector Modelling) IDEF - ICAM Definition based on SADT, ERA	model engineering, using finite set of generic building blocks for computer supported modelling and model based enterprise operation control and monitoring

Fig. 2.2: Evaluation of State of the Art and CIMOSA

This evaluation indicates the difference in scope and content of CIMOSA compared with the State of the Art material analysed. CIMOSA is not a Particular Architecture but a Reference Architecture which provides a set of constructs (Generic Building Blocks, Building Block Types and Partial Models) and computerised support for the development of Particular Architectures for individual enterprises. CIMOSA will support the individual business user in defining and developing his own models as part of an overall Requirements Definition Model. In addition CIMOSA will support enterprise operation by translating the user requirements into a description of CIM system components (resources and executable Information Technology applications). The following table relates some of the State of the Art activities to the different parts of CIMOSA. Only function view and information view are addressed by some of these efforts. Additional references relevant to CIM Architectures are given in Section 6.2.

	Ref.Arch. Gen/Part.		Part.Arch.	F-VIEW	I-VIEW	IIS	Tool
CAM-I DPMM			x	x	x		
NBS AMRF			x	x	?		
ISO TC184 N51	x		x	x			
Purdue	x	x	x	x	x		
ESPRIT							
– EP 34		x	x	x			
– EP 418		x	x	x	?		
– EP 955	?	x	x			x	
– EP 1024		x	x	x			
– EP 2143			?				x
– EP 2165			?				
– EP 2267		x	x			x	
– EP 2277		x	x				x
– EP 2527		x	x		x		
US Governm.							
– CALS	x	x	x	x	x		
– EIF/EIP	recommendation to adopt CIMOSA						
– FOF			x	x	x		
– IDS			?	x			
– IES			?	x			
– IISS						x	
– PDES	x				x		

Fig. 2.3: Relations of State of the Art Activities to CIMOSA

ESPRIT supported projects:

EP 34	Design Rules for Computer Integrated Manufacturing Systems
EP 418	Open CAM Systems
EP 955/2617	Communications Network for Manufacturing Applications (CNMA)
EP 1024/2374	Office Document Architecture (PODA)
EP 2143	Integrated Modelling Support Environment (IMSE)
EP 2165	Integrated Modelling of Products and Processes using advanced Computer Technologies (IMPPACT)
EP 2267	Integrated Systems Architecture (ISA)
EP 2277	CIM for Multi-Supplier Operations (CMSO)
EP 2527	CIM Systems with distrib. Database and config. Modules (CIDAM)

US Government supported projects:

CALS	Computer Aided Acquisition and Logistic Support
EIF	Enterprise Integrating Framework
EIP	EI Program
FOF	Factory of the Future
IDS	Integrated Design System
IES	Integrated Engineering System
IISS	Integrated Information Support System
PDES	Product Data Exchange Specification

2   CIMOSA Architectural Framework

The CIMOSA Architectural Framework contains three major concepts:

1   the CIMOSA Modelling Framework (including the CIMOSA Reference Architecture),
2   the CIMOSA System Life Cycle (including its supporting environment), and
3   the CIMOSA Integrating Infrastructure.

The rest of this section presents an overview of all three major concepts. The following sections are then devoted to a more detailed presentation of each concept.

2.1   Models and Architectures

2.1.1 Definition of Model

- Model: a representation in three dimensions of some projected or existing structure, or of some material object artificial or natural, showing the proportions and the arrangement of its component parts[4]
- Modelling: an additive process, ... corrections are possible during modelling[5]

- Models according to CIMOSA:
    -    are complete representations of enterprise domains detailing their internal processes and the relationships to external agencies (suppliers, customers, government regulatory bodies, etc.),
    -    are multiple subsets (sub-models) of the enterprise model to be derived in order to meet specific needs of individual users,
    -    are provided in two distinct levels of description:

        1) the overall enterprise is represented as an event driven network of domain processes whilst

        2) the individual domain processes are represented as a rule driven network of activities.

Computer Integrated Manufacturing (CIM) requires that all functions of an enterprise work together as an interrelated whole. To ensure that all activities, data and resources of an enterprise are put in proper relationship to each other, it is necessary to model the enterprise in order to identify all those activities, data, resources and responsibilities in an unambiguous way.

Many different representations of the manufacturing enterprise content and structure are required to satisfy the needs of the different users in their day-to-day tasks such as strategic, tactical and operational planning and decision making. CIMOSA provides the necessary constructs to enable these multiple representations to be created and manipulated by those enterprise members who achieve the integration benefits. Such staff have specialist knowledge of their particular field but are not expected to be experts in information technology. For consistency any such multiple representations must be part of, derived from and linked to a common model of the enterprise.

---

[4]   Oxford English Dictionary, 2nd edition, 1989
[5]   Encyclopedia Britannica, 15th edition, 1991

38

A modular approach will allow the very complex nature of an enterprise to be reduced to more manageable proportions by structuring the complexity into a set of interoperating modules. Modularity will also allow for evolutionary model building and model maintenance providing for easy modification of the enterprise (for example its structure, its modes of operation) as well as all the modelled items. To ensure that all such (sub)models (multiple representations) are put in a proper relationship to each other it is necessary to provide a structure within which they can be positioned and their inter-relationships defined. This structure is an architecture.

2.1.2 Definition of Architecture

- Architecture is the art and technique of building, employed to fulfil the practical and expressive requirements of civilised people[6]
- The types of architectures are established not by architects but by society, according to the needs of its different institutions[6]
- Architecture of something is its structure and design[7]

- Architecture according to CIMOSA:
    - the structure and design of something (enterprise domain, process, systems, etc.) = CIMOSA particular architecture
    - the collection of elements which allow to structure and design something in a consistent way = CIMOSA reference architecture
    - the methodology required to use the reference elements for structuring and designing the CIMOSA particular architecture = CIMOSA System Life Cycle Methodology

As mentioned above a structure is required within which to position and inter-relate the multiple representations (sub-models) of an enterprise.

CIMOSA is concerned with modelling real world entities of personnel, software and equipment and the links between them. When modelling such components, different points of view, different aspects and degrees of detail may well need to be considered. To ensure completeness, consistency and a proper separation of concerns it is useful to structure the different viewpoints, aspects and details in a framework. The CIMOSA Modelling Framework defines the common structure for both the CIMOSA Reference and Particular Architectures.

CIMOSA provides a descriptive, rather than a prescriptive, methodology. It does not provide a standard architecture to be used by the whole manufacturing industry, but rather a Reference Architecture from which Particular Architectures can be derived. Such Particular Architectures will fulfil the needs of particular enterprises.

The CIMOSA Reference Architecture provides a common structure to be adopted by individual enterprises as their Particular Architecture. The structure of this Particular Architecture is populated with an unique **particular enterprise model** describing the various processes of the user's enterprise. The CIMOSA Reference Architecture is populated with definitions of all the constructs, and their associated Model Creation Rules, available for use in instantiating particular enterprise models to populate the Particular Architecture (Generic Building Blocks, Building Block Types and Partial Models). Groupings of these constructs exist but they are more of a catalogue of types rather than a model.

---

[6]   Encyclopedia Britannica, 15th edition, 1991
[7]   Collins Cobuild (English Language Dictionary), 1987

2.2 CIMOSA Models

2.2.1 Contents of CIMOSA Models

It is not the intention of CIMOSA to model the entire enterprise just for the sake of modelling. The goals of CIMOSA models are:

- to provide support to enterprise integration,
- to provide a common language within the industry and thus to enforce company & industry standards and terminology,
- to manage or control enterprise processes,
- to enable model based control of enterprise activities and operations.

CIMOSA models should only contain adequate and sufficient information to support the above goals. CIMOSA requires that as a minimum this information concerns:

- the functions to be executed and the way they have to be executed,
- their necessary inputs and outputs in terms of physical objects or information entities,
- the resources needed to execute the functions and the way resource management must be performed,
- the responsibilities and authorities assigned to components of the CIM system and their organisation.

The model will also contain other information that end-users consider relevant to the running of their enterprise. CIMOSA makes use of **integrated** sub-models, i.e. sub-models in which the components (or building blocks) of one sub-model are tightly linked to those forming another sub-model and in which each concept is only modelled once.

2.2.2 Generalities about CIMOSA Models

Within the CIMOSA Modelling Framework (which embraces both the Reference Architecture, the Particular Architecture and the rules to create consistent models) end users, using the terminology of their own specific discipline(s), create a **particular enterprise model** unique to their enterprise. The enterprise is modelled as an event driven network of (domain) processes (see also Fig. 1.7 of Part 1). These processes exchange results produced and used by each other. Domain processes may be defined either as CIMOSA processes representing the business activities of a specific enterprise domain or may be non-CIMOSA processes not further detailed according to the CIMOSA methodology[8]. The internal descriptions of a CIMOSA domain process is represented in Fig. 1.8 of Part 1. Within each process a rule based network of activities provides the (deterministic) means to respond to events; requests from other processes to do something and to produce a result either for the requesting process or for third parties. The rule based network represents the control flow of the process rather than an information flow. This flow of control is expressed in procedural rules allowing to define conditions for branching, synchronisation, etc. Activities are described by their functionalities and their inputs and outputs (function, resource and control.

---

[8] This enables cooperation with existing applications and thereby provides graceful migration from the current operation to more flexible and efficient operations

The network is defined during the modelling process which may be either top-down or bottom-up according to the needs and/or preferences of the user. In the top-down approach, recommended to model To-Be enterprise operations and systems, the domain process is decomposed into lower level processes (see upper part of Fig. 1.8) ending in the network of activities shown in the lower part of the same Fig. Bottom-up modelling would start at the network of activities and aggregate those into higher level processes. Bottom-up modelling would mainly be applied for modelling of As-Is systems for system modifications and enhancements. The level of granularity between event driven and rule based modeling is left to the user's discretion.

Model creation is eased by the provision of common descriptive languages for defining enterprise system requirements and solutions, and by the provision of a range of standard modules which can readily be mixed and matched to build particular enterprise systems (catalogued in the CIMOSA Reference Architecture). The resulting unique particular model embodies all necessary knowledge of the enterprise in a form which can be used directly for the specification of an integrated set of electronic, mechanical, and information technology components necessary for effective realisation of enterprise operations.

The result is an enterprise model which is structured in such a way that specific concerns are decoupled from each other. User requirements are decoupled from implementation aspects such as the actual distribution, storage and processing of information by the three CIMOSA modelling levels. Enterprise activities are decoupled from the flow of control between the activities so that processes can be revised without necessarily changing the installed asset base (resources). This gives the necessary flexibility to adapt rapidly to new challenges from the market place.

At the Particular Architecture Level the different CIMOSA Views are used to ease the representation of different aspects (derived 'sub-models') of the integrated models within the Particular Architecture for an enterprise. There are two groups of sub-models:

- Sub-models at each Modelling Level: These are **integrated** models respectively called **Requirements Definition Model, Design Specification Model** and **Implementation Description Model**.

- Sub-Models derived within each View: These are restrictions (or derived sub-models) of the integrated model respectively called **Function View, Information View, Resource View** and **Organisation View**.

Developing the different sub-models for the Particular Architecture of his own enterprise, the CIM user will start with requirements gathering in the Requirements Definition Model. The system designer will go through requirements optimisation, technology selection and logical restructuring (Design Specification Model needed as a stable base to cope with changes in the other models). Finally the CIM system implementation description (including product selection) will be derived by the CIM system implementor in the Implementation Description Model. The different Views of the model will evolve, during the System Life Cycle, supporting additional structuring and detailing of the model thereby adding new parts and introducing modifications in the course of system use.

CIMOSA therefore supports CIM system design iterations (system maintenance) through its models. This recognizes the aspect of system modification and enhancement as a major concern to CIM system development. Indeed initial CIM system design is a one-time process while CIM system maintenance, i.e. model re-engineering is the real issue in manufacturing enterprises and will occur several times during the CIM System Life Cycle.

References to Formal Reference Base[9] (FRB Item)
B0-6000

2.3   General Description of the CIMOSA Modelling Framework

There are so many aspects and viewpoints to be considered that they cannot be structured in a one dimensional framework. Possible dimensions of a framework for industrial automation can be, amongst others, dimensions of genericity, of applicability, of industrial type, of product type, of enterprise function, together with dimensions for each of these representing ways in which they can change. Dimensions may stand alone but in practice most dimensions are interrelated and are not complete without these relations. It is usual to present different dimensions of a subject on orthogonal axes, so that the axes themselves can be analysed independently and the dependencies can be indicated in the space embraced by the axes. This presentation also allows for the dividing the axes according to sub-dimensions, thus providing for sub-spaces.

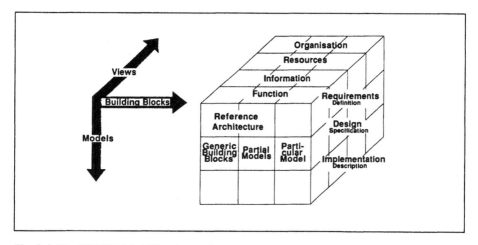

Fig. 2.4: The CIMOSA Modelling Approach

The set of possible models, the structure and behaviour of a model and the different phases of the life-cycle of a model are the key concepts which characterise a model from a generic aspect which is non-application dependant.

For CIMOSA three dimensions, from all possible ones, have been selected for their ability to include all the concepts needed for the modelling of an enterprise (see Fig. 2.4):

---

9   To be ordered from ESPRIT Consortium AMICE Office, Brussels

- one dimension concerned with the life-cycle of the model starting from the statement of requirements to a processable model, this is the dimension of enterprise models,

- one dimension concerned with the structure and behaviour of a model which considers appropriate aspects of an enterprise, this is the dimension of Views,

- one dimension concerned with the degree of particularisation which identifies the set of possible models, this is the dimension of Genericity.

2.3.1 The Dimension of Genericity and Stepwise Instantiation

CIMOSA has defined three Levels of Genericity:
    Generic, Partial and Particular.

Generic Level - a collection (reference catalogue) of constructs which are basic architectural building blocks that can be re-used in various architectural configurations. It includes CIMOSA Generic Building Blocks and Building Block Types for functions, objectives, constraints, services and protocols. Constructs described at this level have the widest application in CIM.

Partial Level - populated with Partial Models. These are incomplete skeletons of models for particular enterprises and are applicable generally to a wide range of industrial sectors, company organisations and/or manufacturing strategies. Partial Models are the prime means by which CIMOSA encapsulates industry needs, and provides a more realistic and usable tool for a particular enterprise.

Particular Level - entirely concerned with one particular enterprise. The CIMOSA Particular Model embodies all necessary knowledge of the enterprise in a form which can be used directly for the specification of an integrated set of manufacturing Technology and Information Technology components.

The Instantiation Process provides for the particularisation of a generic construct to be applied to a specific case according to the needs of the specific case. This particularisation is achieved by restricting selected attributes of those constructs to particular values and possibly aggregating them into constructs more appropriate to the specific application. An instantiated construct inherits the properties of one or more generic constructs with the addition of some specific properties. Instantiation itself is controlled by a set of guide-lines which defines the process steps, constrains the process, and ensures it is applied in a consistent manner.

The **CIMOSA Reference Architecture** contains the Generic and Partial Level of genericity, whilst the **CIMOSA Particular Architecture** contains the Particular Level.

References to Formal Reference Base (FRB Item)			
BO-5000	BO-5100	BO-5200	
BO-5300	BO-5310	BO-5320	BO-5330

2.3.2 The Dimension of Model and Stepwise Derivation

A Modelling Level is a level of abstraction corresponding to one of the main phases of enterprise model development (system life cycle). Each Level is characterised by a specific set of deliverables. CIMOSA has defined three Modelling Levels: Requirements Definition, Design Specification, Implementation Description.

Requirements Definition Level - uses a user friendly language to identify the business requirements of the enterprise, reflecting the objectives of that enterprise (requirements model). Business requirements are concerned with defining WHAT has to be done to fulfil the objectives of the enterprise without regard to the issues of the technology to be employed. These requirements lead to the definition of processes which can be further decomposed using Building Block Types from the Generic Level.

Design Specification Level - uses a computer processable language to identify and quantify, in an implementation independent format (logical model), the technology required to perform the identified processes. It structures and optimises the processes according to the overall enterprise constraints and the selected technology. The result is a computer processable model containing possible design alternatives and able to be evaluated by simulation techniques.

Implementation Description Level - defines in a computer executable form the means of process execution (physical model) by selecting actual vendor products to provide the Information Technology and Manufacturing Technology components (e.g. machines, application programs, human resources) to be used in an integrated and effective realisation to execute the processes as defined by the user's requirements.

The Derivation Process is the way of inter relating the three modelling levels such that each is a representation of one coherent description of the particular enterprise. It is the process of deriving requirements, design and implementation from a common set of objectives. Derivation is a refinement and transformation process from a business description language into a system description language. Derivation itself is controlled by a set of guide-lines which defines steps in the process, constrains the process, and ensures it is applied in a consistent manner.

The Derivation Process has in fact a very *iterative* nature and has not a pure water-fall structure as the CIMOSA "cube" representation might suggest. On one hand engineering of the Design Specification Model might request changes on the Requirements Definition Model. On the other hand the definition of the Implementation Description Model might imply changes on the Design Specification Model and/or on the Requirements Definition Model. This ensures that the final Implementation Description Model remains compliant with the Requirements Definition Model. Thus at the end of the Derivation Process a complete and consistent documentation of the CIM system is available.

References to Formal Reference Base (FRB Item)			
B0-4000	B0-4100	B0-4200	B0-4300

2.3.3 The Dimension of Views and Stepwise Generation

Views are essentially "windows" through which selective aspects of an enterprise can be observed and manipulated. Whilst some particular aspects are emphasised

other extraneous detail is suppressed to avoid obscuring the real issues at stake. CIMOSA Modelling Framework contains four Views:
  function, information, resource, organisation.

Function View - allows observation of the enterprise functionality for operation planning, control and monitoring.

Information View - allows observation of the structure of business information used during enterprise operations for planning, control and decision-making processes.

Resource View - allows observation of the enterprise's assets needed for carrying out the enterprise processes, including the use of the model to manage (control and monitor) these assets.

Organisation View - allows observation of the decision making responsibilities in the enterprise for function, information, resources and for the management of exceptions and decision-making.

The Generation Process defines the process of generating the content of the four Views in a coherent manner to create a concise and consistent Particular Model. Generation itself is controlled by a set of guide-lines which defines the process steps, constrains the process and ensures it is applied in a consistent manner.

A more detailed explanation of the CIMOSA Modelling Framework is presented in Section 3 of this document.

References to Formal Reference Base (FRB Item)			
BO-3000 BO-3400	BO-3100	BO-3200	BO-3300

2.4   The CIMOSA Enterprise and its Environments

In support of the concept of life cycles CIMOSA has defined a set of inter-related environments in which the tasks of modelling (engineering) particular enterprises (System Life Cycle), and operating the enterprise system (using the enterprise model) in order to fulfil enterprise goals (Product Life Cycle), are carried out. These environments and their relationship to the CIMOSA constructs are depicted in Fig. 2.5. This shows the following (A more detailed explanation of the CIMOSA System Life Cycle is presented in Section 4 of this document.):

Content of CIMOSA: this defines the CIMOSA Architectural Framework including the Modelling Framework (Reference Architecture & Model Creation Processes), and the Integrating Infrastructure. This is illustrated in the left hand part of Fig. 2.5.

Enterprise Engineering Environment: in which particular enterprise Domains and their Domain Processes are modelled, built, validated and released for operation in accordance with the procedures defined in the enterprise's System Life Cycle. A set of computerised tools (defined by a CIMOSA compliant Enterprise Engineering Implementation Description Model) ensures that the constructs and guide-lines, contained in the Reference Architecture and the CIMOSA Model Creation Processes, are correctly applied. This is an on-going process, requiring engineering disciplines (illustrated in the middle part of Fig. 2.5).

The computerised tools are specified by a CIMOSA compliant Enterprise Engineering Architecture (constructed by the tool vendor from the CIMOSA Reference Architecture in accordance with the CIMOSA Model Creation Processes and customised to the users needs) which defines the processes of one System Life Cycle. This is illustrated in the top left hand part of Fig. 2.5. Alternative System Life Cycles (tool sets) reflect different methodologies (e.g. waterfall, fast prototyping, concurrent engineering, etc.) for creating CIMOSA conforming Particular Architectures.

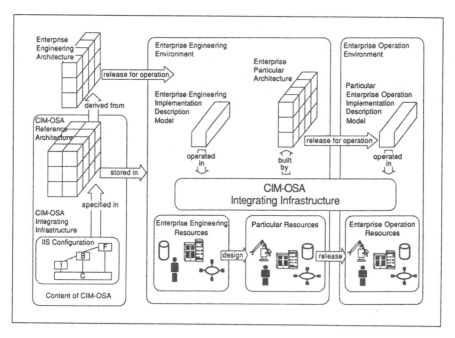

Fig. 2.5: Overview of CIMOSA Environments

Enterprise Operation Environment: in which Domain Processes are carried out and products developed, produced, marketed and sold, orders are issued and received, bills are paid and invoices submitted to customers in accordance with the procedures defined in the enterprise's Product Life Cycle. Support is provided for executing and controlling the Business Processes and Enterprise Activities of each Domain Process contained in the (released) Particular Implementation Description Model by this environment. This is illustrated in the right hand part of Fig. 2.5. The Particular Implementation Description Model is created in the Enterprise Engineering Environment and is transferred to the Enterprise Operations Environment by the Release Process.

Fig. 2.5 shows that both of these Enterprise Environments contain:

1. a common dynamic description of the system, the Released Implementation Description Model;
2. a common infrastructure - the **CIMOSA Integrating Infrastructure**, which provides a common and defined set of services and protocols enterprise wide;

3. the enterprise's **Physical System** in the form of a set of **Resources** (defined as a set of Implemented Functional Entities) providing the functionality required.

Within these two Integrated Environments CIMOSA provides support for the Business, Application and Physical levels of integration.

Business Integration is supported by the use of the Modelling Framework which permits the integration of control (management) of the enterprise's Decision System by means of activities linked into business processes, oriented to the results of the enterprise, and of the resources required to execute the enterprise activities.

Application Integration is supported by the use of the Integrating Infrastructure which provides services to integrate the enterprise's Information System which contains the information required to perform activities. Information is treated as an asset made available and managed system wide. The storage and location of information being transparent to the user (human, machine or computer).

Physical Integration, of the enterprise's Physical System, is supported either by the use of existing networking standards (e.g. OSI, MAP, TOP), or through proprietary networks, to permit the integration of the entities performing the enterprise activities, and of the communication required between all entities. Communications are provided as a common service in which both inter and intra system communication appear the same to the users.

References to Formal Reference Base (FRB Item)			
BO-1100	BO-1200	BO-1300	BO-2100
CO-1000	C4-1300	DO-1000	

2.5 Functional Entities and Functional Operations

The description of the CIMOSA Environments requires a generic element that can be used to describe the functionality of active components (i.e. resources).

Following the OSI-approach, where 7 types of so called Entities are used (Layer 1: Physical Entity --- Layer 7: Application Entity) CIMOSA introduces a generic construct called the Functional Entity. In CIMOSA this is used for the uniform modelling of functionality realized by Human Beings, Machines, Application Programs, Data Storage systems, Communication Services, etc.

The Functional Entity is an active element that can communicate, by means of the message passing principle, with other Functional Entities of a distributed processing system. This forces the designer to organize the complex functionality into autonomous areas which cooperate in a loosely coupled mode. This may sometimes appear inconvenient, but is considered the only way to organize distributable functionality safely. The Functional Entity is an implementation independent functional object able to send, receive, process (modify or interrogate) and even store information. Communication between Functional Entities is transaction oriented. A Transaction is a single bidirectional exchange of messages from a requestor to its responding partner and from the responder to the requestor in that order. CIMOSA distinguishes three major types of Functional Entities, humans, applications and machines. Examples of Functional Entities are human operators, expert systems, database systems, software packages such as CAD systems or MRP packages, NC machines, machining centres, robots, etc.

Functional Entities are integrated into processes via explicit links to Functional Operations. These Functional Operations are atomic, callable functions which can be performed by Functional Entities. They represent the lowest level of functional decomposition in a CIMOSA model at which it is necessary to have control over the autonomous Functional Entities. The functional capabilities of a Functional Entity are completely hidden for its cooperating partners. These capabilities are only visible through the set of Transactions agreed upon between the partner Functional Entities. These set of transactions is conveyed through their common channel.

Functional Entities and their associated Functional Operations may be rather simple or very complex units depending on the modelling detail intended and on the level of control that can be exerted over the autonomous operation of Functional Entities (i.e. an assembly line can be regarded as one entirely autonomous Functional Entity with one Functional Operation 'assemble product' or the individual steps of assembly can be modelled as a set of Functional Operations carried out on an assembly workstation identified as a set of Functional Entities). The exclusively local data access and the clearly defined interaction principle, has a number of advantages for functional design and implementation of information processing systems:

- It enables (and forces) the designer to unambiguously assign responsibilities to autonomous functional objects. In this way each Functional Entity will represent an area of responsibility which it can control autonomously, and which does not need communication with other Functional Entities except such as can be modelled by asynchronous Transactions. This approach will lead to the production of well defined inter-communicating objects.
- It permits concurrent execution of Functional Entities and so enables an easy implementation on distributed DP-equipment.
- It provides asynchronous mode of cooperation allowing robust distributed applications to be constructed.
- It supports common cooperation of Functional Entities, independent of whether the cooperating instances are implemented on the same, or separate target devices. This gives vital design freedom to configure or reconfigure distributed applications.
- It is easy to extend and to modify an overall system.

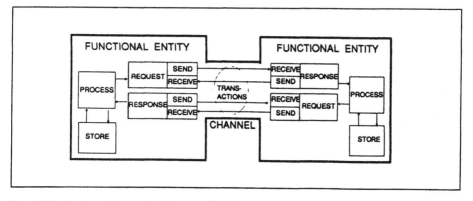

Fig. 2.6: Behaviour of interacting Functional Entities

Fig. 2.6 illustrates the generic behaviour of two interacting Functional Entities. The activities of a Functional Entity always result in a request to be sent to a partner entity or in a response to be re-sent to a partner entity (upon a request sent by this partner). Once a Functional Entity has received a request or a response from a partner it takes full responsibility for this data. The partner then is unable to re-access his issued data.

2.6 CIMOSA Integrating Infrastructure

The CIMOSA Integrating Infrastructure (IIS) is the enabling technology which makes it possible to execute the CIMOSA models, i.e. to control and monitor day-to-day enterprise operations described in the models. It provides a unifying software platform to achieve integration of heterogeneous hardware and software components of the CIM system. The CIMOSA Integrating Infrastructure is made of five entities:

Business Entity: provides generic functions to control the enterprise operations according to the contents of the CIMOSA model.

Information Entity: provides generic functions for data access, data integration and data manipulation.

Presentation Entity: provides generic functions to support the integration of enterprise components (i.e. Resources).

Common Services Entity: provides common services to the other Entities (e.g. message passing, naming, authentication/security, ...).

System Management Entity: provides generic functions to set up, monitor and maintain the Information Technology (IT) components.

A more detailed explanation of the CIMOSA Integrating Infrastructure is presented in Section 5 of this document.

3   The CIMOSA Modelling Framework

The first major concept of CIMOSA to be presented in detail is that of the CIMOSA Modelling Framework including the Reference Architecture. This is presented first in order that the other two major integrated concepts (the CIMOSA System Life Cycle and the CIMOSA Integrating Infrastructure) may be presented and cross referred to the Modelling Framework. This does not imply any one of these concepts is paramount but is simply a way of structuring the presentation of these inter-related concepts.

Requirements:

The CIMOSA approach to an Open System Architecture leads to the identification of a number of requirements to be satisfied by the Reference Architecture and an enterprise's Particular Architecture, its models and their derivations:

■   Models must be derived and optimised for a particular enterprise according to a common reference framework.

- Models should clearly reflect the established enterprise decision making processes, its organisation, its activities, its business processes, its information interchange and its material flows, in a form easily understood by the user and suitable for transformation into a processable implementation.
- Models should be amenable to flexible modification, in order to reflect the changing enterprise environment, constraints and operations, and in particular to be capable of reflecting system implementations which are built in an evolutionary manner (model maintenance).
- Models and their supporting guide-lines should assist and guide the user in the design, implementation and operation phases of systems in a wide range of manufacturing industries.
- The Reference Architecture and its supporting guide-lines should guide the vendor in the design, implementation and marketing of systems and system components.
- Models have to support different people involved in the various phases of modelling an enterprise. It must be possible to re-present the contents of the model to different users according to their specific view of the enterprise through out the system life cycle.
- System engineering support has to assure overall model and system consistency. This design support system must relate new designs, or modification of existing designs, to the existing description of the enterprise system and to provide design choices for new system components.
- System operational support has to provide the integrating mechanism between the many parts of an enterprise, through enterprise-wide information interchange.

User Design Phases of a Particular Architecture using CIMOSA:

These needs presuppose an architectural design which can be arrived at in three distinct, but integrated, phases.

1. To support the **capture of the enterprise's requirements** via a mapping against a common, neutral, supporting reference framework to achieve a consistent set of requirements (this process is termed *Instantiation*).
2. To **organise the captured requirements** in a form in which they can be realised by a **controlled set of Information Technology applications** (we have called this process *Derivation*).
3. To **support the analysis and synthesis of specific aspects** (*Views*) of the enterprise (this process is called *Generation*).

The resultant particular system description must be modular in nature. Such modularity is the key to achieve flexibility, and to enable the identification and context of standards.

3.1 CIMOSA Reference Architecture

The two Reference Architecture levels (Generic Level and Partial Level) of CIMOSA contain all the constructs[10] required to describe (model) the systems of a particular enterprise in an integrated way. The basic CIMOSA constructs comprising the CIMOSA meta-model are defined as follows:

---

[10] Throughout this document the term construct is used as a generic term to cover all forms of modelling entities

50

Generic Building Block (GBB): This is the most abstract form (or super-type) of a modelling construct. Generic Building Blocks form the basic elements of the "modelling language".

Building Block Type (BBT): This is a specialisation (or a sub-type) of a Generic Building Block. Building Block Types are specific words of the "modelling language".

Building Block: This is a (partial or full) instantiation of a Generic Building Block or a Building Block Type. Building Blocks are the sentences expressed in the "modelling language".

Model: This is a consistent aggregation of Building Blocks. This is a consistent set of sentences expressed in the "modelling Language".

Partial Model: It is an incomplete model made of partially or fully instantiated Building Blocks. Partial Models are predefined sentences expressed in the "modelling language".

Furthermore we need to define two other terms: instance and occurrence of a construct.

Instance: It is a user-particularised Generic Building Block or Building Block Type in the Enterprise Engineering Environment (partial or particular instance).

Occurrence: It is copy of an instance to which run-time variables have been added. It is an object of the Enterprise Operation Environment.

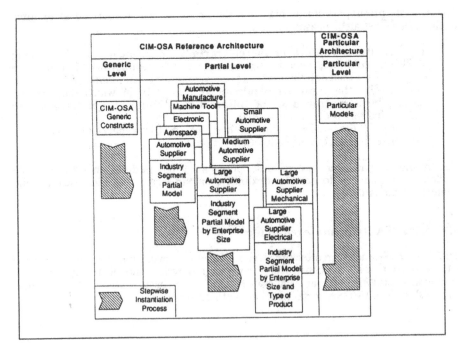

Fig. 2.7: Partial Level

The **Reference Architecture** contains Generic Building Blocks and Building Block Types at the Generic Level and Partial Models at the Partial Level.

The Generic Level is a reference catalogue of basic CIMOSA architectural constructs (Generic Building Blocks, and Building Block Types) for components, constraints, rules, service functions and protocols. Constructs described at this level have the widest application in CIM.

The Partial Level improves the economy of the CIM system design process by providing architectural constructs (the Partial Models) applicable to more specific, but still generic, kinds of enterprises (see Fig. 2.7). Partial Models are like macro-constructs since they represent *re-usable models* for large areas (e.g. Purchasing) or specific aspects (e.g. MRP) of a manufacturing enterprise. These macro-constructs are created from the Generic Building Blocks or Building Block Types of the Generic Level. This partially-instantiated set of Partial Models is also a reference catalogue.

The Generic level is populated with constructs by the Design Authority for CIMOSA (currently ESPRIT Project AMICE but in future the Standards Organisation that inherits the authority for CIMOSA). The Partial level is considered to be an open set populated by AMICE, standardisation bodies, trade associations, component suppliers, and even by internal work in particular enterprises.

For the creation of the **Particular Architecture** instances of both genericity levels of constructs are used. The relationships between the Reference Architecture and the Particular Architecture are expressed in the Instantiation Process of the CIMOSA Model Creation Processes.

The internal structure and the different constructs of the CIMOSA architectural levels are described in the remainder of this text.

References to Formal Reference Base (FRB Item)		
B0-2000	B0-3000	B0-4000

3.2 CIMOSA Modelling Levels

As briefly introduced in Section 2, CIMOSA provides three Modelling Levels to define, prototype, specify and finally describe (part of) the enterprise:

1 the Requirements Definition Modelling Level **defines what is required**, namely the required structure, content, flow of control and capabilities.
2 the Design Specification Modelling Level **specifies what technology is to be employed and how it is to be used** to implement the requirements, namely the detailed design of the functional system (Design Specification Model) in terms of Functional Operations and the employed Resources. Time and system behaviour (using system states and occurrences) are also dealt with.
3 the Implementation Description Modelling Level **describes the actual implementation** in terms of vendors' products (i.e. the Decision System and the Physical System of the enterprise).

In order to provide decision criteria, user inputs have to be provided at each CIM system definition stage (i.e. at the three Modelling Levels). The three modelling levels allow modelling of end user aspects and the CIM system aspects of the

52

enterprise at various abstraction levels. The Requirements Definition Model contains a number of fundamental business aspects (objectives, constraints, functions, information and material, capabilities, resources, rules and organisation) which can be isolated in Views to reduce model complexity. All of these aspects must be accurately reflected in the final Implementation Description Model. Fig. 2.8 shows how the CIMOSA Derivation Process gathers all of these aspects into each Modelling Level.

Analogies to the three Modelling Level approach of CIMOSA can be found in Electronic Circuit Design (Functional, Logical and Physical Design), in Software Engineering (Requirement Analysis, Logical and Physical Design) and in Database Design (Requirements Specification, Conceptual Design, Logical and Physical Database Design). However, these are analogies only in terms of a three phase structuring concept. As will be seen later (Section 4 - System Life Cycle) the content of each of the CIMOSA levels is much richer than any one of these three analogies.

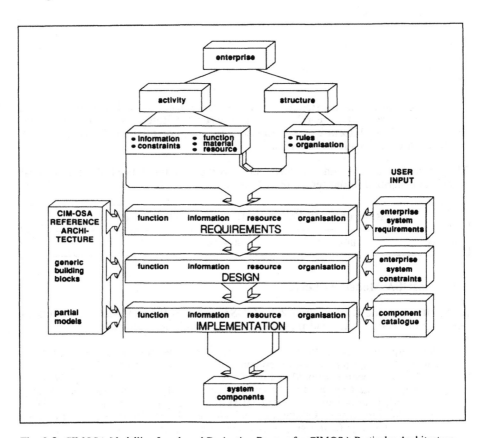

Fig. 2.8: CIMOSA Modelling Levels and Derivation Process for CIMOSA Particular Architecture

CIMOSA analysis starts with requirements definition, then considers all enterprise constraints (business and system capabilities) to provide a globally optimised set of enterprise requirements and ends with system description (component specification, component selection, component implementation, system qualification and release).

To assist the analysis CIMOSA provides a set of generic building blocks for each modelling level the templates for these are presented in Part 3 of this document.

Fig. 2.9 summarises the present list of CIMOSA Generic Building Blocks and their distribution across the different CIMOSA Modelling Levels with attachment to the most relevant View. All the constructs are mapped onto the Generic Level of the CIMOSA Reference Architecture.

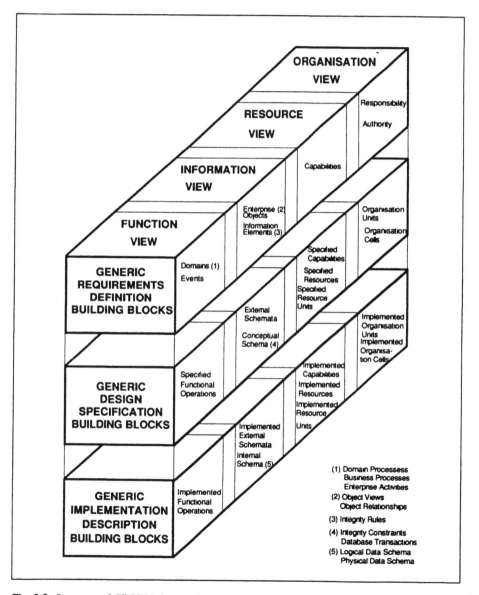

Fig. 2.9: Overview of CIMOSA Generic Building Blocks

The following sections provide the detailed description of each CIMOSA Modelling Level. The full description of these modelling levels and constructs is given in the CIMOSA Formal Reference Base.

References to Formal Reference Base (FRB Item)			
B1-2000	B2-2000	B3-2000	B4-2000

3.2.1 Requirements Definition Modelling Level

3.2.1.1   Purpose

The **Requirements Definition Modelling Level** provides a user friendly language with which to gather and express the business requirements of a particular enterprise from different standpoints (or views). It is also sometimes called the user level.

At the Requirements Definition Modelling Level a **Particular Requirements Definition Model** is produced, by the end user, which states in a business sense and terminology "what" has to be done within the enterprise (or part of an enterprise), but leaving aside technical issues concerning the technology to be used and the details of the actual implementation, in terms of the following aspects:

- functional and behaviour needs,
- information requirements[11],
- resource requirements, and
- organisational requirements.

Particular Requirements Definition Models provide a description of the enterprise system requirements in terms of the enterprise objectives. They also have a relationship with the outside world (environment) since they have to reflect business constraints as well as to recognise the relevant inputs and outputs.

This is the domain of the user and his business requirements. It still leaves options for the system implementation to be chosen at both the Design Specification and the Implementation Description Modelling Levels. The level of details of the model obtained at this level is left to the users but it must state the required basic functionalities and capabilities as well as the objects to be handled. For instance, at the Requirements Definition Modelling Level the requirement may simply be "the automated machining of rotational parts", leaving technical decisions on the type of machines and their supplier to the two other modelling levels. In general, the CIMOSA Particular Requirements Definition Model:

- need not necessarily be complete
- need not necessarily be consistent
- is processable by a computer supported tool for limited on-line consistency checking
- can be entirely described by end-users

This model is later updated according to decisions or choices made at the Design Specification Modelling Level or even at the Implementation Description Modelling Level due to the iterative nature of the Derivation Process. Thus CIMOSA

---

11   The business users' view of required information

maintains a consistent description of requirements, design and implementation aspects of a given enterprise.

References to Formal Reference Base (FRB Item)
BO-4100

3.2.1.2   Users

The requirements modelling level is concerned with the specific needs of those enterprise members who achieve the integration benefits. CIMOSA collectively refers to these as Business Users. They have knowledge in their particular field (E.G. purchasing, production management,) but are not expert in information technology. Therefore they are not required to have knowledge of, nor need they be concerned with, implementation concerns. The Business Users can be further classified into management, process or product engineers, R&D engineers, master schedulers, etc.

3.2.1.3   Constructs

AMICE is using a Process/Activity/Operation approach to support modelling in the Function View across the three modelling levels. This paradigm can be outlined as follows:

Within an enterprise tasks are usually organised into sub-tasks which need to be realised to achieve the business objectives. In the Process/Activity/Operation approach an enterprise is seen as a collection of inter-related but non-overlapping domains, which are subsets of the enterprise. These domains exchange objects between themselves and with other (supplier & client) domains external to the enterprise. Within each domain (unsolicited) real-world happenings and requests to do something will occur. They are described as events of the enterprise. which initiate the execution of (domain) processes. These processes are subdivided into activities interconnected by sets of rules defining the 'flow of control' within the (domain) process. To represent tasks and actions performed within an enterprise CIMOSA forces users to think in terms of Domain Processes, Business Processes, Enterprise Activities and Functional Operations, where Functional Operations define the lowest level of functional granularity. Enterprise Activities are made of Functional Operations while Domain Processes and Business Processes group activities (and may be sub-processes) to form logical chains of activities interconnected by rules. Thus the enterprise is modelled as an event driven network of rule based processes. Functional Operations are ignored at the Requirements Definition Modelling Level and are specified and described at the Design Specification and the Implementation Description Modelling Levels.

The information language proposed to business users is essentially based on the concepts of Enterprise Objects (or simply Objects), Object Views (or external views), and Information Elements. However, to capture more of the semantics of information, concepts of Object Relationships, Object Abstraction Mechanisms and Integrity Rules have been added. Furthermore, Versions and Variants are two constructs used to define Configuration Management requirements on Enterprise Objects.

Domains define portions of the business that are being addressed, establishing the scope of the functional areas subject to CIM system analysis and implementation.

Domains are characterised by means of their Domain Objectives, Domain Constraints, Domain Relationships and their list of Domain Processes.

Domain Objectives are business goals defined in terms of measurable and realistic end results for the enterprise's business to be performed in the Domain.

Domain Constraints are business limitations on measurable and realistic desired end results for the enterprise's business to be performed in the Domain and the operational boundaries imposed by outside forces.

Domain Relationships define the interactions between two related Domains (in terms of Events and Object Views).

Events describe (unsolicited) real-world happenings, timers or requests to do something in the enterprise. There are two types of enterprise events relative to any Domain: those exchanged between one Domain and another (external events) and those originating and handled within one Domain (internal events). Their occurrences are used to activate the processing of the Domain Processes (and possibly the Business Processes) of the enterprise.

Domain Processes are stand-alone processes triggered by nothing but Events and producing defined end results. They encapsulate a well-defined set of enterprise functionality and behaviour to realise clearly defined business objectives (Domain Objectives) under given constraints (Domain Constraints).

Business Processes are user-defined sub-processes of Domain Processes defining pieces of enterprise behaviour. They are made of other Business Processes and/or Enterprise Activities. The prime purpose of Business Processes is to describe the rule based flow of control (or behaviour) within a Domain of an enterprise.

Procedural Rules define the flow of action describing the behaviour of a Domain Process or a Business Process. There are five types of Procedural Rules: forced, conditional, spawning, rendezvous, iteration. (These are components of Generic Building Blocks).

Enterprise Activities define the enterprise functionality as elementary tasks defined by their inputs, their outputs, their function and their required Capabilities. The prime purpose of Enterprise Activities is to describe the "things to be done" (or functionality) within a Domain of an enterprise.

Capability defines technical abilities required by an Enterprise Activity and constraining resource selection.

Objective/Constraint is a, general, unified construct used to describe objectives and constraints of any kind (Domain Constraints, Domain Objectives, objectives and constraints of any kind of enterprise functions).

Declarative Rules describe imposed business rules as formal combinations of objectives and constraints with conditions impacting the behaviour of a Domain Process or of its sub-servant Business Processes and Enterprise Activities.

Enterprise Objects describe generalised entities (or objects) of the enterprise which can thought as a whole. They are composed of sub-objects (i.e. other Enterprise Objects) and/or Information Elements.

Object Abstraction Mechanisms define natural, semantic, links among Enterprise Objects such as generalisation and aggregation. (Not a Generic Building Block).

Object Relationships define application dependent, user-defined, links among pairs of Enterprise Objects.

Object Views describe external manifestations of one or more Enterprise Objects as they are perceived by some group of users or used by Enterprise Activities. They are made up of Information Elements and/or other Object Views. CIMOSA distinguishes between physical Object Views (representing physical objects) and information Object Views (representing information entities).

Information Elements describe elementary, i.e. atomic, pieces of information as perceived by users.

Integrity Rules express user-defined constraints on Information Elements to ensure their consistency.

Versions are configurations of an Enterprise Object created at a given date.

Variants define new types of configuration of an Enterprise Object. They do **not** supersede previous object variants.

Responsibility defines engineering responsibilities for the creation and maintenance of specific modelling activities.

Authority assigns engineering responsibilities for the creation and maintenance of specific modelling activities.

References to Formal Reference Base (FRB Item)			
B0-3100	B0-3200	B0-3300	B0-3400
B1-, B11-series Items	B2-, B21-series Items	B3-, B31-series Items	B4-, B41-series Items

3.2.1.4   Model Creation

Summarising the CIMOSA modelling approach Fig. 2.10 shows the relations between the Generic Building Blocks at the Requirements Definition Modelling Level. These representations remain valid for both the Partial and for the Particular Modelling Levels.

A Domain is made of a non-empty set of Domain Processes and Resources (including Functional Entities) processing real-world objects. Domain Processes are interconnected by Events and the Enterprise Objects exchanged between the Domain Processes. Each Domain Process is made of a hierarchy of Business Processes and Enterprise Activities (See Fig. 2.11). This provides a rule based means to respond to Events. Domain Processes contains at least one Enterprise Activity. The Business Processes just provide a convenient way for users to structure the model as easy manageable (re-usable) blocks to deal with complexity of their model. In fact once completely designed a Domain Process equates to a network of Enterprise Activities, interconnected by Procedural Rules, which can be entered at several entry points under well-defined conditions (starting triggering conditions).

In order to structure the modelling task CIMOSA uses the principle of 'windows' to provide users with selective Views of the enterprise model. As modelling proceeds the user will define, in an iterative manner, building blocks belonging to both the

58

Function and Information Views. (there being no Resource or Organisation View constructs at this level of modelling).

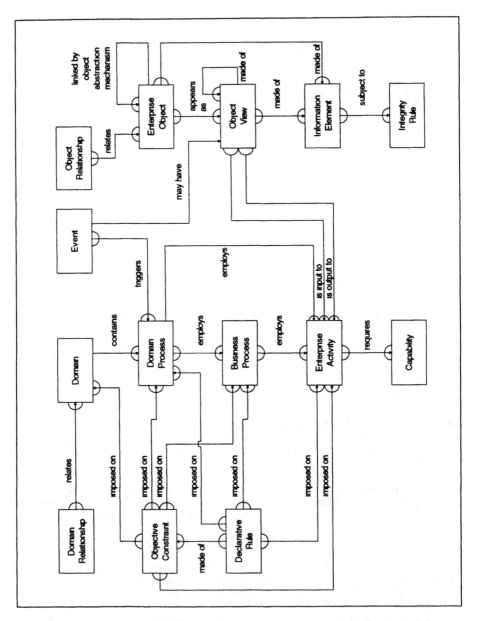

Fig. 2.10: Generic Building Blocks and their Relations at the Requirements Definition Modelling Level

At the Requirements Definition Modelling Level the first step is to establish the Domain(s) to be analysed and to define the Domain's Objectives and Constraints.

The key task is to identify all Domain Processes (i.e. Domain functionalities) of the enterprise that are relevant to achieve the set of objectives. Starting from the Domain Objectives the objects to be produced by the domain functionalities are identified (Domain outputs). Taking into account the Domain Constraints the Domain Objects (Domain inputs) required for the desired outputs are defined. Relations between input and output object(s) define the required Domain Processes. Origins and destinations of Domain Objects (defined as Object Views) together with external Events identify the Domain Relationships with other domains (whether CIMOSA compliant or not).

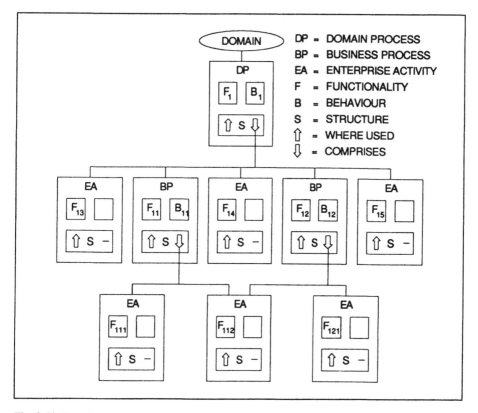

Fig. 2.11: Functional Decomposition at the Requirements Definition Modelling Level

Next, capacity and performance targets, cost constraints and organisational constraints, and so on, are used to detail all the identified Domain Processes. This is done by identifying the lower level Business Processes and Enterprise Activities which are employed, and by defining a set of Procedural Rules for each process describing its behaviour (flow of control between Enterprise Activities). Using the relevant Enterprise Activity construct, for each Enterprise Activity identified, the inputs and outputs (function and control) are defined as well as the Required Capabilities to be provided by the supporting Resources.

Function Inputs, Function Outputs, Control Inputs defined by Object Views are structured and detailed in the Information View. Starting from the Inputs and Outputs of defined Enterprise Activities, Object Views and Information Elements are identified. Then Enterprise Objects and Object Relationships are derived from the definitions of Object Views, and Integrity Rules are expressed on Information Elements to assure information consistency.

The Required Capabilities are defined in the form of:

- Functional Capabilities, i.e. those capabilities required to perform the function of the Enterprise Activity
- Object oriented capabilities i.e. those capabilities related to the object on which the function is performed
- Performance Capabilities, i.e. those capabilities related to the required performance, such as throughput, availability, yield, flexibility, recovery, etc.
- Operational Capabilities, i.e. those capabilities concerned with technical requirements (restrictions, constraints) with respect to the physical realisation of the Enterprise Activity, including requirements from the operational environment with respect to how the Enterprise Activity has to be realised (e.g. operator-less mode of operation or monitoring or reporting capabilities).

References to Formal Reference Base (FRB Item)			
B0-4000	B0-4100	B0-4200	B0-4300

3.2.2 Design Specification Modelling Level

3.2.2.1 Purpose

The **Design Specification Modelling Level** is concerned with technical choices as to **the technology to be employed** to achieve the enterprise goals. It provides an appropriate computer processable language with which to describe and evaluate alternative technical designs in order to select the best available technical solution(s) to provide the total set of required Capabilities as defined at the Requirement Definition Modelling Level and to quantify the total capacity required. At the Design Specification Modelling Level the intention is to quantify the total capacity of a required resource without regard as to product selection or plant layout. Such matters are deferred to the Implementation Description Modelling Level so rendering the Design Specification Model independent of implementation issues and giving the greatest possible flexibility.

The Requirement Definition Model is further detailed in terms of using the chosen technologies producing a logically restructured representation of the required CIM system, the **Particular Design Specification Model**, defined according to business requirements, business constraints and technical constraints. The role of the Design Specification Modelling Level is to decouple the Requirements Definition Modelling Level from the Implementation Description Modelling Level to reduce the impact of changes from one level to the other. It forms a stable base between the business requirements definition and the description of the final system implementation. The modelling is carried out by system designers who optimise the different user requirements from a global enterprise stand-point in terms of business needs and system resource capabilities. Note however that several models can be derived, tested and compared at this level and that the "best" one is selected for implementation. For instance, considering the available Manufacturing Technology and the economical aspects, the decision may be made at this Modelling Level to use a 5-axis machining centre for the automated machining of rotational parts.

The Design Specification model must deal with time and occurrences as well as function, information and resource behaviour to deal with system states. Design activities involved include: resource design, functional design, behaviour design, information system design, resource management definition, organisation structure design, etc. At the Design Specification Modelling Level a Particular Design Specification Model is produced to cover the following aspects:

- Logical grouping of resource objects in terms of Resources, Resource Units and their Capabilities and a detailing of Enterprise Activities in terms of the employed resources (Functional Operations),
- Consistent and optimised grouping of Domain Processes, Business Processes, Enterprise Activities and Functional Operations for each Domain of an Enterprise,
- Consistent and non-redundant grouping of information entities expressed as a Conceptual Schema in terms of entities, relationships and integrity constraints,
- Logical grouping of Organisation Units into Organisation Cells to define the organisation structure and business responsibilities and authorisations.

The resulting Design Specification Model

- must be complete and consistent
- must be transferable into code
- must be executable for simulation purposes, i.e. it must provide a time horizon
- must be detailed and optimised in cooperation between end-users and system analysts

References to Formal Reference Base (FRB Item)
BO-4200

3.2.2.2   Users

The design specification level is concerned with the specific needs of those enterprise members who have the objective to provide to their clients, the Business Users, the system design(s) which best satisfies the users' needs. CIMOSA collectively refers to these as System Analysts. The System Analysts which deal with the Function, Resource and Organization views are also called industrial engineers. Those which deal with the Information View are usually called information analysts.

3.2.2.3   Constructs

The constructs of the Design Specification Modelling Level are used to derive a consistent formal specification from the end user defined enterprise requirements. Constructs inherit properties from the Requirement Definition Level, and when they have been finally refined and transformed into a formal definition they are given the status "Specified" at the Design Specification Level. Constructs forming part of intermediate design solutions are given the status "Alternative". In addition to the specified form of the CIMOSA constructs Event, Domain Process, Business Process and Enterprise Activity the following additional constructs are provided:

62

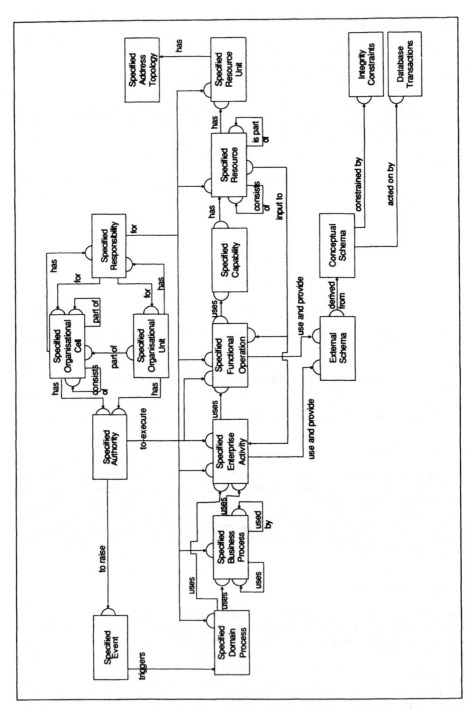

Fig. 2.12: Generic Building Blocks and their Relations at the Design Specification Modelling Level

Specified **Functional Operations** are the basic units of work executed by subsets of Specified Resources known as Specified Functional Entities. When interconnected by a finite algorithm (Activity Behaviour) they specify the internal functionality of Specified Enterprise Activities.

Conceptual Schema is a semantic data model of the CIM Information System with all data redundancies removed. It comprises a data model expressed in terms of the Entity-Relationship-Attribute (ERA) Methodology. It is an information modelling approach used to formally define the semantic data model for the Conceptual Schema, its External Schemata and Integrity Constraints in terms of Entities, Relationships, their Attributes and Abstraction Hierarchies on Entities.

External Schemata represent Object Views in the Design Specification Model involved in the Inputs and Outputs of Specified Enterprise Activities as well as temporary groups of data (called sub-schemata) as used by Specified Enterprise Activities. They are defined in terms of the semantic data model used.

Integrity Constraints formally specify the Integrity Rules expressed at the Requirements Definition Modelling Level in terms of the semantic data model.

Database Transactions specify the dynamic properties of data and information (i.e. data processing operations) as described on Conceptual and External Schemata.

Alternative **Resources** specify alternative design solutions which are evaluated in order to make a technical choice. They provide *defined* **Capabilities** which satisfy the required Capabilities defined at the Requirements Definition Modelling Level.

Specified **Resources** are derived from Alternative Resources by optimisation (making a technical choice) and are needed to make a product choice. They include *specified* Functional Entities which provide the *specified* Capabilities which meet or exceed the *required* Capabilities defined at the Requirement Definition level.

Specified **Capabilities**, provided by *specified* Resources, meet or exceed the *required* Capabilities defined at the Requirements Definition Modelling Level.

Alternative **Resource Units** represent the embodiments of alternative Resources.

Specified **Resource Units** represent the embodiments of Specified Resources.

The specified form of the CIMOSA constructs have the following roles:

Specified **Events** are formally defined specifications of both external and internal Events.

Specified **Domain Processes** are formally defined specifications of Domain Processes. They are defined by their triggering condition, made of Specified Events only, and their Process Behaviour.

Specified **Business Processes** are formally defined specifications of Business Processes. They are defined by their triggering condition and Process Behaviour.

Specified **Enterprise Activities** are formally defined specifications of Enterprise Activities. They are defined by their Function Input, Control Input, Resource Input, Function Output, Resource Output, Activity Behaviour and Ending Status. Activity Behaviour is a finite algorithm specifying the functionality and behaviour of Specified Enterprise Activities. Activity Behaviour is defined in terms of Specified Functional Operations.

Specified **Responsibility** are formally defined engineering responsibilities for the creation, and maintenance of specific modelling activities.

Specified **Authority** are formally assigned engineering responsibilities for the creation and maintenance of specific modelling activities.

References to Formal Reference Base (FRB Item)			
BO-3100	BO-3200	BO-3300	BO-3400
B1-, B12-series Items	B2-, B22-series Items	B3-, B32-series Items	B4-, B42-series Items

3.2.2.4   Model Creation

Summarising the CIMOSA modelling approach the following Figures show the relations between the Generic Building Blocks at the Design Specification Modelling Level (Fig. 2.12). These representations remain valid for both the Partial and for the Particular Modelling Levels. The prime task of the Design Specification Modelling Level is to establish a set of resources which together will provide the total set of Required Capabilities as defined at the Requirements Definition Level. This means that the capabilities of alternative technologies are investigated and the most appropriate "fit" selected whilst taking enterprise constraints into account.

The set of Functional Entities provided by the selected resources are then defined together with their associated Specified Functional Operations. It is then possible to provide a detailed specification of each Enterprise Activity in terms of its Activity Behaviour which is an algorithm employing Specified Functional Operations. This may well lead to a need for further detailing or updating of the functional structure. This means that the structure of some Domain Processes can be changed, that some Enterprise Activities may be further decomposed and become Business Processes, and that some Procedural Rule sets may be reorganised and enriched.

Another task of the system analyst is to add the time dimension into the model. This means that time must be attached to Events, state-transition diagrams must be provided to Enterprise Activities, duration of Functional Operations and Enterprise Activities must be evaluated, and synchronization of occurrences of activities must be considered.

Object Views are translated into External Schemata and then the External Schemata are aggregated to produce a global Conceptual Schema. Alternatively (to provide more user guidance and assure a priori consistency), the Conceptual Schema is defined first from the (a priori defined) Enterprise Object structure and then External Schemata are derived for Object Views. These External Schemata are then used to re-define the Function Input, Function Output, Control Input and Resource Output of the Specified Enterprise Activities and their constituent Functional Operations. From the Conceptual Schema Integrity Constraints and Database Transactions can be formally specified.

All these changes must be reflected in the Requirements Definition Model so that this model remains consistent with the Design Specification Model. However, since several iterations of the Design Specification Model may be maintained at the same time (to concurrently analyse several alternative solutions), the update of the Requirements Definition Model will be required.

Performance analysis of the model, taking into account qualitative and quantitative properties of the model, is used to assist in the evaluation of alternative technology solutions. Qualitative properties deal with structural properties (detection of deadlocks, inconsistencies, dead-ends, etc.). Quantitative properties concern system performance, detection of bottle-necks, etc. These analyses heavily rely on computer simulation of some parts of the model.

References to Formal Reference Base (FRB Item)			
B0-4000	B0-4100	B0-4200	B0-4300

3.2.3 Implementation Description Modelling Level

3.2.3.1   Purpose

The **Implementation Description Modelling Level** is concerned with **product choices as to the implementation of the various technologies** chosen at the Design Specification Modelling Level. It provides all the means to transform the content of the Design Specification Model into a complete computer executable description of the implemented system in terms of all specified, selected and implemented components. Relevant components are selected from CIM vendors' catalogues and will be implemented as the Physical System of the enterprise. These component descriptions together with other relevant information (flow of action, authorities, responsibilities) are the contents of the Implementation Description Model. This is the domain of the implementor and his system implementation.

The CIMOSA constructs at the Implementation Description Modelling Level are logically related to those provided for the Requirements Definition Modelling Level via those of the Design Specification Modelling Level. Thus there will be a fair chance that system components required will already exist in the market place, or can easily be implemented from an existing CIMOSA specification.

Like the two other Modelling Levels, the Implementation Description Modelling Level produces a Particular Model, the Implementation Description Model, which can be accessed via the four CIMOSA Views, which provides further detailing and structuring of the following aspects:

- Operational structure of enterprise functionality defined by means of Domain Processes, Business Processes, Enterprise Activities and Functional Operations
- Operational structure of enterprise information defined by means of an Internal Schema
- Operational structure of enterprise resources (including specifications of Implemented Components)
- Operational structure of the enterprise organisation

The Implementation Description Model (Fig. 2.13) is thus a description of the real world events, objects, processes, activities, resources and organisational units of the enterprise, in terms of all the tangible components used in its CIM system. These components are divided into three groups:

1) **Human Resources** involved in enterprise operations. Since people are an essential component of a CIM system it is necessary to describe them in functional terms. Human resources includes both people and their associated workplans.

2) **Manufacturing Technology** required to process materials, assemble products, pack and move them. Manufacturing Technology includes both machines and their required control programs.

3) **Information Technology** required to process and distribute data for all activities in the enterprise. The Information Technology therefore includes both the host hardware and application programs to be executed by the hardware.

Human Resources	Manufacturing Technology	Information Technology	
Work Plans	Machine Programs	Enterprise Engineering Software	Enterprise Operation Software
Human Skills	Control Programs	Integrating Infrastructure	
		Basic Data Processing Services	
People	Machines	Data Processing Devices	

Fig. 2.13: Components described in the Implementation Description Model

In addition to these operational concerns provision must also be made for the maintenance and revision of the enterprise environment for each operational task. Thus the CIMOSA Enterprise Engineering Environment must also be a component of the installed Information Technology.

The Implementation Description Model is used to describe functionality and behaviour of the Human Resources, Manufacturing and Information Technologies and communication between them. After completion the Implementation Description Model has to be finally released for model based operation, controlling and monitoring enterprise processes. It therefore:

- must be complete
- must be consistent and unambiguous
- is in computer executable form

References to Formal Reference Base (FRB Item)
BO-4300

Human Resources

These embrace all employees of the enterprise who are required to interact with the CIMOSA integrated part(s) of the enterprise:

- people to manage and operate computer - supported enterprise systems or parts thereof (CIM).
- people to design and develop products with computer-aided equipment (CAD).
- people to qualify product design and production with computer-aided equipment (CAQ).
- people to plan and operate product manufacturing with computer aided equipment (MRP/CAM).
- people operating manufacturing technology or performing manufacturing operations like transport, assemble, pack, etc.

Manufacturing Technology Components

These components embrace the widest possible aspects of manufacturing technology:

- machines to shape material - injection moulding, drilling and milling (DNC), flexible manufacturing systems (FMS).
- machines to assemble parts - component insertion machines, bandolier loaders, robots.
- machines to pack products - bottle filling machines, wrappers and fasteners.
- machines to transport goods - automatic guided vehicles, lorries, conveyers.

Many machines including robots, CAD, FMS contain 'intelligence' i.e. computer-like features. However, they are considered to be part of Manufacturing Technology since this intelligence is physically imbedded within the component.

Information Technology Components

These components are categorised under two headings:
Basic Data Processing Resources, and Application Software.

Basic data processing resources include:

- computer hardware
- communications networks
- basic software including microcode and firmware
- operating system software to control computer resources
- database management systems
- language compilers
- 'housekeeping' and other supervisory software
- services of the CIMOSA Integrating Infrastructure

Application software is generally specific to some user task. It can exist in two forms, one designed to be CIMOSA compliant from the start and the other as existing legacy systems surrounded by a 'wrapper' in order to be seen as CIMOSA compliant by the CIMOSA Integrating Infrastructure (see Section 3.3.1).

All Information Technology components are defined by part of the Implementation Description Model.

The **services** of the **CIMOSA Integrating Infrastructure** support the execution of application software by allowing them to run on the host hardware, while keeping application programs and hardware independent of each other. These CIMOSA services also support the Manufacturing Technology components by enabling them to communicate with the host system and to one another (see Section 5).

3.2.3.2   Users

The implementation description level is concerned with the specific needs of those enterprise members who have the objective of making an "executable" model, out of the "processable" one provided by the System Analysts. CIMOSA collectively refers to these as Implementors. By Implementor, we mean the whole category of users which range from the operating systems, communication and data base experts, to the system integrators. The Implementors usually perform the system installation and testing, create configurations (network, processes, other resources). In simple terms, their responsibility is to link the various kind of entities in the CIM environment, in other words the manufacturing and information technology components, complying with CIMOSA.

3.2.3.3   Constructs

The constructs of the Implementation Description Modelling Level are used to derive a consistent description of the real world system from the system analyst's implementation independent (logical) system design. Constructs inherit properties from both the Requirement Definition and Design Specification Levels, and when they have been refined and transformed into a computer executable form they are given the status "Implemented" at the Implementation Description Level. In addition to the implemented form of the CIMOSA constructs Event, Domain Process, Business Process, Enterprise Activity, Functional Operation, External Schema, Resource, Capability, Resource Unit the following additional constructs are provided:

Logical Data Model is (optionally) used to logically restructure the Conceptual Schema and its External Schemata in terms of a given database technology (relational model) before the Internal Schema can be specified.

Internal Schema is a construct, the content of which is derived from the Conceptual Schema of the Information View of the Design Specification Model. Its internal data structure is called a Physical Data Model.

Physical Data Model is the tailored and optimised physical data structure of the Internal Schema as it will be implemented in the CIM system. (Component of Building Block).

The implemented form of the CIMOSA constructs have the following roles:

Implemented **Events** describe how enterprise events initiate action by the physical system of the enterprise.

Implemented **Domain Processes** describe the implemented Domain behaviour.

Implemented **Business Processes** describe the implemented flow of control for a part of the behaviour of a Domain Process.

Implemented **Enterprise Activities** describe the implemented functionality as a control structure of Implemented Functional Operations and indicate physical resources (i.e. Implemented Resources) needed to execute this functionality.

Implemented **Functional Operations** represent the basic units of work (i.e. the basic actions) implemented to realise the functional content of Enterprise Activities. They are executed by active components of the Physical System (Implemented Functional Entities). Implemented Functional Operations consist of the functional description of the specified, selected and implemented components of the enterprise CIM system (static and dynamic). These relate to all Information Technology and Manufacturing Technology components.

Implemented **External Schemata** describe the final implementation form of External Schemata in SQL-like language.

Implemented **Resources** describe physical resources which are derived from Specified Resources at the Design Specification Modelling Level by selection (product choice). They include Implemented Functional Entities.

Implemented **Capabilities** describe capabilities which are provided by Implemented Resources and which comply with Specified Capabilities defined at the Design Specification Modelling Level.

Implemented **Resource Units** describe the embodiments of Implemented Resources.

Implemented **Responsibility** define engineering and operational responsibilities.

Implemented **Authority** assign engineering and operational responsibilities.

References to Formal Reference Base (FRB Item)			
B0-3100 B1-series Items	B0-3200 B2-, B23-series Items	B0-3300 B3-, B33-series Items	B0-3400 B4-series items

3.2.3.4   Model Creation

Summarising the CIMOSA modelling approach the following Figures show the relations between the Generic Building Blocks at the Implementation Description Modelling Level (Fig. 2.14). These representations remain valid for both the Partial and for the Particular Modelling Levels.

At the Implementation Description Modelling Level the actual physical implementation is derived from the system analyst's implementation independent (logical) model by making product and technical choices regarding:

- how the resources are to be provided,
- how and where data is to be stored and
- how the functionalities will be performed

Choosing, from vendors' catalogues, CIMOSA compliant components (Implemented Resources) whose capabilities exactly match or exceed the Specified Capabilities defined by the system analysts.

70

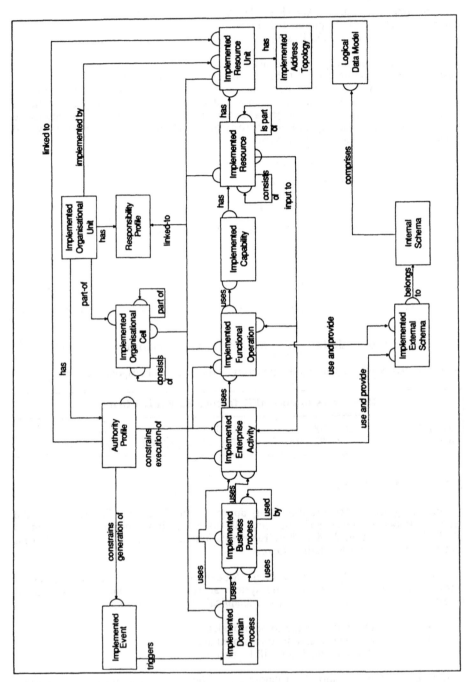

Fig. 2.14: Generic Building Blocks & their Relations at the Implementation Description Modelling Level

The Implementation Description Modelling Level describes the content of the real world system in terms of such components illustrated in Fig. 2.15. Thus all necessary manufacturing and information technology components are defined at this stage (including the services of the CIMOSA Integrating Infrastructure and the supporting data processing equipment). Specified Functional Operations are then mapped onto the Implemented Functional Entities provided by the chosen resources and implementation specific data added to the relevant External Schema, Enterprise Activities, Business Processes.

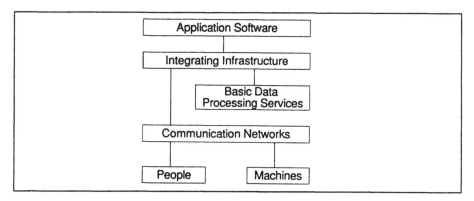

Fig. 2.15: Content of the Implementation Description Model

The physical implementation of the data storage system has to be designed by first deriving a Logical Data Model directly from the Conceptual Schema. This is a normalised data model in relational form. From this the Internal Schema is defined using a SQL-like language. It includes a Physical Data Model defining the data structure of the Information System and the final definition of the Integrity Constraints. External Schemata are finally described as Implemented External Schemata using the SQL view mechanism.

Also the communications network has to be designed and the data processing and manufacturing equipment assigned to nodes, etc. This model is then given to implementors for CIM system implementation (procurement and installation of resources), and used to verify the implementation. Finally it is released for operation.

References to Formal Reference Base (FRB Item)			
B0-4000	B0-4100	B0-4200	B0-4300

3.2.4 Relationships among the main CIMOSA Constructs

Fig. 2.16 shows the main relationships between the basic constructs of CIMOSA.

Function View, Information View, Resource View and Organisation View are four different Views of one and the same model. The Views are not separate unrelated parts of the model but inter-relate by means of relationships between constructs as established in the Reference Architecture.

72

This shows that:

1   an Organisational Unit <u>has</u> Authority <u>to execute</u> Enterprise Activities which operate <u>on</u> Enterprise Objects <u>with</u> the aid of Resources,
2   Object Views of Enterprise Objects <u>are inputs/outputs</u> of Enterprise Activities,
3   Enterprise Activities <u>require</u> Capability <u>provided</u> by a Resource,
4   an Organisational Unit <u>has</u> Responsibility <u>for</u> the design and maintenance of constructs.

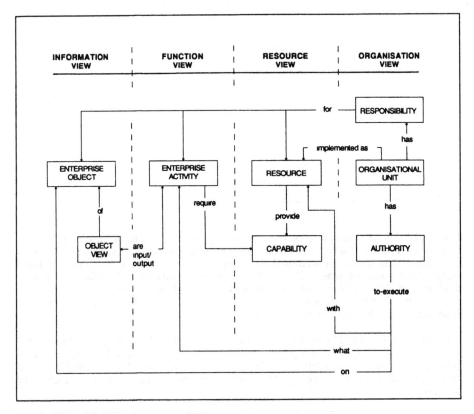

Fig. 2.16: Main Relationships among CIMOSA Constructs

3.3   The CIMOSA Modelling Approach

The major problem with any integration strategy is that of ensuring existing systems and applications can be integrated into any new scheme. It is always necessary to do so in order to preserve current and committed investments in plant and machinery.

3.3.1 Domains and Legacy Systems

The Domain concept provided by CIMOSA is very useful to deal with heritage and legacy systems of the enterprise[12], i.e. systems or models which must be incorporated in the CIMOSA model but must be used as they are (e.g. special manual operations, existing stand-alone automated systems, etc.). In this case they are defined as non-CIMOSA Domains, i.e. only their connectivity with CIMOSA Domains are defined but not their internal structure. Requests (i.e. Events) as well as objects or results (i.e. Object Views) can be sent or received to/from them. Therefore only the Domain Relationships (shared object views) have to be fully defined in CIMOSA terms. In Fig. 2.17 the Manufacturing Orders are related to the two Domain Processes by their Schema representations and the required run time conversions.

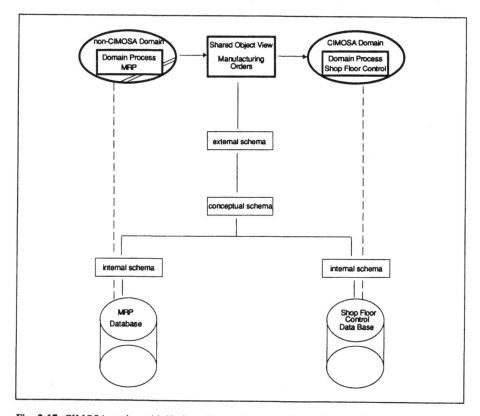

Fig. 2.17: CIMOSA coping with Heritage/Legacy Systems - Domain Process Cooperation

A different way of dealing with legacy systems is to encapsulate them in a CIMOSA Domain as Functional Entities providing well-defined functionalities which can be used by the CIMOSA model (e.g. existing database applications, Bill-of-Materials processors, in-house developed software packages, etc.). A software interface (called a wrapper) needs to be built around them to connect them to the

---

12   see part 4 for more details on enterprise integration with CIMOSA

CIMOSA model via a Presentation Service (see Fig. 2.18). In this case the MRP is directly controlled by the Domain Process Production Control.

3.3.2 Moving from SADT-like Models to CIMOSA Architectures

A number of organisations have already modelled their requirements using IDEF0 or SADT-like techniques. A gateway from these techniques to CIMOSA must be provided to help enterprises capitalise on their previous efforts.

SADT-like techniques essentially concentrate on functional decomposition for the purpose of requirements definition and essentially using one basic construct, the activity construct. They usually end up with a static (i.e. non executable) model with a clear-cut separation of functional and information features (i.e. non-integrated model). CIMOSA provides a much more precise and structured modelling language, enforcing separation of functionality and behaviour modelling and providing well-defined hooks between the Function View and the Information View as well as between the Function View and the Resource View of one integrated model.

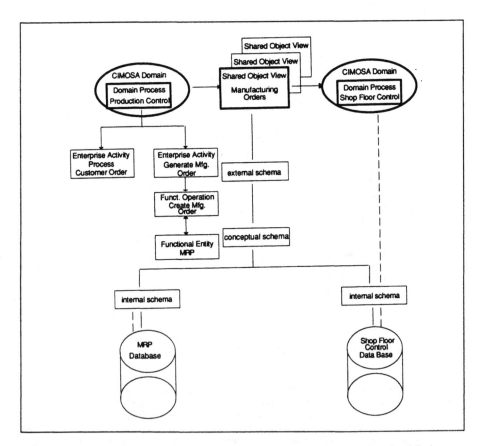

Fig. 2.18: CIMOSA coping with Heritage/Legacy Systems - Encapsulation as Functional Entity

In many cases, what is called the A0 and A1 levels in SADT models usually corresponds to Domains and Domain Processes in CIMOSA Architectures as long as they focus on realisation of major business objectives. Conversely, low-level functionalities in SADT models usually equate to Enterprise Activities in CIMOSA models. Intermediate SADT activities usually have to be restructured in terms of true Business Processes with a well-defined behaviour. Therefore it is possible to migrate from SADT results towards CIMOSA models without loosing too much of previous modelling effort and benefiting from a structured modelling methodology which will end up with a processable implementation model.

3.4   CIM Modelling - State of the Art

Computer modelling of manufacturing systems has two aspects, which are often closely interrelated:

Software systems to build or simulate models

Methodologies which provide different approaches for general system analysis, design and modelling.

State of the art in both fields (Section 6.3 [12] to [18]) has evolved over the years and several schools of thought have developed. CIMOSA has adopted the building block approach and tries to develop a finite set of constructs to enable description of the different aspects of enterprises during the different operational phases. These constructs will be executable by Information Technology to support simulation as well as real time operation of enterprise processes. Therefore CIMOSA is concerned with both Software Systems and Modelling Methodologies.

Modelling methodologies provide structured approaches for model building techniques. The different approaches depend upon the point of view of the model builder. Again different approaches have been chosen by different developers. General modelling methods such as EPOS, PSL/PSA, EXCELERATOR have been available for system analysis and design for many years. Also Computer Aided Software Engineering (CASE) tools have been employed - within limits - to the modelling of manufacturing systems. More specifically the methods (Section 6.4 [19] to [32]) have been applied successfully to manufacturing systems[13].

Some of these methods are supported by computerised tools. Most of them use building blocks of some kind. A method which has employed a more specific set of building blocks aimed at manufacturing modelling is the Integrated Manufacturing Modelling System (IMMS) [31]. The CIMOSA functional modelling approach has been significantly influenced by this work. The GRAI method [29] developed at the GRAI Laboratory of the University of Bordeaux is specially designed for the design and analysis of decision systems of production systems. The GRAI method provides both a modelling methodology as well as tools to apply the method. The M* methodology [32] has been designed to complement GRAI and IDEF methods in the area of information system design and analysis of CIM systems. It is based on an integrated model using high-level Petri Nets and an advanced entity-relationship

---

[13]   Yourdon-DeMarco [19], [20]
    Data Flow Diagrams [21]
    Jackson Method [22]
    SADT [23], [24], IDEF [25], [26], DAFNE [27])
    Petri Nets [28]
    GRAI method [29]
    Entity-Relationship-Attribute approach [30]

model and supports information modelling at the organisation level, conceptual level and implementation level of CIM enterprises. The CIMOSA information modelling approach has been significantly influenced by this work.

4   The CIMOSA System Life Cycle

The second major concept of CIMOSA is that of the CIMOSA System Life Cycle which provides the framework within which to control/manage the activities of creating, maintaining and revising the enterprise models.

4.1   The CIMOSA System Life Cycle

In an analogous way to products, the *enterprise system* which creates those products also goes through a life cycle of development and usage. Whilst today's enterprise systems are in operation, their successors may be in the process of implementation. Strategic business plans under development today will set the stage for the systems implementations of tomorrow. Thus as an enterprise evolves over time the enterprise's systems will go through life cycles. We call the enterprise system life cycle the System Life Cycle. During this System Life Cycle the various Domains, Domain Processes, Business Processes, etc. describing the enterprise's operations are defined, designed and developed.

CIMOSA defines the basic phases of the System Life Cycle in terms which are independent of the modelling methodology employed. CIMOSA does not populate the System Life Cycle with a set of unique processes but leaves it open for tool vendors to define their various proprietary methodologies in a CIMOSA compliant manner. Conformance to the CIMOSA Model Creation processes and the CIMOSA Model Consistency rules ensure that the end result is a CIMOSA compliant particular model.

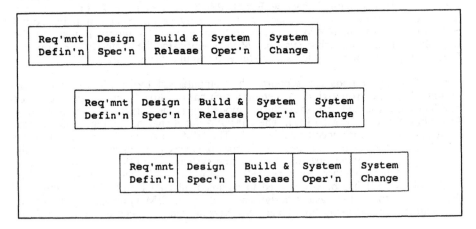

Fig. 2.19: Overlapping System Life Cycles

A single CIM sub-system within a particular enterprise may well be a standard product as far as the vendor of the basic sub-system is concerned, but when customised to a particular enterprise it becomes a one-off product as far as the particular enterprise is concerned. We need therefore to consider the life cycle phases appropriate to one-off products (Note: a different enterprise organisation could well be responsible for executing the tasks of each phase. For example System Operation (execution of product life cycle tasks) takes place in the Enterprise Operations Environment.).

The basic phases of the CIMOSA System Life Cycle (see Fig. 2.19) are:

DP-A: System Requirements Definition
DP-B: System Design Specification
DP-C: System Build and Release
DP-D: System Operation
DP-E: System Change

4.2 Relationships between the Product and System Life Cycles

In order that the tasks associated with each step of the Product Life Cycle may be executed in a controllable manner it will be necessary to define the procedures to be followed. These normally take the form of company standards, work instructions, process sheets, etc. Such procedures would be designed by executing a set of system design tasks which together form the System Life Cycle. Thus the Product and System Life Cycles are intimately inter-related.

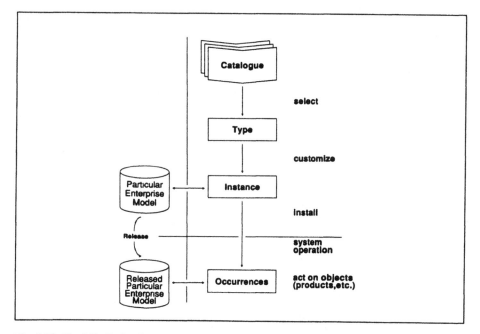

Fig. 2.20: The Life Cycle of a Business Process

In CIMOSA terms life cycle procedures are defined by a set of Domain Processes, Business Processes and Enterprise Activities which describe each task within the life cycle. Whenever it is required to define a new or revised Business Process supporting part of the Product Life Cycle procedures it will be necessary to carry out the tasks belonging to one or more phases of the associated System Life Cycle.

78

These will guide the design/revision processes leading to creation of the new set of enterprise procedures associated with a new version of a Product Life Cycle. The basic System Life Cycle for a CIMOSA Business Process which is part of a particular enterprise model is illustrated in Fig. 2.20. Here it is seen that the creation and execution of a Business Process involves the following basic tasks:

- select an appropriate type of Business Process from the generic level of the Reference architecture;
- particularise the selected Business Process Type by adding enterprise specific parameters to make an instance of the Business Process Type;
- release the Implementation Description Model, which contains the instance, into the operational system;
- add at execution time technical parameters and logistic variables to a copy of the released instance (an occurrence).

This shows that the release process acts as a 'bridge' between the two life cycles.

4.3 CIMOSA Environments

In order to permit the enterprise operations for one task within the Product Life Cycle to be designed/updated without interfering with the execution of current operational tasks CIMOSA has defined two mutually independent execution environments. Execution of Product Life Cycle tasks takes place within the Enterprise Operations Environment and of System Life Cycle tasks within the Enterprise Engineering Environment.

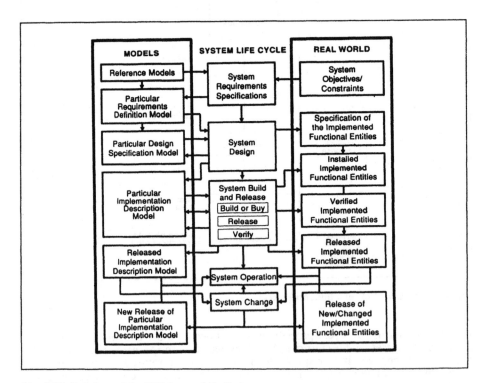

Fig. 2.21: Relations of the CIM System Life Cycle

4.4 Content of the CIMOSA System Life Cycle

Fig. 2.21 presents the CIMOSA System Life Cycle, with its relations to the CIMOSA models and to the real world implementation of a enterprise system. The arrows indicate the starting point of the different life cycle phase and the results they produce at their completion. The two-way arrows indicate iterating phases in the definition process. This diagram is for illustrative purposes only and does not imply that the System Life Cycle is to be implemented as a pure sequential phased process, various modelling methodologies being in practice possible. The rest of this Section outlines the various tasks which must be performed in order to create a complete model of (part of) the enterprise.

In the descriptions which follow, it should be noted that all the activities described within System Requirement Definition, System Design, and System Change are all performed within the CIMOSA Enterprise Engineering Environment, those of System Operation are performed within the CIMOSA Enterprise Operation Environment, whilst those of System Build and Release are not specifically supported by CIMOSA.

4.4.1 Business Objectives Determination

This part is not directly supported by CIMOSA, but it is a prerequisite for the System Life Cycle. Here, the enterprise's business objectives and constraints are determined for that part of the enterprise which is to be modelled and implemented according to CIMOSA. The objectives are specified in terms of such things as markets, product groups and volumes, return on investment (ROI) and profit goals. Constraints may also be imposed such as time scales, investment budgets, and so on.

4.4.2 System Requirements Definition

The first phase, "System Requirements Definition", is primarily concerned with the requirements definition and analysis activities used to build a CIMOSA Particular Enterprise Model. It addresses the parts of the enterprise (domains) to be modelled. This phase establishes a validated, integrated set of requirements for and constraints upon system implementation. While some implementation concerns are inevitably addressed, it is the intention that these concerns are minimised as far as possible so as to concentrate attention on the real underlying needs of an enterprise in a manner minimally compromised by envisaged system realisations. Conversely, where it is desired that the requirements specification is to be formed in a way which is constrained by the current implementation, explicit constraints are introduced during this phase to control the subsequent ones appropriately.

Starting from a set of given enterprise objectives, the contents of the Particular Requirements Definition Model for an enterprise domain are specified. During this process, decisions must be taken regarding the:

- Domain objectives and constraints
- Domain scope, contents and structure
- functional requirements
- information requirements
- capability requirements
- organisational allocations

The task of Requirement Definition can be considered under five headings:- Domain Establishment, Functional Decomposition, Behaviour Analysis, Information Analysis and Verification.

The purpose of the **Domain Establishment** is to identify and define the boundaries and global functionalities of that part of the enterprise which is relevant for achieving the given business objectives. This includes the identification of Domain Processes (global functionalities) which are performed within the Domain, Object Views (i.e. Domain Objects) handled and produced by the Domain, and Domain Relationships with other Domains. The key task in this process is to identify all Domain Processes (i.e. Domain functionalities) of the enterprise that are relevant to achieve the set of objectives.

The purpose of the **Functional Decomposition** is to define the triggering conditions (in terms of Events) and the functional structure of the Domain Processes identified during Domain Establishment, and their further decomposition into Business Processes and Enterprise Activities as input to the Behaviour Analysis phase.

The purpose of the **Behaviour Analysis** is to define the internal behaviour of the Domain Processes and Business Processes which have been decomposed, and thereby defining the dynamic flow of control governing the sets of lower level processes and activities of the Domain.

Here, capacity and performance targets, cost constraints and organisational constraints, and so on, are used to detail the Domain Processes defined during Domain Establishment. Thus, on the basis of a Domain definition, all Domain and Business Processes are decomposed to the level of Enterprise Activities only. In fact the resulting functional model behaves as a network of Enterprise Activities controlled by means of Events.

During this process the following decisions must be taken:

- Choice of the required flow of control (behaviour), considering the performance requirements and the imposed constraints
- Level of detailing (decomposition) of the Business Processes
- Organisational allocations for Business Processes and Enterprise Activities

As a result of the Behaviour Analysis and Functional Analysis the requirements definition of the set of Business Processes and the pool of Enterprise Activities for each Domain Process of the Domain has been completed. This is the basis for the system design. Each of these and all of the following phases are subject to verification (employing some form of type checking and computer simulation) wherever possible.

Information Analysis: Object Views are the links between Function View and Information View. The Domain Objects defined as Object Views during Domain Establishment and the inputs and outputs of the Enterprise Activities, considered to be Object Views, are subject to Information Analysis. Enterprise Objects are derived from Object Views and relationships (Object Relationships and Object Abstraction Mechanisms) are defined. Object Views and Enterprise Objects are composed of Information Elements which represent the smallest unit of information in the requirement definition process. The result of the Information Analysis process is the Particular Requirements Definition Model, Information View .

The purpose of the **Model Verification** is to consolidate the model, i.e. to ensure that the entire Particular Requirements Definition Model of the Domain is satisfactory and represents all the defined requirements:

System Requirements Change

The purpose of the "System Requirements Change" is to handle changes to the Requirements Definition Model which may be necessary because (a) the results of Model Consistency Checking have shown inconsistencies, or (b) the Domain Objectives and Constraints have been changed.

4.4.3 System Design

Purpose of System Design is to specify *HOW* the system requirements (i.e., the *WHAT*) defined in the Particular Requirements Definition Model should be implemented, taking into account the relevant enterprise policies and constraints. In the course of this process, the enterprise model is optimised.

The results of the system design process are:

- the decomposition of the required Enterprise Activities into executable Functional Operations and their Activity Behaviour (algorithm).
- the specifications and selection of the Functional Entities which will provide the required capabilities for the Enterprise Activities and related Functional Operations, data storage and communication;
- the defined location for each of the Functional Entities.

Tasks of System Design have the purpose of specifying quantitative descriptions of the required manufacturing and information technology components using the results of System Requirements Definition. Through material-flow (parts routing) and information-needs analysis, performance analysis, and so on, decisions are taken on such topics as:

- actual means of implementing Enterprise Activities, through selection from available activity parameter sets, and determination of Business Process 'instance parameter' sets, Functional Operations, and Enterprise Activity control structures (Design Specification Model Function View);
- volumes, storage location, internal-schemas, etc., of required information (Design Specification Model, Information View);
- volumes, physical location, performance, etc., of required resources (Design Specification Model, Resource View);
- volumes, location, performance requirements, IIS nodal configurations, etc., for functional components, Functional Operations (Design Specification Model, Resource View);
- responsibilities and authorisation for Domain, Domain Processes, Business Processes, Enterprise Activities, Resources, information, out-of-line situations, etc (Design Specification Model, Organization View);
- material flow models, material storage strategies and information models. (**NB:** models have not yet been defined to express these dynamic 'flow' aspects).

Functional, information and communication system design essentially results from the following tasks:

(1) **Specification of Alternative Component Sets:** identifies possible alternative component sets for the required Capabilities. From this set of alternatives the optimum system design is derived.

(2) **System Optimisation:** includes capacity requirements and flow analysis, and the specification of alternative Logical Cells (which are different clusters of components, allowing the optimisation between flow and performance vs resource utilisation). The results of system optimisation are design specifications which are expressed in the form of a Particular Design Specification Model.

(3) **Selection of the Component Sets:** is the task of selecting a set of actual components which meet or exceed the requirements of the design specifications. This is done considering the enterprise policies and constraints. The final build/buy decisions result in a model describing the total implemented enterprise system, now termed the Particular Implementation Description Model.

4.4.4 System Build and Release

Based upon the results and decisions of system design, System Build and Release is concerned with those activities necessary to bring the system into operation. This involves essentially the procuring (or building) of the necessary new or revised Implemented Functional Entities, integrating them into the existing system, and testing and releasing them for operation. The system build and release process is sub-divided into four lower level steps:

(1) **Build or Buy:** where the enterprise purchases or builds the Implemented Components decided upon during implementation system design and physically integrates them into the existing system. At the completion of build or buy the Implemented Functional Entities and underlying Implementation Description Model are said to be *installed*.

(2) **Verify Implementation:** here, the correct functioning of the installed Implemented Functional Entities, and the correctness of the underlying Particular Implementation Description Model, are verified in a close-to-operational environment. It is expected that the Integrating Infrastructure will, in support of this, provide a set of pseudo-operational facilities for the running of a test environment logically separated from, but physically integrated with, the current operational system. At the completion of this phase the Implemented Functional Entities and underlying Implementation Description Model are said to be *verified*.

(3) **Transfer to Operation:** consists of such activities as operator training and customer acceptance testing, and making the verified Implemented Functional Entities and the underlying Implementation Description Model ready for release into operation. They are then said to be *accepted*.

(4) **Release for Operation:** consists of finally releasing the accepted Implemented Functional Entities and underlying Particular Implementation Description Model for operation. The operational version of the accepted Particular Implementation Description Model is released, from the Integrated Enterprise Engineering Environment, for use by the Integrated Enterprise Operation Environment. It is then termed the *Released* Particular Implementation Description Model.

4.4.5 System Operation

In this phase the released system is operated in order to control the desired product life cycles, under operational support of the Integrating Infrastructure. This is accomplished via the creation, scheduling, and execution of parameterised instances of Business Processes, Enterprise Activities and Functional Operations derived from the underlying Released Particular Implementation Description Model

4.4.6 System Change

Changes to the Enterprise System are required because of change to either the business objectives, the business requirements, the available technology, or because the performance of the system has deteriorated over time.

From the above it can be seen that as the enterprises strive to adapt to an ever changing world, perpetual change becomes the rule and a process to cope with these changes in a controlled and efficient manner is required.

5   The CIMOSA Integrating Infrastructure

The third major concept of CIMOSA is that of the CIMOSA Integrating Infrastructure which not only provides the mechanism to integrate heterogeneous components (resources) but also provides the means to control (manage) the life cycle processes via the execution of CIMOSA compliant enterprise models. According to a definition derived from systems theory, a system is "a set of elements in dynamic interaction organised in accordance with an aim", the CIMOSA Integrating Infrastructure is a system. Its elements are a set of services, and its aim is to be able to execute models conforming to the CIMOSA modeling concepts.

This section presents the rationale which led to the design of the integrating infrastructure, its structure, and the definition of the different services identified.

5.1   Introduction

A number of audiences have been considered in order to develop the integrating infrastructure. These audiences are mainly:

- people who primarily want to know what specific functions are provided by the Services
- manufacturing enterprises who may wish to purchase Service profiles.
- users of the service who want to know how to invoke the Service functions
- vendors who wish to provide integrating infrastructure Service implementations in conformance to the integrating infrastructure service specifications.

The requirements that they put on the development of the integrating infrastructure, and the principle of open systems led us to distinguish two different representations of the integrating infrastructure: its "functional representation" and its "information technology (IT) representation".

The functional representation defines functional blocks which are hierarchically decomposed on two levels, and the structure and the mode of interaction between those blocks. This representation is unique, should be used as a reference and therefore be considered as a standard. It is independent from the current state of available technologies and implementation techniques.

The IT representation is identifying a possible way to implement the functional representation. It is designing a possible solution by identifying the IT components which could satisfy the specifications contained in the functional representation.

In fact, there may be as many "IT representations" as there are possible ways to implement the functional representation of the CIMOSA integrating infrastructure. We thereby provide a hosting mechanisms to take advantage of new technologies and still maintain the characteristics of an open systems environment.

CIMOSA provides the specifications of the components of the functional representation, and their mode of interaction, which constitute also the hosting mechanism. This mechanism is the only part of the IT representation that is of interest to CIMOSA. Using these specifications, vendors will have the possibilities to develop competitive edges in an open systems environment which is addressing the needs of the users.

References to Formal Reference Base (FRB Item)
C4-3120   C4-3205

5.2   Generic Functional Requirements

The CIMOSA Integrating Infrastructure is an information technology based infrastructure which supports a manufacturing environment while executing what has been described in a CIMOSA conformant model. From this general statement, we can derive the rationale for the first level of decomposition of the integrating infrastructure. We will here briefly outline the operation of a generic manufacturing enterprise and relate these to this decomposition.

Events and Behaviour Management

A typical manufacturing enterprise is subject to a great number of events, generated internally or externally, to which it has to react. To support this, the integrating infrastructure must be capable of behaving to events in a specified fashion. It should rely, for this purpose, on the definition of a domain model. The integrating infrastructure then uses this model to orchestrate the manufacturing processes of the enterprise. This highlights two basic requirements on the Integrating Infrastructure:

- It should accept events, and be able to relate them to relevant domain models;

- It should be able to interpret the behaviour described in the domain model, in order to launch and monitor successfully the identified processes on a set of available and appropriate resources.

This is the aim of a set of components of the Integrating Infrastructure called the "Business Services". These services use mainly the information presented in the function view and resource view of a CIMOSA model for this purpose.

Manufacturing Resources Management

Typical manufacturing resources, recognised as types by CIMOSA, for which the Integrating Infrastructure needs to be able to establish a dialogue with, are applications, machines and humans. The integrating infrastructure must be able to support all computerised applications used in the manufacturing processes. It must interact with manufacturing machines or devices at the shop-floor level to instruct them (e.g., by loading an NC tape) of the operations to be performed, to accept responses from them (e.g., load tool requests) and to be informed when the operations are completed or when a failure has occurred. It also needs to allow the humans, through a VDT (Visual Display Terminal), to interact on the processes, to instruct, receive or provide information.

These basic requirements are met by the set of components of the Integrating Infrastructure called the "Presentation Services". These services use mainly the information contained in the resource view of a CIMOSA model for this purpose.

Information Management

All enterprises handle a wide variety of information (e.g., orders, schedules, work in progress, NC tapes) and the integrating infrastructure must be capable of providing this information to the requestors in a transparent fashion, hiding the location of the data (e.g., local or remote), the filing method (e.g., database management system, file systems) and the manner in which the data are assembled (possibly from a number of database).

These basic requirements are ensured by the set of components of the Integrating Infrastructure called the "Information Services". These services use mainly the information contained in the information view of a CIMOSA model for this purpose.

Communication Management

Enterprises are also developing network infrastructures to link computer systems and machines together. They support message and information exchanges between systems and/or machines and are needed for the CIMOSA IIS to be active. The liaison with these infrastructures is one of the main roles of the "Common services" of the CIMOSA Integrating Infrastructure.

To summarise, the CIMOSA Integrating Infrastructure reacts to enterprise events by executing a CIMOSA conformant model. The CIMOSA Integrating Infrastructure hides the location, storage and physical placement of information and resources from the requestor of the information, and manages the link with the underlying communication infrastructure. The CIMOSA Integrating Infrastructure can also be considered as an entity per-se. It should therefore contain specific services to be able to configure and manage the use of its services. Those specific services are called the "System Management Services".

The function, information and resource views of a CIMOSA model have been mentioned in liaison with the presentation of the main components of the CIMOSA Integrating Infrastructure. The organisation view, not yet mentioned, is not the prime focus of any one of these components but will be used by each of them in the course of executing a CIMOSA model.

5.3   First Level of Decomposition of the Integrating Infrastructure

As briefly outlined in the last paragraph, the CIMOSA Integrating Infrastructure consists of five interacting sets of services, these sets being called entities. Fig. 2.22 shows the set of these entities. In the following sections we will give the

86

definition of an "entity" and detail it for each identified entity of the CIMOSA Integrating Infrastructure.

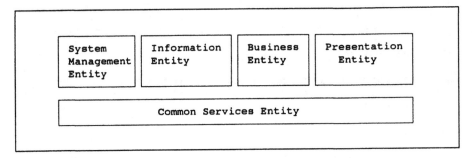

Fig. 2.22: First level of decomposition of the CIMOSA Integrating Infrastructure
.

- The Business entity, to provide event and behaviour management
- The Presentation entity, to provide manufacturing resource management
- The Information entity, to provide information management
- The Common services entity, to provide communication management
- The System Management entity, to provide system management

References to Formal Reference Base (FRB Item)		
C4-3200	C4-3210	C4-5000

5.3.1 Definition of an Entity

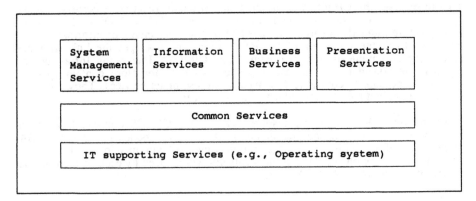

Fig. 2.23: Implementation of the CIMOSA Integrating Infrastructure Services

An entity is defined in terms of functionalities and is providing the context in which individual services, the second level of decomposition of the integrating infrastructure, will be specified. Therefore an entity is intentionally more abstract than a service. The distinction between the entity and a service is comparable to the distinction made in [OSI][14] reference model between "layers" and "service elements", which are defined within layers. Entities belong to the "functional representation" of the integrating infrastructure. Only the services which compose these entities will be mapped onto underlying services, as shown on Fig. 2.23, for their implementation ("IT representation").

References to Formal Reference Base (FRB Item)		
C4-3205	C4-3210	C5-3215

5.3.2 The Business Entity

Goal: Provide generic functions to initiate, monitor and control Enterprise operations, in accordance with the particular Enterprise model, by processing the corresponding executable model.

Functionalities:

- support event driven enterprise operations,
- support coordination, sequencing and synchronization of Enterprise operations,
- manage enterprise resources,
- support flexible changes of enterprise operations.
- allow human interventions to deal with exceptional events (with the aid of the "Presentation entity").

According to CIMOSA, complex applications will be decomposed into a set of domain processes containing functional operations which will, at the end, be executed by selected resources according to the description of the enterprise behaviour. The Business Entity allows to initiate the reactions of the enterprise to events through the selection of appropriate processes, to interpret the description of the behaviour, to select and locate the resources on which the enterprise operations will be executed, and to monitor this execution in cooperation with the Presentation entity. The services which compose the Business Entity are further detailed in section 5.5.4 below.

References to Formal Reference Base (FRB Item)
C4-5010

5.3.3 Information Entity

Goal: Provide generic functions necessary for information access, integration and manipulation.

Functionalities:

- Support system wide access to enterprise information
- Provide transparent access to heterogeneous data storage means

---

[14]   [OSI] ISO 7498 Information Processing Systems, Open Systems Interconnection; Part 1 "Basic Reference Model".

- Maintain consistency and integrity of enterprise information
- Support flexible change of enterprise information
- Support definition and manipulation of relevant enterprise information
- Support system data as well as user data
- Support different types of data:
    - alphanumeric and
    - file type data
- Support definition and enforcement of information access rights.

The Information entity is basically fulfilling the requirement of transparent and system-wide access to heterogeneous data storage and file systems. It allows to hide heterogeneity and distribution, and to handle information requests generated using the CIMOSA modeling language. Schema or data conversion, depending of their nature, are done directly by the integrating infrastructure, or indirectly, but transparently, through external converters. The services which compose the Information Entity are further detailed in section 5.5.5 below.

References to Formal Reference Base (FRB Item)
C4-5020

5.3.4 Presentation Entity

Goal: Provide generic functions to support the integration of enterprise components.

Functionalities:

- Support interactions between the integrating infrastructure and enterprise resources,
- Present heterogeneous resources in a homogeneous fashion to other infrastructure services,
- Provide access to external components
- Integrate existing applications.

Presentation functions are necessary when interactions take place between the integrating infrastructure and external components. *Human beings* and *machines* are typical components of the enterprise requiring presentation.

Presentation for *human* requires a set of particular functions related to the ability of human user to take initiatives and decisions, and to its comfort when accessing functions and information. The integration of existing application can be achieved at various degree (see definition of integration). The minimum level of integration is the support of interactions allowing the basic control of an existing application by an integrating infrastructure (e.g. start, get end status). More integration may require some co-operation with other entities of the framework (e.g. sharing of data) but will always be managed through the Presentation entity. The services which compose the Presentation Entity are further detailed in section 5.5.6 below.

References to Formal Reference Base (FRB Item)
C4-5030

5.3.5 Common Services Entity

Goal: Provide common services to the other entities.

Functionalities:

- Exchange messages between the services of the infrastructure,
- Manage messages (e.g priority, ...),
- Provide for transparencies required by other entities.
- Provide common services (e.g naming, time management, authentication, ...).

The functions provided by the common services entity are offered to the other entities. The other entities have the choice to use or not those functions, unless this choice impacts interoperability. When it is impacted, this choice is specified and published within the service specifications. The services which compose the Common services Entity are further detailed in section 5.5.7 below.

References to Formal Reference Base (FRB Item)
C4-5040

5.3.6 System Management Entity

Goal: Provide generic facilities to set up, maintain, monitor the components of the integrating infrastructure.

Functionalities:

- distribute and install new release of components of the integrating infrastructure,
- Set up and configure these components for run time operations,
- Start and operate these components,
- Reconfigure and report on security,
- Perform error logging and performance measuring on the components,

Distributed computing has created unique system management needs as well as network management needs. The network and management software should allow to perform any operational support or management task remotely. It should be possible to perform all IT system management tasks, from operational control to capacity planning using the network as a management tool, not just as a communication path. The Services of the System-Management entity have to support all management functions applicable to configuration management, fault management, performance management, accounting and security. This entity is used to access system management functions, with the support and coordination of other entities. Coordination is extended to interactions with the enterprise engineering tools, when distribution and installation of new release of models is supported by a particular integrating infrastructure.

References to Formal Reference Base (FRB Item)
C4-5050

5.4   General Properties of an Integrating Infrastructure

The common services and the system-management entities are already introducing the reader to some of the general properties of an integrating infrastructure. By properties we mean those attributes or qualities which an Integrating Infrastructure should exhibit. These properties have been kept in mind when defining the structure of the CIMOSA Integrating Infrastructure, and its second level of decomposition and should also be used by the vendors when designing possible implementations:

- distribution
- openness
- portability and connectivity support
- portability of an integrating infrastructure
- conformance/compliance to standards
- reliability
- performance
- migration support

References to Formal Reference Base (FRB Item)			
C4-3110	C4-3600	C4-3610	C4-3620

5.4.1 Distribution

For various reasons computer applications, machines, human resources are installed on or linked to various computers, which themselves are more or less connected by communication networks. In the process of integration, the resulting global CIM system will most naturally be distributed on (the) various computers: an integrating infrastructure ought to support such a distributed system. As a consequence an integrating infrastructure will itself be distributed. This is the case for the CIMOSA Integrating Infrastructure.

5.4.2 Openness

When putting together various pieces of software to constitute a system, including an integrating infrastructure, it is of interest for the enterprise, in that case for the system analyst and the implementor, that he is offered a large choice of appropriate components, which can be put together in a variety of ways. This flexibility should allow him to adjust the system to his needs. A system characterized by the fact that it can easily be built by putting together existing individual components, and similarly modified or extended, will be called "open". Such a characteristic should obviously be aimed at for an integrating infrastructure. Minimum requirements to reach that openness is the existence of standards describing the functions and components, generally through the related interfaces, standards which ought to be public, maintained, and well accepted.

AMICE is developing a base for standardisation, frameworks, definitions and specifications, in order to build a true CIM Open System Architecture. Its intention is to propose a framework for CIM integrating infrastructures, and the integrating infrastructure service specifications as specific standards. Acceptance of openness will lead to the need for portability of components from one system to another.

5.4.3 Portability and Connectivity Support

It is of interest that the entities which interface with the integrating infrastructure be portable (software), or easily connectable (machines) with respect to that integrating infrastructure. An integrating infrastructure should be designed as to favour these portability and connectivity. A necessary requirement for portability and connectivity is that the concerned interface be well defined and generally accepted, that is that it conforms to some standard. Completion of the generic ISO standards on portability is a prerequisite for any specific development in this area within AMICE.

5.4.4 Portability of an Integrating Infrastructure

Beside the fact that it supports portability of the components which are interfaced to it, it may be a requirement that an integrating infrastructure itself is portable in some aspect (OS, language, ...) with respect to the platform it runs on (see 5.4.1). The conclusion on standards given above applies to this property as well.

5.4.5 Conformance/Compliance to Standards

Conformance to standards is necessary to realize the two properties above, distribution, openness and portability. Hence it is expected that every integrating infrastructure will be defined in respect to some standards. The definition of the CIMOSA Integrating Infrastructure make specific references to available standards when appropriate (see also 5.6).

5.4.6 Reliability

Reliability refers to the ability of a system to provide continuously an adequate service. Beside the needs to use reliable components to start with, reliability covers techniques (globally covered under the name fault resistance or fault tolerance) used to cope with the effects of the failure of a component. Some of those techniques are to retry operations (until success, and if not possible, leaving the system in a known state and reporting), to duplicate entities (services, data), to organise some interactions as transaction (when possible, e.g. for data), etc.

The various services offered by an integrating infrastructure should be reliable. The technique used for this should be chosen appropriately for the area concerned: e.g. transaction service for an information service, retry for a communication service, etc. Reliability is defined for each individual service of the CIMOSA Integrating Infrastructure.

5.4.7 Performance

It is clear that the user expects its integrating infrastructure to be as performing as possible, given the current state of the technology. This property applies principally to the possible implementations of an integrating infrastructure. It is therefore not directly the concern of AMICE for the definition of the CIMOSA Integrating Infrastructure.

5.4.8 Migration Support

Migration means here time-migration, i.e. the move from one system to a modified one as time goes by. This is an absolute requirement for today's manufacturing, first to support the existing, then to make the process of integration easier because progressive. This is one of the reason that led to the identification of the System-Management entity in CIMOSA.

5.5 Second Level of Decomposition of the Integrating Infrastructure

The second level of decomposition of the integrating infrastructure, after the level of the entities, corresponds to the level of the services. Until now, the CIMOSA Integrating Infrastructure has been defined quite abstractly by a set of five blocks of services (entities) and a list of properties. We will here introduce the notion of services and the techniques used to specify them. We will end up by describing each service identified by CIMOSA.

5.5.1 Principle of a Service

Introduction

CIMOSA uses the principles defined in [DOAM][15] for its IIS service definitions.

Complying with this definition three levels of detail are applied for the specification of the CIMOSA Integrating Infrastructure services:

- The abstract service
- The possible distribution of the service
- The application interface

References to Formal Reference Base (FRB Item)
C4-3200

The Abstract Service

A service comprises a number of functions which all together provide the functionalities of the service. It can have a state, i.e. information which is maintained by the service between executions of functions. Functions are described in terms of WHAT is offered by the service, not WHO can request them nor HOW they are executed. Their specifications are detailed in a service definition and a protocol specification, as is explained below. The DOAM distinguishes roles that a service can have in an interaction. The first roles identified are the role of x-servers, and the role of x-clients. The x-server is the component which provides part or all the functions specified at the service definition. The x-client is any requestor of an x-server. The x-client and the x-server interact according to an x-access-protocol (see Fig. 2.24).

The **service definition** describes the interactions between the x-client and the x-server. It focuses on the semantic of the information exchanged, and not on its syntactical representation. The x-access **protocol specification** deals with the syntactical representation of the information exchanged and the exchange rules. It

---

[15]   [DOAM]   ISO/IEC DIS 10031-1 Distributed Office Application Model.

contributes to the definition of the interoperability between different implementation of the integrating infrastructure.

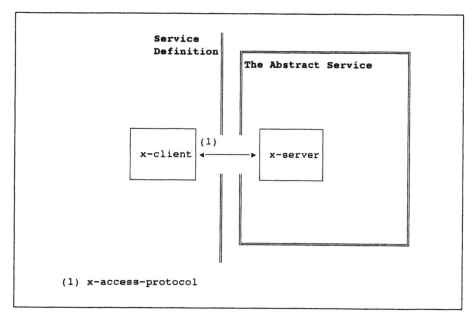

Fig. 2.24: The Abstract Service

Distribution of the Service

The full set of functions specified at a service definition may be provided by a set of servers of the same type constituting a system of servers (e.g. It is possible that a server would not be able to fulfil alone a client request. This server will have to request a peer server to perform this task or part of it). Those servers interact with each other through a peer protocol which is called x-system-protocol.(see Fig. 2.25)

The possible distribution of a service requires the definition of interactions between servers. x-system protocol specification describes those interactions, but it does not affect the service definition where the service is considered as a whole.

x-Application-Interface

It is now the time to introduce the third role identified in the Distributed Office Application Model, and to distinguish between the requestor of a server, i.e the x-client, and the user of a service, the x-user:

- The x-user is issuing a request.
- The x-client is processing it to the server.

By definition the x-user is co-located with the x-client. Interactions between the x-user and the x-client take place through the x-application-interface. The x-server may be local or remote to the x-user, but this organization is transparent to the x-user due to the processing performed by the x-client (see Fig. 2.26).

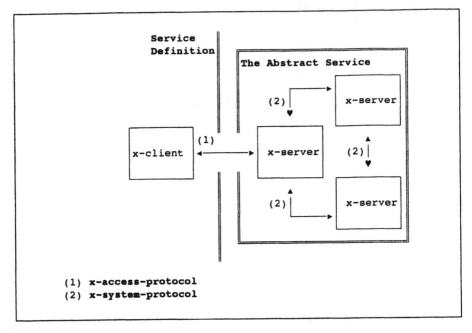

Fig. 2.25: System of Servers

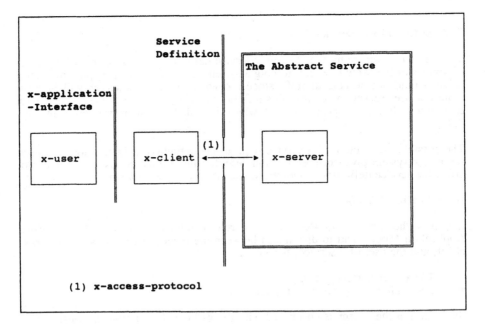

Fig. 2.26: The x-Application-Interface

The application interface defines the actual access to the service. In other words it defines how an application acting as user of a service, can access the service to request execution of functions. The scope of the application interface is limited to the access to the service, and does not deal with general data processing issues (e.g. issues of accessing operating systems, ...).

Besides the actual access to the functionality, the application interface provides for:

- transparency of service provision,
- possibility of local optimisation,
- selection of required service functional subsets,
- portability of components acting as users (when the application interface is adopted as an industry standard).

There are two ways to specify an x-application-interface:

- by an Interface Definition Notation (IDN) which is independent of any programming language, or
- by an Application Program Interface (API) which includes a binding to a particular programming language. (API may include conformance statements).

Other Aspects of the Principle of Service

This user-client-server model is a model of interaction. The user, client, server behaviours are not permanent properties, but roles valid during interactions. For example, an x-server can have the role of an y-user during an interaction. This internal behaviour of the x-server is not visible in its service definition but allows cooperation between services.

The x-application-interface is offered to any x-user, and leaves the freedom to the client on HOW to establish interactions with the server. When those interactions are local (without networking activity), vendors may use this freedom to improve the performance of their implementations.

When those interactions are remote (with networking activity), they impact directly the interoperability between clients and servers. Therefore the mechanisms or the services used to support interactions, must be specified (e.g mapping on ACSE, or ROSE, or a reliable message queueing service) and are documented in the Protocol Specification.

References to Formal Reference Base (FRB Item)
C4-3220

5.5.2 Principles Relevant for the Service Identification

Services are refinement of entities by detailed grouping of functions. Some fundamental assumptions or rules have been used for their identification:

- A service may consist of distributed servers.

- Boundaries between services have to comply to available Reference Models if some reference model is applicable in the area of concerns, or differences with the reference model have to be documented.
- Define the borders between services in order to isolate the impact of changes in technology within one service only.
- Grouping rules should be based on cohesion, i.e. based on how services are "clustered" together. As such there is functional, sequential, communicative, procedural, temporal, logical and coincidental cohesion.
- Create a boundary where a minimum of connectivity to other services appears.

References to Formal Reference Base (FRB Item)
C4-3225

5.5.3 Service Specification

As can be derived from the DOAM, the full specification of a service is made of:

(1)- A service-definition
(2)- A protocol-specification
(3)- An Interface-definition

We will not enter here into the details of each technique used for each of these three parts of a full service-specification. We will concentrate thereafter on the service-definition as much as it helps for the presentation of each service in the next paragraphs (5.5.4 to 5.5.7). A special case should be made for the System Management services. Their description will not be presented as they are currently being developed within AMICE.

References to Formal Reference Base (FRB Item)
C4-3220

5.5.3.1 Conventions for Service Definition

The service-definition presents the higher level of abstraction from the different specifications of a service. It documents the functions which are provided by the service. The elements of a service-definition described here, are close to those recommended by the ISO in [Guide][16].

All services of the CIMOSA Integrating Infrastructure are described using the same model of interactions as introduced previously. As we have seen, this model formalizes the paradigm of client server computing. It introduces the relationship between users of the service and the service itself. Each service definition is therefore only focusing on:

- The identification and grouping of functions (functional unit, Service subset), using in this process the definition of "Service objects".

---

[16]   [Guide]   ISO/IEC JTC1/SC21 N4118 Methodology and guide-lines for the development of Application Layer Protocols.

- the definition of each of the functions offered by the service, including the description of parameters (inputs/outputs, data types, range of values, default value).
- the definition of the behaviour of the service, by means of allowed sequences of functions (using State Transition Diagrams - STD - defined for each service-object).
- the context in which the service will interact with its partners.

As the service definition hides the potential usage by the service of functionality provided by an other service, this context is documented in an annex and is not normative. The different levels of grouping of functions defined for the integrating infrastructure are:

- Functional Units which represent small meaningful groupings of Functions. The rule for such groupings is that a particular member of a group would not be useful if the other members were not also available. **Service object** is the abstraction used to support this grouping.
- Service subsets are logical grouping of Functional Units that include a kernel Functional Unit and any other set of Functional Units.

References to Formal Reference Base (FRB Item)
C4-3300

5.5.3.2   Service-Objects

The Service Object captures part of the static and dynamic aspects of a service (e.g. attributes and behaviour). Their identification supports the definition of the service-functions. The service acts as an object manager, while the service object acts as a managed object. Some Service Objects may map with a CIMOSA modelling construct. Such a service object is the representation of an occurrence of the construct seen from the service perspective.

Business Processes and events are, for example, represented as service-objects in the CIMOSA Integrating Infrastructure. Some other Service Objects may represent something which is relevant for the service, but which is not visible in enterprise modelling. An example of this kind would be IT mechanisms such as a semaphore or a transaction.

Service-Objects are used to share the semantics between the service and its clients, rather than the relationship by itself, this later being defined by the DOAM.

Description of Object Behaviour

The dynamic aspects of a Service Object are described by means of a State Transition Diagram, which depicts how an Object behaves. Only its externally visible behaviour is relevant for this dynamic description. The States of the Service Object correspond to the set of allowed values for its attribute "status". Transitions mark each allowed sequence of states, and are linked, through causality, to the definition of the functions of the service. The State Transition Diagram, indeed, shows the possible sequence of operations which is accepted by the Service Object, therefore the allowed sequence of functions which is provided by the service.

Description of Object Attributes

The static description of a Service Object consists of a list of several attributes of different categories. For each attribute, its possible range of values is given in one of the forms: enumeration, acceptance rule, range, reference to other defined attributes.

The following categories of Service Object attributes have been identified:

Service Object

− identification
− status
− references
− other attributes

Where:
identification are attributes which contains data that are used to identify the object (e.g. names, system-wide unique identifiers, ..).
status are attributes which determines the allowed states of the object. Several statuses may be necessary to define completely an object (e.g. life cycle status, execution status, ...)
references are attributes which contains a pointer to other objects.
other attributes are ... any other attributes.

References to Formal Reference Base (FRB Item)
C4-3310

5.5.3.3   Service Functions

The **Functions** are the basic "units of processing" that are offered by the Services of the CIMOSA Integrating Infrastructure. They describe the interactions:

- between a service and its clients.
- between any servers belonging to the same service.

The key principle for the specification of functions is to describe basic capabilities in abstract terms, i.e. implementation independent terms.

Components of a Function: Request and Response

The detailed description of a Function is done by the means of two basic primitives: the Request and the Response. A Request (known as Argument, in other standards) is issued by a client to invoke some Function (named in other standards procedure or operation). The form of the Request is specific to the Function. A Response (known as Result or Result/Error, in other standards) is issued by a service to complete some Function previously invoked by a client of that service. A Response may be positive (+) or negative (-) as appropriate to the circumstances.

The form of the Response is usually specific to the Function. However, most negative Responses are common to several Requests. One or more parameters may be associated with a primitive and each of these parameters has a defined range of values. Parameter values associated with a primitive are passed in the direction of the primitive. The use of these two primitives does not impose any specific implementation of the Functions. Primitives are conceptual, and should be distinguished from programmatic calls to the service.

Description of Functions

The specification of each Function consists of a (textual) description of its objective, and of a description of its static and dynamic aspects.

Static Aspects - Parameters

The static description of the Function consists of Request and Response parameters, including the range of values taken in one of the forms: enumeration, citation, acceptance rule, range, reference to other defined parameters ... This description starts with the **Function Name**, followed by the list of all its **Request** and **Response** Parameters. This is depicted in Fig. 2.27. The presence of each parameter in the corresponding primitive (i.e. Request or Response) is described by one of the following values:

M   parameter is mandatory for the primitive;
C   parameter is conditioned by other parameters of the environment;
S   parameter is a selection (i.e. choice) from a collection of two or more possible parameters.
O   parameter is a user option;

All Parameters can be defined by a structured list of sub-parameters.

```
Function Name

Parameter Names          Code        Value

Request
    Parameter A          (M)         A1, A2, ... An
    Parameter B          (M)
        Sub-parameter B1 (M)         Bi:Bj
        Sub-parameter B2 (O)         <expression>

Response
    Positive             (S)
        Parameter X      (M)         "same as param.C"
        Parameter Y      (C)
    Negative             (S)
        Parameter Z      (M)         Z1, Z2, ... Zn


M: Mandatory                              C: Conditional
S: Selection (between 2 or more parameters)   O: Optional
-----------------------------------------------------------
```

Fig. 2.27: Function Description (static aspects)

Dynamic Aspects - Actions

The dynamic description of the Function is provided for information only, and therefore is not normative. This description covers the "externally visible" behaviour of the service when performing the Function, covering both normal and exception behaviours as well as status updates of Service Objects, if any. This dynamic description illustrate how sequences of interactions are related in time. It takes the form of a structured and (when possible) sequential list of events and actions. Among those actions, the service may request the execution of functions by another service.

A graphical summary of what a service definition looks like is shown in Fig. 2.28.

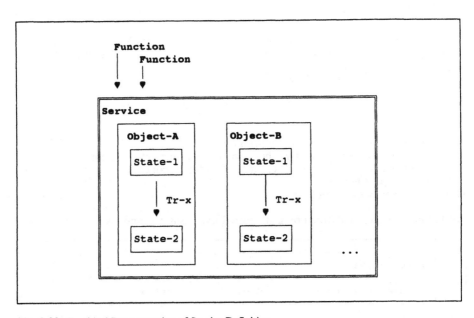

Fig. 2.28: Graphical Representation of Service Definition

References to Formal Reference Base (FRB Item)			
C4-3320	C4-3330	C4-3340	C4-3350

5.5.4 The Business Services

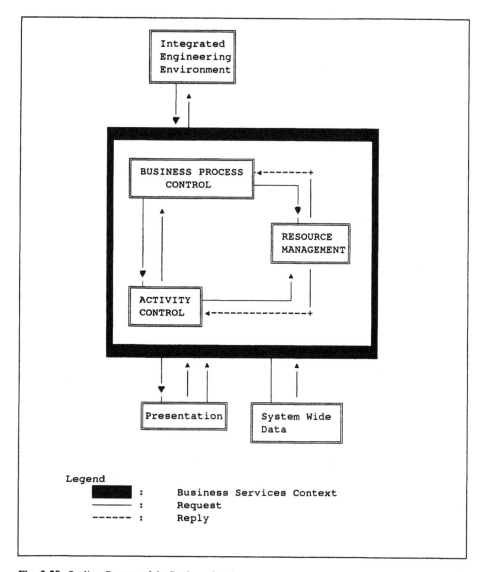

Fig. 2.29: Outline Context of the Business Services

The Business Services provide those functions required to "execute the enterprise model" which contains both the function view (i.e function and behaviour) and the resource view, that is they manage the execution of Business Processes and Enterprise Activities and the reservation and allocation of resources. Additionally, they provide the following general purpose functions:

■   provide status information on Enterprise Activities, Business Processes and Resources.

- modify set-up (i.e. configuration) parameters (e.g. models, occurrences, scheduling windows, etc.).
- report out of line situations.

The Business Services include:

- **Business Process Control (BC)** which manages and dispatches the execution of Business Processes and Enterprise Activities by interpreting the Procedural Rule Sets. The Business Process control service is acting on two different service-objects:
  - The "event" service-object
  - The "Business Process" service-object
  the definition of which is derived from the corresponding modeling constructs.

- **Activity Control (AC)** which controls the execution of Enterprise Activities by dispatching the Functional Operations which are carried out by the Resources.
  The Activity Control service is acting on two different service-objects:
  - The "Enterprise Activity" service-object
  - The "Functional Operation" service-object
  the definition of which is derived from the corresponding modeling constructs.

- **Resource Management (RM)** which reserves and dynamically schedules the Resources used by the Enterprise Activities to perform their Functional Operations.
  The Resource Management service is acting on three different service-objects:
  - The "Resource unit" service-object which contains the static and dynamic attributes of the resource unit defined in the resource view,
  - The "Resource pool" service-object which corresponds to a cell (physical and permanent) of resource units with the same attributes and behaviour,

Fig. 2.29 is representing the context of the Business services. An example of the way the Business Services interact with each other demonstrated in Fig. 2.30. The actions outline how the services of Business Services interact with each other and with other CIMOSA Integrating Infrastructure services. The simplifying assumption adopted is that the triggered Domain Process is made of a number of sequential Enterprise activities.

The simplified sequence of actions are:

- An Event triggers Business Process Control to create a Domain Process occurrence.
- Business Process Control requests Resource Management to schedule the Business Process occurrence.
- Resource Management creates a schedule for this Business Process occurrence. It creates start and end dates for each Enterprise Activity and, if required, will allocate a Resource Capacity (optional).
- when the first Enterprise Activity reaches its start time, Business Process Control will ask Activity Control to execute it.
- Activity Control will control the processing of each Functional Operation which makes up the Enterprise Activity.
- Activity Control asks Resource Management to acquire Resource Units for a Functional Operation.
- Resource Management assigns Resource Units to the Functional Operation.

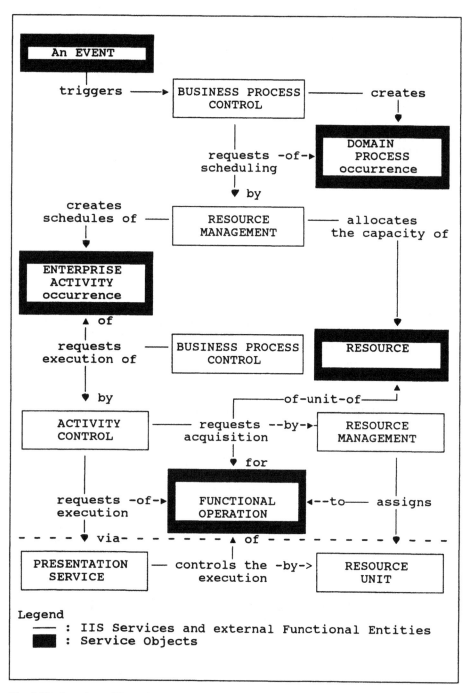

Fig. 2.30: Overview of B Services at Work

104

- Activity Control now requests the relevant (human, machine, application) Presentation service to execute the Functional Operation.
- Presentation service controls the execution of the Functional Operation.
- After the execution of the Functional Operation, the relevant Presentation service reports the results back to Activity Control.
- Activity Control starts the next Functional Operation (if any). After the last Functional Operation has been completed, Activity Control reports this to Business Process Control.
- Business Process Control then asks Activity Control to execute the next (if any) Enterprise Activity. When the last Enterprise Activity is complete, Business Process Control will create an end Event for this Business Process occurrence.

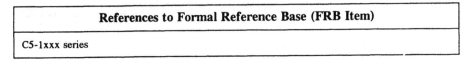

References to Formal Reference Base (FRB Item)
C5-1xxx series

5.5.5 The Information Services

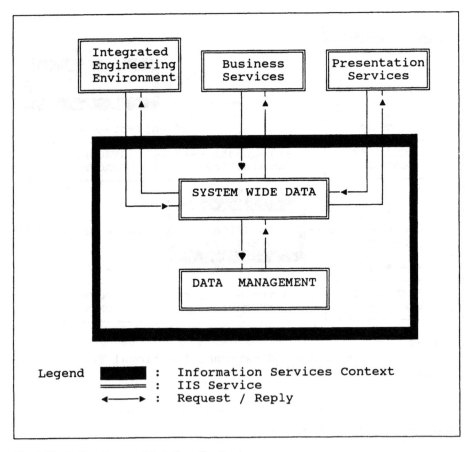

Fig. 2.31: Outline Context of the Information Services

The Information services provide all generic functions for data access, data integration, and data manipulation. They consist of the System-Wide-Data service (SD) and the Data Management service (DM) as two cooperating services handling data requests transparently. Fig. 2.31 shows the context of the Information services. The Information services are supporting the use of existing storage systems, thereby protecting the huge investments made in this area by manufacturing enterprises. Additionally, they provide the general purpose functions to:

- support flexible changes of the information of the enterprise, data definition, configuration (product version and variant), and the definition and enforcement of data access and rights;
- maintain data consistency and integrity

The Information Services include:

- **System Wide Data Service (SD)** which provides a unified data access to its clients through the definition and use of Implemented External Schemas (SQL views or files).
  The data requests are expressed according to a global data relational and file structure, in SQL for database data and in a high level file language for file type data. These requests refer to Implemented External Schemas which may comprise data distributed on several CIMOSA system nodes; the distribution aspect is hidden to the user.
  The data requests are split by System Wide Data into a set of local sub requests according to the data distribution. These local requests are expressed in SQL or file language. Each local request is passed to the corresponding Data Management which is the interface to the storage system containing the local data.

- **Data Management (DM)** which is responsible to present any storage system in a unified way to System Wide Data. For database data, Data Management has to translate when necessary the local request expressed in SQL into the transaction language of the corresponding database.

The System Wide Data service (SD)

In more detail the characteristics of the System Wide Data service are the following. This service is a generic data service for all the data needed in a CIMOSA enterprise, that is it is used both for the enterprise data as well as the data stored and used owing to CIMOSA modelling and CIMOSA model execution (the "CIMOSA data").

This service has been structured according to 2 main types of data: database data and file type data, covering easily all data found today in an enterprise[17]. But the intended service is global over those 2 types of data: the needed feature of consistency enforcement is obtained through the usual concept of transaction, but here a single transaction can be composed of any association of database data requests and file requests.

For the database data, SQL, well normalized today, has been chosen as the unified access method used by the SD service, in line with the modelling in the Information View, which ended up with a relational model at the Implementation Level. In line

---

[17]   It is likely that this will evolve to a single approach, object oriented like, when a large enough consensus, implying normalized description and access method, is obtained for the latter.

with this choice, the SD service for its database part is patterned upon (and will be mapped to) RDA (Remote Database Access) in its SQL specialization, where RDA is the recent ISO norm for access of remote databases.

For the file service part, the SD functions are similar to a high level file service, and as such can be mapped to the ISO norm FTAM, but also to several de facto norms (FTP, ...). An existing distributed file system (NFS, AFS, ...), although a priori more powerful, can also be used to support that part of the SD service.

Finally to obtain the SD global service for database data and file type data, where a single transaction combines both types of requests, some layer of functions must be added above the functions of a DB and of a file system, restraining and combining them in the appropriate way.

As said above, the SD user is relieved of any concern about location and distribution of the accessed data. The data requested are referred to through their external schema, coming for the modelling, and the Information Services are in charge of finding then the right DB(s) or file store(s) and their node(s) (there may be several to be accessed). For database data, this means that an SD server may have to split a single data request it receives in several sub-requests, each sent to a different DB, and, when reading, reassemble the partial results on the way back. As such, the SD service encompasses the distribution kernel of today distributed databases.

For file type data, there is obviously no splitting of request, SD just determines which file store, on which node, holds the file (or will receive the file) and routes the request to the appropriate DM server. Then the file is transferred directly between the SD client and the file store governed by DM, and appropriate return information is passed back to SD to close properly the transaction.

Finally the potentially distributed nature of the data manipulated make it imperative for proper transaction handling that the 2 phases commit technique be used. The addressed SD server will be the coordinator, coordinating the DM servers involved in that transaction. The Information Services also relieves the user of concerns about replicated data. Assuming some data is replicated in the system (this is specified during the modelling), the Information Services will take care that, when modifying data, every replicate is modified, and when reading, a single, appropriate copy is read. SD is the major actor for this.

As a further feature associated to replicated data, is the possibility that 2 replicates, although conceptually equivalent, do not have the same format; but, since equivalent, a converter (program, tool, ...) is available allowing to go from one format to the other. The Information Services are providing a structure so that such a conversion is automatically handled, unknown to the user, when needed. This applies only to file type data.

The Data Management service (DM)

As said, inside the Information Entity, the Data Management service, is in charge of presenting various storage means to SD in a unified way. In practise, it means that, if needed, it has to convert the database requests it receives, in SQL form, into the appropriate variant, or even according to a fundamentally distinct type of data storage for the local database.

Furthermore, Data Management will handle the conversion between replicates when needed; it will have to take care of the name mapping when necessary (from CIMOSA global names, unique CIMOSA wide, which are used by SD, to local names proper to the local storage systems, names which are not necessarily unique across the whole system). DM ought also to be able to maintain local consistency (if the local storage system does not already has this feature), and behave as a partner in 2 phase commitment coordinated by SD.

Standardization

From the ISO RDA standard which is the appropriate one to support the SD and DM services for database data, the notion of dialogue has been retained, and is used in both the SD and DM services: a dialogue is a basic relationship between an SD user and its server (respectively a DM user and its server), containing one or several transactions. It may be used for connection establishment and severing, but need not to. It will be used for resource opening and closing.

Service Objects

The service-objects manipulated by the two services are the following:

The SD-Dialogue Object

It identifies a cooperative relationship between a System Wide Data user and a System Wide Data server of the System Wide Data service. This relationship may include one or several, although not concurrent, (SD) transactions.

The Implemented External Schema Object

It identifies an implemented external schema (an SQL view or a set of files) which may comprise data distributed on several nodes.

DM-dialogue Object

It identifies a cooperative relationship between an SD server, seen as a DM user, and a DM server. All interaction between them occur within the context of the dialogue which may include one or several DM transactions.

Storage Group Object

It identified an existing data storage mean (database, file, set of files) which is located on a given CIMOSA node.

References to Formal Reference Base (FRB Item)
C5-3xxx series

5.5.6 The Presentation Services

The Presentation Services provide those functions required to control the execution of Functional Operations by the heterogeneous Enterprise resources, namely the Machine Functional Entities, the Application Functional Entities and the Human Functional Entities as described in the CIMOSA Resource View. Additionally, they provide the following general purpose functions:

- provide status information on the Functional Operations and Functional Entities allocated to the Functional Operations.
- allocate/relinquish resources to/from Functional Operations

108

- set-up the resources in order to allow the execution of the Functional Operations.

The Presentation Services include:

- Machine Dialogue Service (MD) which controls the execution of Machine Functional Operations.
- Application Dialogue Service (AD) which controls the execution of Application Functional Operations.
- Human Dialogue Service (HD) which controls the execution of Human Functional Operations.

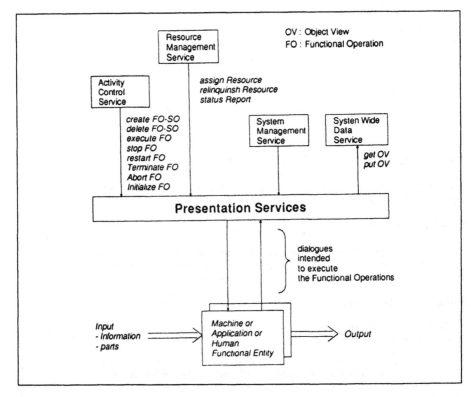

Fig. 2.32: Context of the Presentation Services

The Presentation Services will accept recipes or scripts to convert Functional Operation requests in concrete processing steps. These scripts have to be provided by the engineering department of the enterprise organisation. They are modified or replaced when new Functional Operations are required. The scripts describing the execution of FO's are outside of the scope of the CIMOSA modelling. The run-time interpretation of these scripts is therefore optional and will generally be embedded in the control engine of the associated resource. The usage of MMS to support the interaction between Machine Dialogue and Machine Functional Entities is, for example, recommended but not mandatory.

The Presentation Services will accept multiple and concurrent Functional Operations. It will control their concurrent execution and manage the potential Functional Operations conflicts (same resources, for example). The resources (external Functional Entities) must be allocated by System Management to one (and only one) Dialogue Server of the Presentation Entity. Consequently, all Functional Operations defined for a Functional Entity have to be called from this server. The allocation of the resources to the servers is anyway transparent for a client of the Presentation Entity as well as the access to the relevant server. Fig. 2.32 represents the context of the Presentation services.

Service-Objects manipulated by the Presentation Services

One type of service-object is manipulated by all of the Presentation services. It is the "Functional Operation" Service Object. It contains the static and dynamic attributes of the Functional Operation defined in the function view. Other Service Objects that do not stem from the CIMOSA modelling are required to specify the various Presentation Services. These specific Service Objects will include for instance "Dialogue Objects" representing the "scripts" that are applied to translate the request of a Functional Operation in concrete data/material processing steps. But the concrete representations of these Dialogue Objects are outside the scope of CIMOSA since the languages intended to express these scripts are resource dependent.

Generic Functions of the Presentation Services

Each Presentation service is offering generic functions. These functions are linked to:

- SU-FU   Set Up operations
- RM-FU   Resource Management operations
- OC-FU   Operation Control operations

SU-FUSet Up Operations

These functions are intended to create, delete, and initialize Functional Operation Service Objects. Initializing a Functional Operation enables the allocated resources to execute the processing steps that are required to execute the Functional Operation. It consists of the following functions:

- Create Functional Operation Service Object
- Delete Functional Operation Service Object
- Initialize Functional Operation Service Object

RM-FU   Resource Management Operations

These functions allow the clients of the Presentation Services to allocate and de-allocate resources to Functional Operation occurrences (represented in the CIMOSA Integrating Infrastructure as Functional Operation Service Objects). It consists of the following functions:

- Assign Resource to Functional Operation
- Relinquish Resource of a Functional Operation

OC-FU   Operation Control Operations

The purpose of these functions are to control the execution of a Functional Operation. The functions that can successfully be invoked depend on the nature of the Functional Entity executing the Functional Operations. So, if the Functional Entity is for instance not interruptable, there is little point in issuing a "stop" or "terminate" Functional Operation. It consists of the following functions:

- Execute Functional Operation
- Stop Functional Operation
- Restart Functional Operation
- Abort Functional Operation
- Terminate Functional Operation

The Machine Dialogue Service

There are various kinds of programmable manufacturing devices in the shop floor. These can be roughly divided into two categories

- special purpose devices (including)
    - Robot Controllers
    - Numerical Controllers for machine tools

- general purpose devices (including)
    - Programmable Controllers
    - Process Monitoring and Control Systems

Programmable Controllers and Process Monitoring and Control Systems are the basic equipment used to implement all the various control task required to store, move and convert physical quantities in the manufacturing floor. Especially Programmable Controllers are available in many performance classes and therefore comprise more than 90 % of the machine specific control equipment used in the shop floor.

In an overall manufacturing system interworking of all these machine controllers has to be organized into one co-operating system. There are many structural principles to organize the co-operation. One possibility is a multi level hierarchical control structure. We can distinguish two areas:

(1)   the level of station/ machine controllers

       These are directly associated with the machines and the physical process. These are modelled in CIMOSA as Machine Functional Entities.

(2)   the level of supervisory controllers (Shop Controller and Cell Controller)

       In CIMOSA this kind of control is implemented in the Integrating Infrastructure. Thus the CIMOSA Integrating Infrastructure has to act as client of the Machine Functional Entities.

Within the CIMOSA Integrating Infrastructure it is the Machine Dialogue Service which takes the role of the client of Machine Functional Entities. The main purpose of the Machine Dialogue Service is to:

- dynamically configure channels to the Machine Functional Entities
- install and remove programs
- on-line changes of programs (remote configuration)
- control programs (start, stop etc.)
- data-input and output with executing programs
- diagnosis and exception handling with both devices and programs

The Application Dialogue Service

The range of the CIM applications is very wide: CAD (Computer Aided Design), CAM (Computer Aided Manufacturing), PPC (Production Planning and Control), FDC (Factory Data Collection), PMS (Production Management System), book-keeping, stock management, computer aided maintenance... In an overall manufacturing system, all these applications have to be organized into one co-operating system. Following the case, an Application Program can be implemented as:

- a set of (local or remote) procedures
- a (local or remote) Process under the control of an Operating System
- a set of (local, remote or distributed) interworking Processes

But in the present context, we need only to know which entities interact, and which procedures and processes could be considered as Application Functional Operations. An Application Functional Operation is indeed a basic controllable unit of information processing not required to be further decomposed. The start of an Application Functional Operation is hereafter outlined:

- Activity Control asks Application Dialogue to arrange a given Application Functional Entity.
- Application Dialogue installs the Application Functional Entity if needed.
- Activity Control requests Application Dialogue to start an Application Functional Operation to be executed by an Application Functional Entity previously installed.
- The parameters to be transferred to the Application Functional Entity could require a schema conversion. System Wide Data performs this schema conversion on behalf of Application Dialogue.
- Application Dialogue invokes the Application Functional Operation with the appropriate parameters.

The Human Dialogue Service

The purpose of the Human Dialogue Service is to provide the functional capability through which a human operator can interface with a CIMOSA system. The requirements Satisfied by the Human Dialogue Service are:

(1) Integrate human work by supporting the execution of Human Functional Operations defined in the CIMOSA Enterprise Model.
(2) Allow authorized personnel to enter Events as defined in the CIMOSA Enterprise Model.
(3) Allow authorized personnel to intervene manually in order to change the model controlled execution of Business Processes arbitrarily.

References to Formal Reference Base (FRB Item)
C5-2xxx series

5.5.7 The Common Services

The Common Services are introduced to provide common solutions to issues common to the previous services. Most of those issues are raised by the distribution, by communication and by associated transparencies. The definition of the Common services is not straightforward but indirect:

- Common services are not executing an enterprise model but support the model execution by the Business, Information and Presentation services.
- Common services are not impacted by the results of enterprise modeling.
- Common services allow to extend generic IT resources to CIM specific resources.
- Common services may already be provided by supporting IT platforms.
- Use of the Common services is not mandatory for other CIMOSA Integrating Infrastructure services but the functionality of the Common services shall not be repeated in other CIMOSA Integrating Infrastructure services.

The boundary between application-oriented and common oriented services is indeed difficult to define. This is an issue that has also been recognised in the basic Reference Model of Open Distributed Processing. The Functionalities currently seen for the Common services cover:

- Communication:
  - exchange of messages between the components of the CIMOSA Integrating Infrastructure,
  - queue management of these messages,
- Services for:
  - naming
  - registration
  - security
  - time

But the Common services may have to be extended according to new Functionalities identified as being commonly needed.

The Communication Service (CS)

The Communication Service is managing the exchange of messages between the constituents of the CIMOSA Integrating Infrastructure. CS relieves the CIMOSA IIS Clients and Servers from the necessity to handle vendor specific interfaces to communication processing environments.

CS provides the facilities required for communication in a distributed CIMOSA system. It allows all IIS Clients and Servers to communicate with each other without any knowledge whether the partner resides on the same or on a different computer. It ensures secure message transfer, e.g. message recovery and redelivery in case of communication line failure, sender abort, receiver abort or other failures. It comprises synchronous and asynchronous communication and handling of message queues throughout the whole CIMOSA system. Functions described for CS effect two types of objects:

- CS_USER object.
  It encapsulates information related to the registration of an IIS Service as a CS user.
- MESSAGE object.
  It encapsulates information related to the data units exchanged.

Communication Modes of CS

CS provides unidirectional message transfer as well as bidirectional request/response pairing. For the second case two synchronization modes are supported, the asynchronous and the synchronous communication mode. In the asynchronous mode an IIS Client sends a request to an IIS Server and continues, without waiting for the response resulting from his request. Upon return of the reply CS relates it to the initial request and delivers it to the IIS Client as soon as inquired by the Client. In the synchronous mode the requesting IIS Client does not continue its work but waits for the response from the IIS server. In order to allow for selective reception of messages, CS users may specify the type of a message to be send out and may request a certain type of messages to be received.

Transparency Features for CS

To ease communication between IIS Clients and Servers the users of CS shall not be bothered with certain communication problems. Therefore the functions of CS are provided to its users transparently with respect to the following:

- Location transparency: The local or remote location of an IIS Client or Server is hidden. Invocations are routed to the correct location.
- Access transparency: The way of accessing an IIS partner is independent from whether it is local or remote available.
- Migration transparency: IIS Clients and Servers do not need to know if the communication partner is moved from one location to another.
- Replication transparency: IIS Client may be unaware of which server of an IIS Service is going to provide the requested service.
- Concurrency transparency: The existence of concurrent IIS Clients/Servers of an IIS Server/Client is made invisible for the IIS Clients/Servers.

Security Requirements for CS

CIM systems have to be protected against interference by accidentally or intentionally getting information out of or intruding into the system.

Therefore communication partners have to be checked on their true identity (authentication). Access to an IIS Client or Server will only be granted, if the authorization of the accessing IIS Client/Server agrees with the preconditions required to access the IIS Service. Unauthorized reading and understanding (data confidentiality) as well as modification (data integrity) of data packets to be transferred shall be prevented.

Naming and Registration of IIS Clients and Servers

Unambiguous naming and addressing of IIS Clients and Servers are ensured throughout the whole system. Abstract names are mapped onto the respective communication address information. Accurate registration of the participating communication partners is a precondition for communication in a dynamically configurable distributed system. This information has to be registered in accordance with the needs for CIMOSA System Management tasks, e.g. for security management. Registration of different types of default servers of an IIS Service eases the provision of the transparencies mentioned above and the implementation of distributed IIS Services significantly.

The other Services of the "Common services" Entity

One service has been identified for each of the other functionalities of the "common services" entity.

References to Formal Reference Base (FRB Item)
C5-4xxx series

5.6 CIMOSA Integrating Infrastructure and Standardisation

For its operation, the Integrating Infrastructure will be supported by a set of Information Technology means, structured in most cases as an open Distributed Processing System. This leads to consider the relations between the CIMOSA Integrating Infrastructure and both types of standards those leading to complete platforms (1,2,3) and those focussing on the definition of individual services (4,5,6):

(1) the "ODP - Reference-Model" standard which is in preparation within ISO,
(2) platforms developed by consortia which have a fair chance to become de-facto standards, such as OSF-DCE now incorporated into the "Common Application Environment" of X/Open,
(3) connected frameworks such as STEP,

(4) elements of the ISO layer 7, such as MMS, FTAM or RDA,
(5) specific reference models such as the Reference Model for Data Management,
(6) methods or languages of specifications.

The CIMOSA Integrating Infrastructure and ODP

ODP mentions in its "field of Application": "Industrial-Process Control Systems, Command and control systems, Business Interchange Systems, Engineering Development Systems,". All these applications are involved in the concept of CIM. There is therefore a common interest between ODP developments and the CIMOSA Integrating Infrastructure definition.

We have to consider that ODP is not in the area of application of basic standards but in the area of Framework and Reference model developments. Its documents are guide-lines for the development of further standards, and define the overall structure of systems. So when comparing the Integrating Infrastructure and ODP today, we can only consider: the methods, the definitions, the generic concepts of ODP.

The CIMOSA integrating infrastructure is developed in parallel with ODP-RM with the best possible consistency. When this Framework will be reconsidered in accordance with the standardization Directives, the infrastructure will be put in line with the issued ODP standards, and generally all related IT standards. The position of the CIMOSA Integrating Infrastructure in the ODP-RM and the relative positions of the CIMOSA Integrating Infrastructure and ODP-RM developments can still be qualified and the CIMOSA Integrating Infrastructure should be considered as a set of "Application specific functions" (Ref:ODP:B:7.0.3, 7.0.4, 7.0.5, 7.1.1).

The CIMOSA Integrating Infrastructure and OSF-DCE

OSF-DCE is providing a set of services easing the development of applications in a distributed and heterogeneous environment. Its adoption by X/Open should allow its progressive standardisation. It has been chosen to support the prototype of the CIMOSA Integrating Infrastructure implementation (AMICE phase III).

The CIMOSA Integrating Infrastructure and ISO Layer 7

The definition of individual CIMOSA Integrating Infrastructure services may be supported by specific standards available within the ISO layer 7. This is especially the case for the Information services and the Machine Dialogue service which are supported by the definition of RDA/SQL and FTAM, respectively MMS. CIMOSA does not intend to re-invent in areas where developments have occurred, and is taking advantage of them as much as they support the definition of the Functionalities of the CIMOSA Integrating Infrastructure services identified. This is true for ISO standards, as well as for other sources.

5.7 Co-Existence with Legacy Systems

CIMOSA Integrating Infrastructure specification allows for the coexistence of CIMOSA conformant products and non-CIMOSA conformant systems which include legacy systems. This allows manufacturing enterprises to progressively replace legacy systems based on business criterion (e.g., no longer appropriate for the business) and not just on technological criterion.

The CIMOSA Integrating Infrastructure allows a set of possible solutions depending on the objective to be reached. If information sharing is not an aim or a constraint of the integration of the considered legacy system, it could simply be addressed as an Application Functional Entity through the Application Dialogue service. Its access would be incorporated in functional decompositions. It could also continue to be accessed through human interventions which will not be specified in a model, but could take advantage of the services of the CIMOSA Integrating Infrastructure to access to other resources. The CIMOSA Integrating Infrastructure is therefore a platform of development, and migration of the application would need to be specified.

The highest level of integration is what CIMOSA defines as 'Business Integration'. This level of integration implies a CIMOSA model of the enterprise and would require legacy system to be re-engineered and re-specified in CIMOSA enterprise models.

5.8 Integrated Infrastructures - State of the Art

The most important papers and reports related to CIM Implementation Architectures have been analyzed and compared with the CIMOSA IIS concepts (Section 6.5 [33] to [41]).

The major impact of the current standardisation effort is seen in the lower level of the IIS services (Communication and Information Services). The analysis also indicates that there are no similar activities, which address the IIS services necessary to implement the Particular Implementation Models. This is especially true for the upper level services (Business and partially for the Presentation Services). Generic concepts from OSI and ODP activities will be observed closely and adapted when appropriate.

6 References

6.1 CIM Architecture - State of the Art

[1] ICAM project 1105: Conceptual Design for Computer Integrated Manufacturing
[2] CAM-I DPMM: Discrete Parts Manufacturing Model
[3] NBS AMRF: Automated Manufacturing Research Facility
[4] ISO TC 184/SC5/WG1 N51: Ottawa Report on Reference Models for Manufacturing Standards
[5] ESPRIT Pilot Project 34: Design Rules for Computer Integrated Manufacturing Systems
[6] ANSA: Advanced Networked System Architecture
[7] ICEIMT Proceedings, MIT Press 1992 (Intern. Conference on Enterprise Integration Modelling Technology, Hilton Head/SC, USA, June 1992)

6.2 CIM Architecture additional State of the Art

[8] A Synthesis of Factory Reference Models, Ind. Techn. Inst., Ann Arbor/Mich.,USA Sept.1987
[9] CEN/CENELEC evaluation report on CIM architectures N40, Nov.1988
[10] CIM Reference Model Committee, Purdue University, IJCIM, Vol.2/#2,1989
[11] T. J. Williams, A Reference Model for Computer Integrated Manufacturing from the Viewpoint of Industrial Automation, 11th IFAC World Congress, Tallinn, USSR, August 1990

6.3 Enterprise Modelling - State of the Art

[12] Modelling in Manufacturing - State of the Art; AMICE internal Document R03349430D; 1988.
[13] G. Stemmer; MFSP, ein Verfahren zur Simulation komplexer Materialflussysteme; Krausskopf, Mainz; 1977.
[14] O. Järvinen, H. Konrad; Object-oriented modelling of production activity control systems; Proceedings of the 4th CIM Europe Conf., 18-20 May 1988; 353-364.
[15] Y-L. Chang, R.S. Sullivan, J.R. Wilson; Using SLAM to design the Material Handling System of a Flexible Manufacturing System; Int. J. Prod. Res.; Vol. 24, No. 1, 1986; 15-26.
[16] A.A.B Pritsker; Introduction to Simulation and SLAM II; Halsted Press (2nd edition); New York, NY; 1984.
[17] C.D. Pegden; Introduction to SIMAN with Version 3.0 Enhancements; State College (Systems Modeling Corporation); 1985.
[18] W. Dangelmaier, B.-D. Becker; SIMPLE and EXCON - A new Object Oriented Simulation System with Expert System Support; Fraunhofer-Institut für Produktionstechnik und Automatisierung; Stuttgart.

6.4 Enterprise Modelling Methodologies - State of the Art

[19] T. DeMarco; Structured Analysis and System Specification; Yourdon Press; 1978.
[20] E. Yourdon; What Ever Happened to Structured Analysis?; DATAMATION, June 1, 1986; pp. 133-138.

[21] C. Gane, T. Sarson; Structured Systems Analysis: Tools and Techniques; Prentice Hall; 1979.

[22] M. Jackson; System Development; Prentice Hall; 1983.

[23] D.T. Ross, Structured Analysis; Proc. Intern. CAM Congress, CAM-I Inc. Arlington/Tx; 1974; 338-421.

[24] D.T. Ross; Structured Analysis: A Language for Communicating Ideas; IEEE Transactions on Software Engineering, Vol. SE-3, No. 1; 1979.

[25] Introduction to IDEF; SoftTech Inc., Waltham/Mass. 1979.

[26] R.R. Bravoco, S.Y. Yadav; A Methodology to Model The Information Structure of an Organization; Computers in Industry 6; 1985; 354-361.

[27] DAFNE (Data and Function Networking) An Integrated Methodology boosting SADT capabilities; ITALSIEL; 1985.

[28] J.L. Peterson, Petri Net Theory and Modelling of Systems; Prentice-Hall; 1982.

[29] G. Doumeingts, B. Vallespir, D. Darricau, M. Roboam; Design Methodology for Advanced Manufacturing Systems; Computers in Industry 9; 1987; 271-296.

[30] P.P.S. Chen; The Entity-Relationship model: toward a unified view of data; ACM Trans. on Database Systems, Vol 1, No. 1; 1976.

[31] H. Engelke, J. Grotrian, C. Scheuing, A. Schmackpfeffer, W. Schwartz, B. Solf, J. Tomann; Integrated Manufacturing Modeling System; IBM Journal of Research and Development, Vol. 29, No. 4; 1985; 343-355.

[32] F. Vernadat, A. Di Leva, P. Giolito; Organization and information system design of manufacturing environments: the new M* approach; Computer-Integrated Manufacturing Systems, Vol. 2, No. 2; 1989; 69-81.

6.5 Integrated Infrastructure - State of the Art

[33] NBS AMRF: Automated Manufacturing Research Facility

[34] IISS (Integrated Information Support System)

[35] ANSI paper on Information Resource Dictionary System

[36] MAP, TOP and CNMA Specifications

[37] ISO/IEC JTC1:
- Open System Interconnection (OSI)
- Distributed Transaction Processing (DTP)
- Remote Database Access (RDA)
- Reference Model of Data Management (RMDM)
- Distributed Office Application Model (DOAM)
- Information Resource Dictionary System (IRDS)
- Application Layer Structure (ALS)
- Remote procedure Call (RPC)
- Remote Operation Service Element (ROSE)
- The Directory
- ESTELLE and LOTOS
- Abstract Syntax Nr.1 (ASN1)
- Open Distributed Processing(ODP)
- Portable Operating System Interface for Computer Environments (POSIX)

[38] ISO TC 184:
- Manufacturing Message Specification (MMS)
- Standard for Exchange of Product Data (STEP)

[39] CCITT:
- Distributed Application Framework (DAF)

[40] ECMA:
- Support Environment for Open Distributed Processing (SE-ODP)

[41] DIN Technical Report 15: Many existing and emerging standards in the area of CIM like NC processing, Machine interfaces, graphic language and text/graphic interchange formats.

6.6 CIMOSA General References

[42] Beeckman, D. (1989), Intern. Journ. of CIM, 2, 94-105
[43] ESPRIT Consortium AMICE, (1987), Public Document (private publication)
[44] ESPRIT Consortium AMICE, (1988), Public Document (private publication)
[45] ESPRIT Consortium AMICE, (1989), Open System Architecture for CIM, Springer Heidelberg
[46] Klittich, (1990), Intern. Journ. of CIM, (to be published)
[47] Kosanke, K., Vlietstra, J., (1989) Proceedings IFIP, 759-770 (2 papers)
[48] Kosanke, K., T. Klevers, (1990). Journ. Computer Integrated Manufacturing Systems, 3, 47-52
[49] Vernadat, Jorysz, (1990), Intern, Journ. of CIM (2 papers, to be published)

Part 3

User Guide on Requirements Definition Model

Part 3 provides a general user guidance for the use of the Open System Architecture for CIM (CIMOSA) in enterprise modelling. The current version is on requirements definition only. This user guide is based on the current status of the work on CIMOSA being undertaken by the ESPRIT Consortium AMICE. The examples provided are taken from a project case study carried out at Aerospatiale.

1   Introduction

Business Requirements Definition results in a CIMOSA Requirements Definition Model which expresses all the business function, information, resource and organisation needs of the CIM system to be implemented in the enterprise under consideration. This model defines what has to be done in a business sense from the business users point of view without reference to specific implementation options or decisions.

The Requirements Definition Model should be entirely described by end-users to really capture his view of the business needs. To build that model, CIMOSA therefore provides a set of Generic Building Blocks which are easily understandable by business users, and cover the important aspects of a manufacturing system. The Generic Building Blocks can be considered as an elementary modelling language used to model a specific aspect of the enterprise. The Generic Building Blocks used to build a CIMOSA Requirements Definition Model are the following:

> Domain (Function View)
> Domain Objective/Constraint (Function View)
> Domain Relationship (Function View)
> Event (Function View)
> Domain Process (Function View)
> Declarative Rule (Function View)
> Business Process (Function View)
> Enterprise Activity (Function View)
> Enterprise Object (Function View & Information View)
> Object View (Function View & Information View)
> Information Element (Information View)
> Integrity Rule (Information View)
> Abstraction Mechanism (Information View)
> Object Relationship (Information View)
> Capability (Function View & Resource View)
> Responsibility (Function View & Organisation View)
> Authorisation (Function View & Organisation View)

Building Blocks for information, resource and organisational aspects are used in more than one view. For example, Object Views are first identified in the Function View and then further described, structured and detailed in the Information View (Information Analysis). Requirements Definition Models can be represented in two ways:

- in structured textual form using description templates of the Generic Building Blocks;
- in graphical form using the graphical representation of the same Building Blocks (optional).

CIMOSA has defined a description template for each Generic Building Block. In some sense, documenting a Requirements Definition Model consists in filling in the blanks in the templates. Templates can be filled in progressively when business users go along the different phases of the System Requirements Definition, or at the end of the System Requirements Definition when all information is available. It is important to note that a Requirements Definition Model must not necessarily be complete and consistent. It will be logically re-structured, optimised and simulated at the Design Specification Level before being translated into an Implementation Description Model which is computer executable on the Integrating Infrastructure for model based operation control and monitoring.

As an example for a CIMOSA template, the description template for the Building Block "Objective/Constraint" is provided. The template in its generic form provides at its left side the items to be described and on its right site the relevant information to be provided by the user. For consistent description of the Generic Building Blocks most entries are mandatory. Optional information is identified as such.

Template: OBJECTIVE/CONSTRAINT (generic)

TYPE:	[relevant category-select from list <name>]
IDENTIFIER:	[OC-<Unique Identifier>]
NAME:	[name of the Objective/Constraint in the form: <noun1> <noun2> <noun3> where <noun1>: subject of objective or constraint <noun2>: either <target> or <constraint> <noun3>: object of objective or constraint]
DESIGN AUTHORITY:	[name of person and department with authority to design/maintain this particular instance]
DESCRIPTION:	[textual description. Mandatory]
SUBJECT:	[<identifier> / <name> of Enterprise Object instance which is subject of objective or constraint. optional]
TARGET:	[<identifier> / <name> of Information Element of Enterprise Object instance which is target of objective/constraint. Only used if SUBJECT entry is defined]
VALUE:	[<value1> / <value2> where <value1> = lower limit <value2> = upper limit Note: If only one value is given <value2> must contain <minimum> or <absolute>. Only used if SUBJECT entry is defined]
VALIDITY:	[date from: <yy.mm.dd.> / date to <yy.mm.dd.> where any date can be replaced by <unlimited>. Optional]
INHERITED FROM:	[list of <identifier> / <name> of Objective/constraint instance from which this Objective/Constraint instance is inherited]

The level of details of a Requirements Definition Model is left to the user but it must state the required basic functionalities, information and capabilities as well as objects handled and organisation structure needed. An example of the use of the Objective/Constraint template is given below. Here the information required has been provided for a manufacturing related activity concerned with implementation of a new Motor Assembly Line. Subject and Target are defined using information view identifiers (EO = Enterprise Object, IE = Information Element) taken from an AMICE project case study. The example also identifies the inheritance from higher level definitions (OC-23).

Template: OBJECTIVE/CONSTRAINT

OBJECTIVE/CONSTRAINT

TYPE:	Constraint / system design /investment
IDENTIFIER:	OC-IN1234
NAME:	INVESTMENT CONSTRAINT MOTOR ASSEMBLY
DESIGN AUTHORITY:	J. P. Smith / Manufacturing engineering
DESCRIPTION:	Investment for motor assembly is limited to Ecu 5,000, 000 for new product line.
SUBJECT:	EO-IN4481 / INVESTMENT
TARGET:	IE-111 / Inv_Amount
VALUES:	ECU 5, 000, 000 / maximum
VALIDITY:	unlimited / 90.09.30
INHERITED FROM:	OC-23 / MOTOR ASSEMBLY PLANT CONSTRAINT

The System Requirements Definition is split into six phases:

System Requirements Definition

- Domain Establishment
- Behaviour Analysis
- Operational Analysis
- Information Analysis
- Organisation Analysis
- Consistency Checking

During **Domain Establishment** business users have first to define the Domain to be modelled and identify the set of Domain Processes representing the business that should be done within the Domain. A CIMOSA Domain represents a sub-set of the enterprise to be analysed and for which a CIMOSA compliant Particular Model will be created. In other words, a Domain describes a part of an enterprise and its relationships with the outside environment from a high-level management point of view.

The second phase of the System Requirements Definition deals with the Domain Process **Behaviour Analysis**. It is concerned with functional decomposition of Domain Process(es) into Business Processes and Enterprise Activities which cooperate together to achieve the desired objectives. Domain Process behaviour analysis leads to the identification of the control flow connecting Enterprise Activities. Business Processes are structuring the Domain Process behaviour into subsets of Procedural Rules Set.

Operational Analysis defines all Inputs and Outputs (Function, Control and Resource) of the Enterprise Activities as Object Views. This includes the required resource capabilities and the authorised responsibilities.

The purpose of the **Information Analysis** is to capture the information needs of an enterprise expressed in the operational analysis in an Enterprise Object structure and to provide sufficient details (Information Elements) to allow the consistent derivation of these Information Requirements into the Information View of the Design Specification Model.

Organisation Analysis defines Organisation Centers and Organisation Structure of the enterprise starting from definition of responsibilities and authorisation. Thus allowing to establish decision-making processes based on responsibilities defined for processes, functionalities, information, resources, etc. to be defined in the Function View.

Consistency Checking verifies the consistent definition of the various points of view (Function, Information, Resource and Organisation) described in a Requirements Definition Model. In general, a Consistency Checking must be performed between any two Views of CIMOSA. For example the Function View and the Information View are related by means of Object Views. All Function Inputs, Function Outputs and Control Inputs must be described as Object Views in the Information View. If information needed for an Enterprise Activity is not described as an Object View in the Information View, this is an inconsistency. It is assumed that the Consistency Checking will be done automatically by CAEE tools. It is not developed in the present version of User Guide

2 Domain Establishment

Using CIMOSA to elaborate the Requirements Definition Model of an enterprise one starts with defining the modelling Domain. CIMOSA views an enterprise as a dynamic system made of communicating Domains (sub-systems e.g. subcontractors will be particular Domains[1]) containing Domain Processes, consuming or simply using Events and Enterprise Objects (perceived as Object Views). In other words, a complete CIMOSA enterprise can be perceived as a federation of Domains generating and receiving Events and sharing Enterprise Objects[2].

Domain Establishment can be split into several steps:

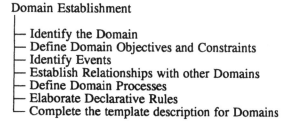

A prerequisite for CIMOSA Domain Establishment is that enterprise's business objectives and constraints are determined for the part of the enterprise (Domain) to be modelled. This requires to decompose the enterprise's objectives & constraints in objectives and constraints of the Domain. The result of the Domain Establishment phase is presented as a set of Domains each defined by a description template. The description template provided by CIMOSA for Domain description is shown below:

---

[1]   Note: a subcontracting enterprise can be constrained by several clients and must therefore behave as being a Domain included in several enterprises.

[2]   Note: in general, different Domains have different views on the same Object.

124

The Generic Building Blocks used in Domain Establishment are:

Domain
Domain Objective/Constraint
Domain Relationship
Event
Domain Process
Declarative Rule
Enterprise Object (further defined in § 2.4)
Object View (further defined in § 2.4)

Template: DOMAIN (generic)

DOMAIN

Part 1:   DOMAIN DESCRIPTION

TYPE: [relevant category - select from list]

IDENTIFIER: [DM-<unique identifier>]

NAME: [name of Domain in the form <adjective>
                                 <noun>, where
                                 <noun> relates to functionality,
                                 <adjective> relates to scope]

DESIGN AUTHORITY:
                                 [name of person & department with authority
                                 to design/maintain this particular instance]

DOMAIN DESCRIPTION:
                                 [short textual description of objectives and
                                 constraints of Domain and of Domain
                                 Processes required to achieve objectives]

CIMOSA COMPLIANT: ['yes' or 'no']

Part 2: DOMAIN COMPONENTS

DOMAIN OBJECTIVES·
                                 [non-empty list of identifiers and names
                                 separated by / of objective/constraint
                                 instances describing objectives to be fulfilled
                                 by Domain instance]
DOMAIN CONSTRAINTS.
                                 [list of identifiers and names separated by / of
                                 objective/constraint instances describing
                                 constraints imposed on Domain instance]

Template: DOMAIN DESCRIPTION (continued)

DOMAIN PROCESSES:	[non-empty list of identifiers and names separated by / of Domain Processes performed by Domain instance. Can be left empty if CIMOSA compliancy is 'no']
BOUNDARY:	[non-empty list of identifiers and names separated by / of Domain Relationship instances between this Domain instance and other Domain instances]
OBJECT VIEWS:	[non-empty list of identifiers and names separated by / of all Object View instances, occurrences of which can be received, used or sent by occurrences of Domain instance. Can be left empty if CIMOSA compliancy is 'no']
EVENTS:	[non-empty list of identifiers and names separated by / of all Event instances, occurrences of which can be received, used or sent by occurrences of Domain instance. Can be left empty if CIMOSA compliancy is 'no']

The description template of a Domain can be associated with other templates to describe in detail the components of a Domain: Domain Objective/Constraint, Domain Relationship and Event. Domain Processes will be defined using its template during the Behaviour Analysis phase.

2.1   Identify a Domain

Domains describe a part of an enterprise and its relationships with the outside environment from a high-level management point of view. One distinguishes a CIMOSA Domain from non-CIMOSA Domains. A CIMOSA Domain represents a sub-set of the enterprise to be modelled and analysed. CIMOSA aims at breaking down the classical boundaries created by Taylorism in enterprise organisation structures. To achieve this goal some Domain identification principles are proposed:

- Domain Boundaries do not map to the organisational structure or physical units of a company, such as departments or plants. Instead one must think in terms of process networks rather than in terms of function responsibilities. Never cut across a management, operational and/or support business processes by a Domain boundary.

- Start CIMOSA with a well defined Domain, i.e. one containing full management, operational and support processes. Then expansion can be made in two ways:
  (1) make it bigger to include other Domain Processes;
  (2) decompose further an Enterprise Activity.
- If a Domain external process is often triggered by an internal process, include this external process in the Domain in order to reduce events between Domains.
- Avoid isolated function-oriented Domains and "big islands of automation" by grouping as many closely inter-related Domain Processes as possible into one Domain.
- Domains are not allowed to overlap, i.e. two distinct Domains can not share a common Domain Process.

Non-CIMOSA Domains only need to be identified and can be incompletely described. The internal details of non-CIMOSA Domains are hidden and only their exchange with CIMOSA Domains (Events and Object Views) must be precisely defined. For example, in the Aerospatiale case study, CIMOSA Domain and non-CIMOSA Domains are identified as follows:

CIMOSA Domain:

- FMS (Flexible Manufacturing Shop)

non-CIMOSA Domains:

- PRODUCTION CONTROL
- MANUFACTURING ENGINEERING
- QUALITY ASSURANCE
- PROCUREMENT
- PLANT STORAGE
- MAINTENANCE

2.2 Define Domain Objectives and Constraints

For each Domain the Domain Objectives and Constraints must be defined. Domain Objectives and Constraints are either obtained on enterprise level directly from management authorities (directors, top managers, department heads, and the like) or are derive from the high level ones.

Domain Objectives define the business goals and expected achievements imposed on the Domain, i.e. measurable and realistic desired end results for the enterprise's business. Domain Objectives can be expressed in terms of:

- goals (budget, profit, revenue, return on investment)
- strategic business plans (product groups, product prices, product volumes..)

Domain Constraints describe enterprise constraints imposed on the Domain, expressing conditions restraining the range of possibilities of some enterprise processes or entities within that Domain. Domain Constraints can be expressed in terms of:

- limitations (investment limits, personnel limits, given locations, supplier availability, time requirements)

■ policies (scope of enterprise - make or buy, size of plants, plant location, supplier constraints, etc.)
■ risk taken or accepted.

Domain Objectives and Constraints influence the definition of Domain Processes. Domain Objectives and Constraints will be further decomposed into the Objectives and Constraints of Domain Processes. CIMOSA provides description template for Objectives/Constraints. Each Domain Objective and Constraint must be described using the relevant template. As an illustration example, the main Objectives and Constraints of the FMS Domain in the Aerospatiale case study are defined below. The main constraint imposed on this FMS Domain is the constraint on resources. All developments leading to proposals of new machines need a justification based on the return-on-investment and flexibility gain.

1°: maximize productivity and flexibility
2°: minimize cycle time and work-in-process
3°: improve quality and labour conditions.

An example of the description template for Domain Objective n°2 identified above is shown below:

Template: DOMAIN OBJECTIVES/CONSTRAINTS

```
DOMAIN OBJECTIVE/CONSTRAINT

TYPE:                tbd
IDENTIFIER:          DO-02
NAME:                Objective of cycle-time
DESIGN AUTHORITY:    DE/BO
DESCRIPTION:         Domain Processes must be analysed by taking
                     into account objective of minimizing cycle
                     time: complete cycle for each batch is
                     expected to be divided by 2 and work-in-
                     process by 3.
SUBJECT:
TARGET:
VALUES:
VALIDITY:            from < build-time > to < run-time >

INHERITED FROM:      /
```

Some of these Objectives and Constraints will be taken into account in the Generation Process (e.g. the Objective minimising Batch volume dictates the process structure) and in the Derivation Process (e.g. the Objective of Flexibility dictates constraints on the resource choices). Some other will be translated in Declarative Rules to be applied for decision making activities (run-time decision rules).

2.3   Identify Events

An Event describes real-world happenings or requests to do something in the enterprise or in its environment. It can carry information (defined as an Object View) and it triggers the execution of one or more Domain Processes by initiating the processing of their associated set of Procedural Rules. This will result in the activation of a group of Business Processes and/or Enterprise Activities, which together comprise the Domain Process. CIMOSA provides a Generic Building Block "Event" to describe those real-world happenings. The sources of Events in a CIMOSA model are limited to:

- Resources (e.g. machine failure, error detection, management orders etc.)
- Enterprise Activities (e.g. request to do something, list of orders, error detection, etc.)
- Domain for Events coming from outside the model (e.g. management orders, customer requests, etc.).

Two kinds of Events are used in CIMOSA:

- Endogenous (or internal) Events: An Event occurring within a Domain. Endogenous Events are generated by Enterprise Activities or Resources within the Domain.
- Exogeneous (or external) Events: An Event occurring in another Domain but requires processing within the particular Domain. It crosses the boundary of the Domain and is therefore involved in at least one Domain Relationship.

An Event is defined by:

- the identification of its source,
- the event type,
- a textual description of the event,
- an identification of the Domain Process to be triggered

Examples of Events can be the following:

- Timer (i.e. clock times) indicating when certain enterprise actions have to be performed (e.g. time = 5:00 p.m.).
- Requests or orders (i.e. solicited happenings) such as arrival of an order, a customer request, a management order, etc.
- Unsolicited happenings such as a signal indicating a machine failure, an alarm, etc.

Defining Events consists in identifying real-world happenings which must be dealt with during the enterprise operation. For the illustration purpose, let us see how Events (EV-xx) are identified in the Aerospatiale case study.

- Some spare parts are urgently needed somewhere: EV-03
- A manufacturing order can not be accepted: EV-98
- A manufacturing order is accepted, trigger a Machining Process: EV-10
- A machine fails during the machining: EV-02
- A maintenance is needed: EV-99
- A maintenance action is finished: EV-04
- etc...

CIMOSA provides a description template to fully describe an Event. An example of the description template for Event "EV-02" is given below.

Template: ENTERPRISE EVENTS

ENTERPRISE EVENT: RESOURCE EXCEPTION

TYPE:	Happening / Non-deterministic
IDENTIFIER:	EV-02
NAME:	RESOURCE EXCEPTION
DESIGN AUTHORITY:	DE/BO
DESCRIPTION:	During performance of Operational Enterprise Activities, any status change (to/from abnormal situation) of employed resource has to raise this Event.
GENERATED BY:	Operational Enterprise Activities
TRIGGERS:	DP-02 / EXCEPTION MANAGEMENT
RELATED OBJECT:	none

2.4   Establish Relationships with other Domains

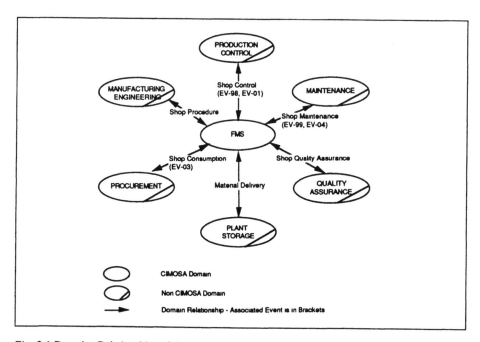

Fig. 3.1 Domains Relationships of the FMS Domain

CIMOSA views a manufacturing system as a set of Domains communicating with each other. Therefore relationships between Domains must be clearly defined. The Domain Relationship defines the interactions and exchange of the Domain being considered with another Domain. A Domain Relationship indicates Events and Object Views which can be exchanged between two Domains, specifying those received and produced by the Domains. An Object View is one particular description of an Enterprise Objects as it is perceived by a user according to his stand-point. An Enterprise Object being a generalised entities (concrete or abstract) of the enterprise (ex. Machine, Production Plan etc.) may be described by many Object Views. Object Views and Enterprise Objects are defined in the Information Analysis phase. Here, only the names of Object Views involved in Domain Relationships are identified. In the Aerospatiale case study, the relationships between the CIMOSA Domain FMS and non-CIMOSA Domains are shown in Fig. 3.1. Only those Object Views and Events involved in the Relationships are mentioned which are important to develop the case study (see following table).

RELATIONSHIP NAME	INVOLVED OBJECT VIEWS	EVENT
Shop Control	Manufacturing order	EV-98 EV-01
Shop Procedure	Process Plan Part Program	
Shop Consumption	Cutter	EV-03
Material Delivery	Part	
Shop Maintenance	Machine	EV-04 EV-99
Shop Quality Assurance	Inspection Procedure and Report	

Template: DOMAIN RELATIONSHIP

```
DOMAIN RELATIONSHIP: SHOP CONTROL

TYPE:                tbd
IDENTIFIER:          RL-08
NAME:                SHOP CONTROL
DESIGN AUTHORITY:    DE/BO
DESCRIPTION:         Through this relationship, PRODUCTION
                       CONTROL Domain receives a synthetic
                       view of Shop Capacity and Work-In-
                       Progress in FMS Domain.
DOMAIN 1 NAME:       FMS (Flexible Manufacturing Shop)
DOMAIN 2 NAME:       PRODUCTION CONTROL
INVOLVED OBJECT VIEWS:
                       - OV-015: Shop
                       - OV-016: Shop workload
INVOLVED EVENTS:     EV-98 /
                     EV-01 /
```

CIMOSA provides a description template to define a Domain Relationship with an example for the Domain Relationship "Shop Monitoring" shown above:

Domain Boundaries defined by means of Domain Relationships might need to be modified during the following steps. A typical example is that it might be necessary to enlarge the Domain by including "external" functions to avoid breaks in natural processes and to limit Events between Domains in order to improve the Domain consistency and contribute to reduction of Taylorism-based functional areas.

2.5 Define Domain Processes

Domain Processes define functionalities and behaviour of a Domain. These processes are stand-alone processes triggered by Events and governing the execution of Enterprise Activities (i.e. basic functionalities), according to so called Procedural Rules and Declarative Rules producing a defined result. CIMOSA is basically a Process oriented, Event-driven approach. The definition of Domain Processes is tightly dependant on the identification of Events which solicit actions in the Domain. The business user must ask the following question during the Events and Domain Processes definition:

what can happen (Events) and, what has to be done about these happenings (Domain Processes)

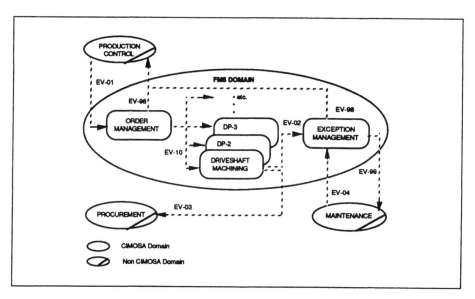

Fig. 3.2 Domain Processes of the FMS Domain

Talking about happenings, the term "exception" can hardly be ignored. Two types of exception must be distinguished:

- Normal exception: which must be included in the process body by calling an enterprise function according to a particular ending status (if... then),

- Abnormal exception: which cannot be foreseen (e.g. machine failure); in that case, the process is suspended but some decisions have to be made elsewhere.

As a Domain Process is only triggered by an Event, Events must be identified before defining Domain Processes. In general, whenever there is an Event identified, there must be a corresponding Domain Process defined. However, an Event can be used to trigger several Domain Processes within an enterprise. A Domain Process can be triggered by means of several Events. Therefore, there is no one-to-one mapping between Events and Domain Processes. In the Aerospatiale FMS Domain, the following Domain Processes are defined to react to the Events previously identified:

- ORDER MANAGEMENT: The need of spare parts is addressed to the Production Control Domain which raises an EV-01 (manufacturing order) to trigger the ORDER MANAGEMENT Domain Process to plan manufacturing of spare parts. If the manufacturing order can not be accepted, an EV-98 is raised to trigger an associated Domain Process in the Production Control Domain. If the manufacturing order is accepted, the EV-10 is raised to trigger the DRIVESHAFT MACHINING Domain Process.

- DRIVESHAFT MACHINING (1 to 69): Triggered by EV-10, the DRIVESHAFT MACHINING Domain Process produces the parts according to the manufacturing order received. The FMS produces 69 types of parts manufactured in small to medium batches (typically 50). DRIVESHAFT MACHINING are long transformation processes composed of 10 to 20 transformation steps from raw material to finished parts. In fact, each type of part has a specific process plan which defines the steps to be executed in order to perform the batch transformation. In the case study, each process plan is modelled as a Domain Process: DRIVESHAFT MACHINING, (DP-1,..., DP-69).

- EXCEPTION MANAGEMENT: Triggered by EV-02 coming from the DRIVESHAFT MACHINING Domain Process, the EXCEPTION MANAGEMENT Domain Process deals with problems which have occurred during the execution of the DRIVESHAFT MACHINING Domain Process.

Fig. 3.2 shows how the FMS Domain Processes are triggered by Events. In the Aerospatiale FMS Domain, up to 71 Domain Processes are defined:.

ORDER MANAGEMENT
EXCEPTION MANAGEMENT
DRIVE SHAFT MACHINING:
- DP - 1
- DP - 2
- DP - 3
- ....
- DP - 69

Each Domain Process should be assigned the Objectives and Constraints which can be obtained by decomposing the Domain Objectives and Constraints in Objectives and Constraints of the Domain Processes. A Domain Process may have, optional Inputs and Outputs for Function, Control and Resources. Examples of Function Input and Output of the Domain Process "DRIVESHAFT MACHINING" are:

Function Input:	Driveshaft_Batch_Material
	Driveshaft_Batch_Status0
Function Output:	Driveshaft_Batch_Material
	Driveshaft_Batch_Status4

There is not a fixed behaviour relationship between Domain Processes. This means that Domain Processes are not linked by Procedural Rules (see Behaviour Analysis), but instead have to be considered as entities of functionality which are, in the time domain, independent from each other. In the example, it is not possible to state that after execution of the "DRIVESHAFT MACHINING" Domain Process, the "EXCEPTION MANAGEMENT" Domain Process will become active. This may happen, when a function of Domain Process "DRIVESHAFT MACHINING" fails, but it will (hopefully) not always be the case.

When defining Domain Processes, it is important to define them in such a way that they have a limited number of interactions between them. Domain Processes are "isolated" entities of functionality. The reason is that each Domain Process is at the root of a functional decomposition hierarchy. Inside such a hierarchy, where functions are linked by Procedural Rules, it is easy to follow and understand the control flow. Between different Domain Processes, control flows by sending and receiving events, which makes it much more difficult to follow the control flow. Therefore, interactions between Domain Processes should be minimised. Each Domain Process defined in a Domain, is related to Domain Objectives defined by business users. When starting further modelling of the Domain Processes, business users should start with the Domain Process(es) reflecting the most important objectives of the Domain. In the example, this would be Domain Process "DRIVESHAFT MACHINING". In fact, the prime objective of Domain "FMS" is to produce parts.

2.6 Elaborate Declarative Rules

Having identified the Domain Processes and having decomposed the Domain Objectives/Constraints in the Objectives and Constraints of Domain Processes, business users must define under what conditions objectives and constraints can be combined and applied, in terms of Declarative Rules. Declarative Rules are (complex) combinations of business objectives and constraints applicable to the execution of Domain Processes, as well as conditions on Business Processes and/or Enterprise Activities. To define Declarative Rules first, write down a list of objectives and of constraints applicable to the Domain Process considered. Then define logical combinations of objectives and constraints listed above to form conditions to be verified. Objectives and constraints can be connected by AND, OR and NOT operators. Finally, the Declarative Rule is defined in form of IF (set of conditions) THEN (set of rule elements). An example of a Declarative Rule described by template is provided above[3]. This example can be applied for a parts manufacturing Business Process which can serve regular customers or the army. Again EO identifies the related Enterprise Objects onto which the Declarative Rules are imposed and OC defines the Objectives and Constraints imposed on the Enterprise Objects. The Declarative Rules themselves are expressed as a set of conditions combining objectives and constraints and a set of IF-THEN-ELSE rules which are defined for the different conditions identified.

---

[3] Note: The same description template is used during the Behaviour Analysis phase to define Declarative Rules imposed on Business Processes and Enterprise Activities.

Template: DECLARATIVE RULE

```
DECLARATIVE RULE

TYPE:                Part Manufacturing
IDENTIFIER:          DR-102
NAME:                Quality Manufacturing Rule
DESIGN AUTHORITY:    J.J. Smith / Process Design

IMPOSED ON:          EO-34 / Product Quality
                     EO-52 / Supplier
                     EO-56 / Customer
COMPRISES:

   OBJECTIVES:       OC-20 / Scrap Rate < = 10%
                     OC-21 / Scrap Rate < = 5%
                     OC-22 / Scrap Rate < = 2%

   CONSTRAINTS:      OC-50 / Customer_Type = Defense
                     OC-51 / Customer_Type = Regular
                     OC-70 / Supplier_Type = "ABC"
                     OC-51 / Supplier_Type = "XYZ"

SET OF CONDITIONS:   C1: OC-20 AND OC-51
                     C2: OC-21 AND OC-50
                     C3: OC-22 AND OC-50

SET OF RULE ELEMENTS:
                     IF C1 THEN OC-70, OC-71 APPLY
                     IF C2 THEN OC-70, OC-71 APPLY
                     IF C3 THEN OC-71 APPLY
```

2.7 Complete the Description Template of Domains

At the end of the Domain Establishment phase, all the information needed to fully describe a Domain must be available[4]. The Domain description template is supposed to be filled in progressively. As an example, the FMS Domain of the Aerospatiale case study is described in the following:

---

4   Note: Each Domain Process will be defined by a description template at the end of the Behaviour Analysis phase, when all the Business Processes and/or Enterprise Activities employed by that Domain Process are identified.

Template: DOMAIN

```
DOMAIN (This example is incomplete)

Part 1:                  DOMAIN DESCRIPTION
TYPE:                    Production/Shop/Batch oriented
IDENTIFIER:              DM-01
NAME:                    Flexible Manufacturing Shop (FMS)
DESIGN AUTHORITY:        DE/BO
DESCRIPTION:             FMS is a Domain assigned to Production of a
                         wide range of cylindrical parts defined by
                         their dimensions and material types. Parts
                         will be manufactured on a medium-sized
                         batch basis. Quality control and traceability
                         are part of shop responsibility
CIMOSA COMPLIANT:        Yes

Part 2:                  DOMAIN COMPONENTS

DOMAIN OBJECTIVES:       DO-01/ maximize productivity and flexibility
                         DO-02/ minimize cycle time and WIP: cycle
                         time for each batch is expected to be divided
                         by 2 and WIP by 3
                         DO-03/ improve quality & labour conditions

DOMAIN CONSTRAINTS:
                         DC-01/ Constraint on Resources
                         DC-02/ Constraint on new investment

DOMAIN PROCESSES:        DP-01/ ORDER MANAGEMENT
                         DP-02/ EXCEPTION MANAGEMENT
                         DP-03/ DRIVESHAFT MACHINING
                         DP-04/
                         .....
                         DP-69/

DOMAIN BOUNDARY:         RL-01/ Manufacturing Order Release
                         RL-02/ Procedure Receipt
                         RL-03/ Consumable Receipt
                         RL-04/ Raw Material Receipt
                         RL-05/ Inspection Procedure Receipt

OBJECT VIEWS:            OV-015: Shop
                         OV-016: Shop workload

EVENTS:                  EV-03 / Some spare parts urgently needed
                         EV-98 / A manuf. order not accepted
                         EV-10 / A manuf. order accepted, trigger a
                            DP
                         EV-02 / A machine fails
                         EV-99 / A maintenance is needed
```

3   Behaviour Analysis

The purpose of the "Behaviour Analysis" is to define the behaviour of Domain Processes. Domain Processes will be further decomposed into Business Processes and/or Enterprise Activities, thereby defining the dynamic flow of control governing the set of Business Processes and/or Enterprise Activities of a particular enterprise Domain.

During the Behaviour Analysis, a business user will make use of Business Processes and Enterprise Activities already available in the Partial Models at the Partial Architecture Level. If he could not find the partial models suitable to represent his requirements, Generic Building Blocks will be directly used to define Business Processes and Enterprise Activities satisfying his requirements. He must try to make them as general as possible to facilitate their reusability.

The Behaviour Analysis phase can be split into several steps as follow:

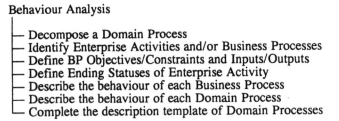

Behaviour Analysis

— Decompose a Domain Process
— Identify Enterprise Activities and/or Business Processes
— Define BP Objectives/Constraints and Inputs/Outputs
— Define Ending Statuses of Enterprise Activity
— Describe the behaviour of each Business Process
— Describe the behaviour of each Domain Process
— Complete the description template of Domain Processes

In general, each step is based on the result achieved at the previous step, but the process of the Behaviour Analysis may require several iterations steps to reach the final result. The final result of a Behaviour Analysis is composed of:

- a functional structure of each Domain Process
- a set of Business Processes
- a pool of "identified Enterprise Activities"

Domain Process decomposition results in the functional structure; a Business Process defines the Behaviour; and an Enterprise Activity defines basic functionality. At the end of the Behaviour Analysis phase, all the Domain Processes and their employed Business Processes must have been defined by description template. Enterprise Activities are just simply identified, they will be fully defined in the Operational Analysis phase.

3.1   Decompose a Domain Process

When a Domain Process is triggered by an Event, a set of tasks must be done to react to that event. Decomposing a Domain Process consists in identifying these tasks in terms of hierarchically structured functions. A function thus obtained can be a Business Process or an Enterprise Activity depending on its position in the hierarchy. The decomposition of a Domain Process must be made without any concern about the nature of these functions (Business Process or Enterprise Activity) before the complete decomposition is finished. One continues the decomposition until elementary tasks are identified. These elementary tasks are considered as basic functionalities of the Domain. Examples of basic functionalities could be: SCHEDULE WORKSHOP, MONITOR WORK-IN-PROGRESS, REPORT SHOP STATUS, SET-UP MACHINE, MAINTAIN WORKSTATION etc.

As an example, a CIM related Domain Process could be 'Production Planning'. It could be broken up into four functions (Business Processes/Enterprise Activities): 'Accept Customer Order', 'Schedule Production', 'Verify Capacity' and "Plan Raw Material". Each function can be further decomposed if necessary into lower level Business Processes/Enterprise Activities. Such a Domain Process would be triggered by the Event 'Customer Order' and would produce the result 'Production Schedule'. Fig. 3.3 shows graphically an example of such a decomposition. In practice, the result of a Domain Process decomposition can also be represented in a simple textual form (see below).

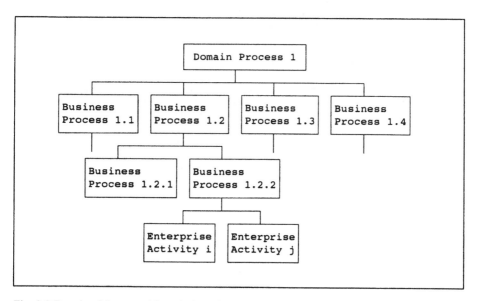

Fig. 3.3 Functional decomposition of a Domain Process

Let us see an example of how to decompose the Domain Process "DRIVESHAFT MACHINING" developed in the Aerospatiale case study. This Domain Process groups together all the machining tasks necessary to produce a batch of Driveshaft parts. The automation level of workstations is very unequal: complexity of part clamping often requires human handling but some turning centers are equipped with handling robots. Transport between stations and the automatic warehouse is performed by AGV's carrying parts and tools by means of pallets. The first level of decomposition allows to identify 9 Business Processes:

Domain Process 1 : DRIVESHAFT MACHINING

— Business Process 1.1: INPUT PARTS
— Business Process 1.2: SH-PREMILLING SUPPORT
— Business Process 1.3: DS-HEAD PREMILLING
— Business Process 1.4: DS-SHORTENING SUPPORT
— Business Process 1.5: DRIVESHAFT SHORTENING
— Business Process 1.6: TOOLSET PREPARING
— Business Process 1.7: DRIVESHAFT MILLING
— Business Process 1.8: DRIVESHAFT INSPECTION
— Business Process 1.9: OUTPUT PARTS

138

It may happen during a decomposition that one finds it necessary to merge several Domain Processes initially defined at the Domain Establishment phase, into one Domain Process. In this case, one should go back to the Domain Establishment phase to re-define Domain Processes, and then continue the Behaviour Analysis. When decomposing a Domain Process, the objectives and constraints assigned to that Domain Process must also be decomposed so that each enterprise functionality has its own Objectives/Constraints. An objective/constraint imposed on a function might influence the way of the further decomposition of that function. It may also be required at the Design Specification Modelling Level to make design choices. At the Requirements Definition Modelling Level, Objectives and Constraints can be combined together with conditions to form Declarative Rules which will constrain the run-time execution of these functions.

3.2 Identify Enterprise Activities and/or Business Processes

Enterprise Activities represent elementary tasks of the enterprise, therefore, they are at the lowest level of a functional decomposition. At this step, business users only need to identify these Enterprise Activities without specifying their inputs and outputs. Any enterprise functionality identified between the Domain Process level and Enterprise Activity level is called "Business Process". In other words, a Business Process describes pieces of enterprise behaviour at all levels of a functional decomposition hierarchy except the top and bottom levels. If a function at the lowest level which is supposed to be an Enterprise Activity, needs to be broken down into more detailed functionalities, then it becomes a Business Process. In this case, it is necessary to re-consider the functional decomposition hierarchy.

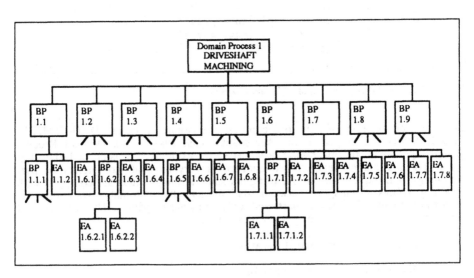

Fig. 3.4 Hierarchy of DP "DRIVESHAFT MACHINING"

It must be understood that a hierarchical definition does not mean that any given Business Process and/or Enterprise Activity is assigned to only one parent Domain Process and/or Business Process. Any Business Process or Enterprise Activity can be employed by any other process regardless of its relative positions in a function hierarchy. In the above example, the Enterprise Activity "STORE" is used by two Business Processes: BP-1.1. and BP-1.6.2. The Business Process "MOVE

PALLET" is used by two other Business Processes: BP-1.6 and BP-1.7. Thus Business Processes and Enterprise Activities can be re-used in a particular CIM system leading to economy of design.

In fact, once completely defined, a Domain Process equates to a network of Enterprise Activities triggered according to well defined conditions. Thus the most important Building Blocks in the Function view at the Requirements Definition Level are Domain Process and Enterprise Activity. The Business Process just provides a convenient way to structure Behaviour (Procedural Rules) and Enterprise Activities into easy manageable blocks to deal with complexity of the model. The Business user may have already noticed that the main differences between a Domain Process and a Business Process are:

(1)   a Domain Process has no parent structure,
(2)   a Business Process is never triggered by events,
(3)   Domain Processes are triggered by nothing than events.

Further detailing the example given above, the enterprise functions employed by the Domain Process "DRIVESHAFT MACHINING" can be either Business Processes or Enterprise Activities according to their position in the functional hierarchy (The graphical representation of the functional structure of this is shown Fig. 3.4):

```
Domain Process 1:    DRIVESHAFT MACHINING
├─ Business Process 1.1:    INPUT PARTS
│    ├─ Business Process 1.1.1:    PALLETISATION
│    └─ Enterprise Activity 1.1.2:    STORE
├─ Business Process 1.2:    SH-PREMILLING SUPPORT
├─ Business Process 1.3:    DS-HEAD PREMILLING
├─ Business Process 1.4:    DS-SHORTENING SUPPORT
├─ Business Process 1.5:    DRIVESHAFT SHORTENING
├─ Business Process 1.6:    TOOLSET PREPARING
│    ├─ Enterprise Activity 1.6.1:    ANALYSE TOOLSET
│    ├─ Business Process 1.6.2:    MOVE PALLET
│    │    ├─ Enterprise Activity 1.6.2.1:    TRANSPORT
│    │    └─ Enterprise Activity 1.6.2.2:    STORE
│    ├─ Enterprise Activity 1.6.3:    CHECK TOOLSET POTENTIAL
│    ├─ Enterprise Activity 1.6.4:    CREATE TOOL
│    ├─ Business Process 1.6.5:    DESTROY TOOLSET
│    ├─ Enterprise Activity 1.6.6:    CHANGE CUTTER
│    ├─ Enterprise Activity 1.6.7:    MEASURE TOOL
│    └─ Enterprise Activity 1.6.8:    DEFINE TOOL POTENTIAL
├─ Business Process 1.7:    DRIVESHAFT MILLING
│    ├─ Business Process 1.7.1:    MOVE PALLET
│    │    ├─ Enterprise Activity 1.7.1.1:    TRANSPORT
│    │    └─ Enterprise Activity 1.7.1.2:    STORE
│    ├─ Enterprise Activity 1.7.2:    SET-UP MACHINE
│    ├─ Enterprise Activity 1.7.3:    UP-DATE ORDER
│    ├─ Enterprise Activity 1.7.4:    LOAD PART
│    ├─ Enterprise Activity 1.7.5:    UNLOAD PART
│    ├─ Enterprise Activity 1.7.6:    MILL DRIVESHAFT
│    ├─ Enterprise Activity 1.7.7:    VERIFY DRIVESHAFT
│    └─ Enterprise Activity 1.7.8:    TEAR DOWN MACHINE
├─ Business Process 1.8:    DRIVESHAFT INSPECTION
└─ Business Process 1.9:    OUTPUT PARTS
```

Sometimes, the decomposition of a Domain Process results in only one level of hierarchy, such as the Domain Process "ORDER MANAGEMENT" developed in the Aerospatiale FMS case study. In this case, all functions can be directly considered as Enterprise Activities.

Domain Process - ORDER MANAGEMENT

    — Enterprise Activity 1: UPDATE PRODUCTION SCENARIO
    — Enterprise Activity 2: UPDATE SHOP CAPACITY
    — Enterprise Activity 3: SCHEDULE
    — Enterprise Activity 4: ANALYSE SCHEDULE

It may be helpful to know that an Enterprise Activity will be further decomposed (only one more level of detail), at the Design Specification Modelling Level, into Functional Operations which are the smallest pieces of tasks controlled by CIMOSA. A Functional Operation is executed by a Functional Entity specified in the Resource view at the Design Specification Modelling Level. Therefore, another criteria to control functional decomposition is to continue the decomposition until it is possible to identify Enterprise Activities made only by Functional Operations (each one executed by just one Functional Entity).

3.3   Define BP Objectives/Constraints and Inputs/Outputs

Having finished the identification of Business Processes, one has to define the Objectives and Constraints for each Business Process. Those can be obtained by decomposing the Objectives and Constraints of its parent Domain Process or Business Process. Some of the Objectives/Constraints will be applied during the Model development, others can be derived in Declarative Rules which will constrain the run-time execution of Enterprise Activities. Objectives, Constraints and Declarative Rules are described in the same way as done in the Domain Establishment Phase.

At the Requirements Definition Modelling Level, a Business Process can have, optional Input/Output for Function, Control and Resource. e.g. Function Inputs/Outputs allow to document at this early stage in the modelling process the desired end result (Function Output) of the Business Process, and the required Function Inputs to produce that result. These Inputs/Outputs are mainly defined as Object Views during the Information Analysis. As an illustration example, the Function Inputs/Outputs of the Business Process "DRIVESHAFT MILLING" can be identified as follow:

    Function Input: Driveshaft_batch_material
                             Driveshaft_batch_status2

    Function Output: Driveshaft_batch_material
                             Driveshaft_batch_status3

3.4   Define the Ending Status of an Enterprise Activity

Before describing the behaviour of each Business Process using Procedural Rules, the Ending Status of each Enterprise Activity must be identified. An Ending Status of an Enterprise Activity is a value describing one of the possible termination states of that Enterprise Activity. An Ending Status is needed for a Procedural Rule to determine which Enterprise Activity should be further triggered to continue the execution of the Business Process or Domain Process.

It is important to distinguish an Ending Status from an Event. An Enterprise Activity can generate an Event which triggers a different Domain Process. The Ending Status of an Enterprise Activity is used by its parent Business Process or Domain Process to determine what is the next Enterprise Activity to be triggered within the same Domain Process. The list of all possible Ending Status values for each Enterprise Activity must therefore be established in the CIMOSA model, if the behaviour of the enterprise is to be fully defined. There are no restrictions on the number of Ending Statuses defined for an Enterprise Activity (minimum number 1).

The Ending Status of a Business Process is the logical function of Ending Statuses of its employed Enterprise Activities. Several cases are possible:

- if Business Process BP1 always finishes by Enterprise Activity EA1, the Ending Status of BP1 is the Ending Status of EA1.
- if Business Process BP1 finishes by either Enterprise Activity EA1 or Enterprise Activity EA2, then the Ending Status of BP1 is given by (Ending status of EA1 or Ending Status of EA2)
- if Business Process BP1 finishes by both EA1 and EA2, then the Ending Status of BP1 is given by (Ending Status of EA1 AND Ending Status of EA2)

Remark: There is no Ending Status for Domain Processes because they are not used anywhere in the CIMOSA model. As an example for defining simple behaviour of the Business Process "TOOLSET PREPARING", the Ending Status value of its employed Business Processes and Enterprise Activities are[5]:

Enterprise Activity 1.6.1: ANALYSE TOOLSET	- DONE
Business Process 1.6.2: MOVE PALLET	- DONE
Enterprise Activity 1.6.3: CHECK TOOLSET POTENTIAL CREATE	-
	- RENOVATE
	- REACHED
Enterprise Activity 1.6.4: CREATE TOOL	- DONE
Business Process 1.6.5: DESTROY TOOLSET	- DONE
Enterprise Activity 1.6.6: CHANGE CUTTER	- DONE
Enterprise Activity 1.6.7: MEASURE TOOL DONE	-
Enterprise Activity 1.6.8: DEFINE TOOL POTENTIAL	- DONE

3.5 Describe the Behaviour of Business Process(es)

The behaviour of a Business Process defines the sequence of activation of Business Processes and/or Enterprise Activities employed by that Business Process. Before describing the behaviour of a Business Process, the Procedural Rule construct must be first presented. Procedural Rules are formal statements of the intended flow of actions associated to Domain Processes and Business Processes. The formal statement has the form:

'Wait for one or more Business Processes / Enterprise Activities to end with a specific status and then trigger one or more Business Processes / Enterprise Activities'.

Expressed in a general form the Procedural Rule can be written as a set of conditions and a related action:

---

5   Note: If the Enterprise Activity completes with an unspecified value exception handling has to be invoked.

WHEN (triggering condition) DO action

There are 5 types of Procedural Rule defined in CIMOSA[6]:

- **Type Process Triggering**: Process Triggering rules are used as first rules in a set of Procedural rules and define the triggering conditions of the Domain / Business Process.

    WHEN (Event_a)   DO EFy
    WHEN (START)   DO EFx
    WHEN (ES (EFx) = value 1)   DO EFy

    where
    EFy: Business Process or Enterprise Activity
    ES (EFx):   Ending Status of enterprise function x
    value a: represents a possible value for the ending status

- **Type Forced**: Forced Procedural Rules cause the next Enterprise Activity or Business Process to be activated independent of any status information.

    WHEN (ES (EFx) = any)   DO EFy

- **Type Conditional**: Conditional Procedural rules cause the activation of one of a defined number of Enterprise Activities or Business Processes according to the value of an Ending Status.

    WHEN (ES (EFx) = value_1)   DO EF1
    WHEN (ES (EFx) = value_2)   DO EF2
    WHEN (ES (EFx) = value_3)   DO EF3

- **Type Spawning**: Spawning Procedural rules cause the activation of two or more defined paths of Enterprise Activities or Business Processes in parallel.

    WHEN (ES (EFx) = value_1)   DO EF1 & EF2 & EF3

    Type Rendezvous: Rendezvous Procedural rules cause, firstly, a wait for all of the paths activated by a defined Spawning Procedural Rule to be completed and, secondly, for one or more Enterprise Activities or Business Processes to be activated.

    WHEN (ES(EF1)=value_1 &
           ES(EF2)=value_2 &
           ES(EF3)=value_3)   DO EF4

To define the behaviour of a Business Process, it is important to understand the role of the Business Process. The pool of Enterprise Activities represents the complete enterprise functionality. A Business Process defines how these Enterprise Activities have to be triggered in order to produce the desired result. Enterprise Activities do not belong to any Business Process but are employed by one or several processes via their associated Set of Procedural Rules. This relationship allows Enterprise Activities to be shared between different Business Processes and ensures a separation of functionality (Enterprise Activities) and behaviour (Business Processes) making it possible to revise behaviour, in order to meet changing circumstances, without altering the installed functionality. As an illustration

---

6   Note: Combination of these basic rules and loops (iterative execution of a subset of rules) are allowed.

example, the behaviour of the Business Process "TOOLSET PREPARING" developed in the Aerospatiale case study is presented below. Recall that this Business Process is decomposed as:

Business Process 1.6: TOOLSET PREPARING

- Enterprise Activity 1.6.1: ANALYSE TOOLSET
- Business Process 1.6.2: MOVE PALLET
- Enterprise Activity 1.6.3: CHECK TOOLSET POTENTIAL
- Enterprise Activity 1.6.4: CREATE TOOL
- Business Process 1.6.5: DESTROY TOOLSET
- Enterprise Activity 1.6.6: CHANGE CUTTER
- Enterprise Activity 1.6.7: MEASURE TOOL
- Enterprise Activity 1.6.8: DEFINE TOOL POTENTIAL

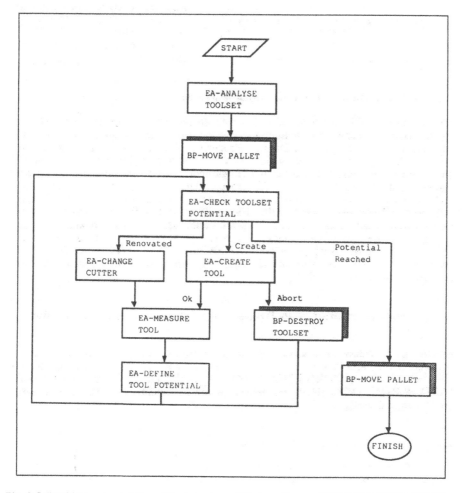

Fig. 3.5 Graphical representation of the behaviour of Business Process "TOOLSET PREPARING"

This Business Process behaviour is described in a textual representation given in the following (and shown in a graphical representation in Fig. 3.5):

```
WHEN (START)                                    DO ANALYSE TOOLSET
WHEN (ES(ANALYSE TOOLSET) = Done)               DO MOVE PALLET
WHEN (ES(MOVE PALLET) = Done)                   DO CHECK TOOLSET POTENTIAL
WHEN (ES(CHECK TOOLSET POTENTIAL) = Renovate)
                                                DO CHANGE CUTTER
WHEN (ES(CHECK TOOLSET POTENTIAL) = Create)
                                                DO CREATE TOOL
WHEN (ES(CHANGE CUTTER) = Done)                 DO MEASURE TOOL
WHEN (ES(CREATE TOOL) = Abort)                  DO DESTROY TOOLSET
WHEN (ES(CREATE TOOL) = Ok)                           DO MEASURE TOOL
WHEN (ES(MEASURE TOOL) = Done)                  DO DEFINE TOOLSET POTENTIAL
WHEN (ES(DEFINE TOOLSET POTENTIAL) = Done)
                                                DO CHECK TOOLSET POTENTIAL
WHEN (ES(DESTROY TOOLSET) = Done)               DO CHECK TOOLSET POTENTIAL
WHEN (ES(CHECK TOOLSET POTENTIAL) = Potential Reached)
                                                DO MOVE PALLET
WHEN (ES(MOVE PALLET) = Done)                   DO FINISH
```

3.6 Describe the Behaviour of a Domain Process

Having finished the behaviour description of all the Business Processes and having identified all possible Ending Statuses of each Enterprise Activity, one can start describing the behaviour of a Domain Process. A Domain Process behaves like a stand-alone dynamic object which has a structure (defined by functional decomposition hierarchy) and behaviour (defined by Procedural Rules describing how it reacts to external stimuli, i.e. Events). There must be one Procedural Rule set for each Domain Process[7]. As an illustration example, consider again the example of Domain Process "DRIVESHAFT MACHINING" developed in the Aerospatiale case study. In certain sense, one can say that Domain Process behaviour is the sum of all Business Processes behaviour plus the explicit definition of Event interactions (triggering point BP/EA in the DP[8]). All events have to be external to the DP described and all triggering points should be identified in the DP-PRS (sum of all BP-PRS's).

3.7 Complete the Description Template of a Domain Process and a Business Process

At the end of Behaviour Analysis, template description of the Domain Process and the related Business Process should have been finished. The template description of the Domain Process "DRIVESHAFT MACHINING" and of the Business Process "DRIVESHAFT MILLING" are shown below as examples (including the DP procedural rule set).

---

[7]   Note: Domain Processes are independent of one another, and are linked to other Domain Processes by events rather than by Procedural Rules.

[8]   Note: Enterprise Activities are not yet completely defined, but will be further described by a description template in the Operational Analysis Phase.

Template: DOMAIN PROCESS

DOMAIN PROCESS: DP-03, DRIVESHAFT MACHINING

TYPE:	Operational/Produce/Small Batch Machining
IDENTIFIER:	DP-03
NAME:	DRIVESHAFT MACHINING
DESIGN AUTHORITY:	DE/BO/ME
OBJECTIVE:	
CONSTRAINT:	
DECLARATIVE RULE:	
DESCRIPTION:	From a batch of raw Driveshaft (status 0), this Machining Process generates a batch of finished (from the Domain point of view) Driveshaft (with status 4).

EVENT:	EV-10/ ACCEPTED ORDER

FUNCTION INPUTS:	Driveshaft_Batch_Material
	Driveshaft_Batch_Status0
FUNCTION OUTPUT:	Driveshaft_Batch_Material
	Driveshaft_Batch_Status4
CONTROL INPUT:	
CONTROL OUTPUT:	
RESOURCE INPUT:	
RESOURCE OUTPUT:	

ENDING STATUS:	done (batch completion)

COMPRISES:	BP-3.1: Input parts
	BP-3.2: SH-Premilling Support
	BP-3.3: DS-Head Premilling
	BP-3.4: DS-Shortening Support
	BP-3.5: DRIVESHAFT Shortening
	BP-3.6: Toolset Preparing
	BP-3.7: Driveshaft Milling
	BP-3.8: Driveshaft Inspection
	BP-3.9: Output parts

PROCEDURAL RULES:

WHEN (Event_10)   DO INPUT PARTS & SH_PREMILLING SUPPORT

WHEN (ES(INPUT PARTS) = done & ES(SH_PREMILLING SUPPORT = done)
                                         DO DS_HEAD PREMILLING & DS_SHORTENING SUPPORT

Template: DOMAIN PROCESS (continued)

```
WHEN (ES(DS_HEAD PREMIL.) = done &
    ES(DS_SHORTEN. SUPPORT) = done)
                                    DO DRIVESHAFT
                                        SHORTENING &
                                    TOOLSET PREPARING
WHEN (ES(DRIVESHAFT SHORTEN.) = done &
    ES(TOOLSET PREPAR.) = done)   DO DRIVESHAFT
                                        MILLING
WHEN (ES(DRIVESHAFT MILLING) = done)
                                    DO DRIVESHAFT
                                        INSPECTION
WHEN (ES(DRIVESHAFT INSPECTION) = done)
                                    DO OUTPUT PARTS
WHEN (ES(OUTPUT PARTS) = done )   DO FINISH
```

Template: BUSINESS PROCESS

```
BUSINESS PROCESS: BP-3.7, DRIVESHAFT MILLING
TYPE:                Operational/Produce/Small Batch Machining
IDENTIFIER:          BP-3.7
NAME:                DRIVESHAFT MILLING
DESIGN AUTHORITY:    DE/BO/ME MANUFACTURING
                     ENGINEERING

OBJECTIVE:
CONSTRAINT:
DECLARATIVE RULE:
DESCRIPTION:         Business Process performs milling of a
                     Driveshaft batch and updates status of
                     associated Manufacturing Order.
– FUNCTION INPUT:    OV-33: Driveshaft_Batch_Material
                     OV-67: Driveshaft_Batch_Status2
FUNCTION OUTPUT:     OV-33: Driveshaft_Batch_Material
                     OV-68: Driveshaft_Batch_Status3

CONTROL INPUT:
CONTROL OUTPUT:
RESOURCE INPUT:
RESOURCE OUTPUT:
ENDING STATUS:       done (completion status)
COMPRISES:           EA-3.7.1: ANALYSE toolset
                     BP-3.7.2: Move pallet
                     EA-3.7.3: Check Toolset potential
                     EA-3.7.4: Create tool
                     BP-3.7.5: Destroy toolset
                     EA-3.7.6: Change cutter
                     EA-3.7.7: Measure tool
                     EA-3.7.8: Define tool potential
PROCEDURAL RULES:
```

4   Operational Analysis

Enterprise Activity describe the operations required to produce the defined Outputs from the Inputs provided (see Fig. 3.6). The functionality of an Enterprise Activity will be further decomposed at the Design Specification Modelling Level into a set of Functional Operations to be executed by Human, Machine or Application Functional Entities. After the "Behaviour Analysis" has been completed, the set of identified Enterprise Activities must be specified. The third phase of the System Requirements Definition aims at defining all Inputs and Outputs of these Enterprise Activities.

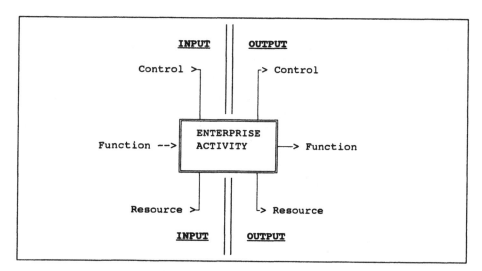

Fig. 3.6 Enterprise Activity Inputs and Outputs.

The Operational Analysis is split in the following steps:

Operational Analysis

- Define Function Input/Output
- Define Control Input
- Define Control Output
- Define Resource Input
- Define Resource Output
- Describe Required Capability (Resource View)

4.1   Define the Function Input/Output

The Function Input of an Enterprise Activity is a set of Object Views on Enterprise Objects which are operated on by the functionality of that Enterprise Activity. These Object Views can come from the Function Output of another one of the Enterprise Activities of the Domain or from the outside, i.e. from another Domain via a Domain Relationship. Similarly the Function Output of an Enterprise Activity is a set of Object Views produced as a result of the operations performed on its Function Input under the constraint of its Control Input. As an example, typical Function Input and Output of a Customer Order Processing activity are defined in reference to a customer order, the product file and the customer file. This will be indicated in the Function Input entry and Function Output entry of an Enterprise Activity:

FUNCTION INPUT: - OV-1 / Customer_Order
                         - OV-2 / Product_File
                         - OV-3 / Customer_File

FUNCTION OUTPUT: - OV-10 / Validated_Order
                         - OV-11 / Product_Request
                         - OV-12 / Pending_Customer_Bill

where Customer_Order, Product_File etc. are names of Object Views.

When defining Function Input and Output as Object Views on Enterprise Objects, it is useful to distinguish two major classes of Object Views - physical and information. Physical Object Views are concerned with concrete objects of the Enterprise (e.g. raw materials, workpieces, end products, etc.). Information Object Views are concerned with abstract entities of the enterprise (e.g. documents, forms, files data, etc.). In the Aerospatiale case study, the Function Input and Output of the Enterprise Activity "CREATE TOOL" is an example of physical Object Views. It resembles a Cutter, a Holder and Intermediate Elements to form a Tool.

FUNCTION INPUT: - OV-051-00: Holder
                         - OV-053-00: Cutter
                         - OV-052-00: Intermediate Elements

FUNCTION OUTPUT: - OV-031-02: Cutting Tool

Another example of the Function Input and Output of the Enterprise Activity used by the Domain Process "ORDER MANAGEMENT" is concerned with information Object Views.

EA-110: ANALYSE SCHEDULE

FUNCTION INPUT: - OV-103-04: Proposed workplan
                         - OV-110-00: Simulation Results

FUNCTION OUTPUT: - OV-103-03: Release Workplan

According to the nature of Function Input and Output (physical Object Views or Information Object Views) the flow of information and the flow of materials can be derived from the CIMOSA model from the definition of the Enterprise Activities. These two flows are independent of the flow of control represented by the set of Procedural Rules governing the sequence of execution of the Enterprise Activities of the model. In some cases, it is not easy to distinguish a Function Input from a Control Input. One criteria is that a Function Input is processed during the execution of the Enterprise Activity, while a Control Input is not processed.

4.2   Define the Control Input

A Control Input contains information used to control or to constrain the execution of an Enterprise Activity but not being processed by the Enterprise Activity. In other words, a Control Input is defined as a set of Object Views which will be used to direct (i.e. constrain) or pass run-time information to the operations of an Enterprise activity, and not be transformed by the operations of the Enterprise

Activity (e.g. part identification, manufacturing schedules, NC programs etc.). In some cases, a Control Input may be interpreted as constraints on the operations, which contain such information as rules, instructions, company policies, e.g. the Enterprise Activity can only be used within certain quantity limits, or allowable scrap rate. The Object View of a Control Input can come from Function Output of other Enterprise Activities, outside Domains or be associated to the Events involved in the triggering of the Domain Process employing the Enterprise Activity. An example of Control Input:

A machining activity is constrained by the instructions of a given NC-Programme. This NC-Programme is an Object View produced as the Function Output of another activity "PREPARE NC-PROGRAMME and used as Control Input of this Machining activity. In the Control Input it is refereed to as:

CONTROL INPUT: - OV-1 / NC-PROGRAMME

The Object View OV-1 / NC-PROGRAMME will be further described in the Information Analysis.

In the Aerospatiale case study, the Enterprise Activity EA-1.6.4 "CREATE TOOL" is executed according to the rules provided by the definition of the Formal Tool. In other words, "Formal Tool" defines the functionality and standard characteristics of a cutting tool. The Control Input is therefore defined as:

EA-1.6.4: CREATE TOOL

CONTROL INPUT: - OV-031-02: Formal Tool

The Enterprise Activity "CREATE TOOL" is employed by Business Process "Toolset Preparing" whose role is to generate a Toolset i.e. the set of tools required by a workstation operation.

4.3   Define the Control Output

The Control Output of an Enterprise Activity provides a set of Events, occurrences of which could be generated by occurrences of an Enterprise Activity or of its employing processes. During its execution an Enterprise Activity can raise Events, which can in turn activate the processing of Domain Processes within the same Domain (endogenous Events) or in other Domains (exogeneous Events). The list of such Events is provided by the Control Output of an Enterprise Activity.

As an example, let us consider a Machining Monitoring Enterprise Activity. This activity compares the actual machining operations status with the planned schedule. In case of significant deviations the activity can trigger a Domain Process for re-scheduling, raising an Event EV-01 called Re-scheduling Request. If no other Event can be generated by this activity its Control Output is then denoted by:

CONTROL OUTPUT: - EV-01 / Re-scheduling request

In the Aerospatiale case study, the Enterprise Activity EA-1.6.4. CREATE TOOL also controls the minimum level of local stock for cutters and can therefore generate an Event EV-03 to the PROCUREMENT Domain.

EA-1.6.4: CREATE TOOL

CONTROL OUTPUT: - EV-03

For the FMS Domain, the Enterprise Activity ANALYSE SCHEDULE either validates the new workplan to trigger (EV-10) Domain Process DRIVESHAFT MACHINING, or generates a request for capacity modification, or generates an Event (EV-98) to PRODUCTION CONTROL Domain to inform that it is impossible to fulfil the actual Production Scenario.

EA-110: ANALYSE SCHEDULE

CONTROL OUTPUT: - EV-10
                        - EV-98

In some cases, no Event is generated by an Enterprise Activity, the Control Output is therefore left undefined.

4.4   Define the Resource Input

Resource Input defines the required resources (or a set of resources) for the execution of an Enterprise Activity. At the Requirements Definition Modelling Level, if the analysis concerned is the to-be analysis, the required resources may be unknown. In this case, the Resource Input must be left undefined. If business users perform the as-if analysis, the Resource Input of an Enterprise Activity is the Resource being used to execute that Enterprise Activity. In case of to-be analysis where Resource Input is left undefined, Required Capability to execute that Enterprise Activity must be identified. The identified Required Capability will be further documented in the Resource View at the Requirements Definition Modelling Level.

In the Aerospatiale case study, the Enterprise Activity "MILL DRIVESHAFT" needs a milling machine to execute that Enterprise Activity. As the final choice of a milling machine will be made at the Design Specification Modelling Level, only Required Capability is identified:

EA-511: MILL DRIVESHAFT

REQUIRED CAPABILITY: - RR-95: Milling Machine class 1

The Required Resource Capability "Milling Machine class 1" will be described in detail in the Resource View. Other examples can be found in the Aerospatiale case study concerning the human resource. The Enterprise Activities "CREATE TOOL" and "ANALYSE SCHEDULE" both need human resources for their execution. As the qualification of the human resource needed for those two Enterprise Activities is different, Required Capability is different. In the case study, human resources are also classified and documented in the Resource View.

EA-164: CREATE TOOL

REQUIRED CAPABILITY: - Human resource/Shop Operator Class 3

EA-110: ANALYSE SCHEDULE

REQUIRED CAPABILITY: - Human resource/Shop Management Class 1

Business users should express as explicit as possible their requirements on the resources, although the final design choice is made at the Design Specification Modelling Level. In many cases, the use of one type of resource rather than another reflects strategic orientation and politics of a company. For example the Director of an enterprise may impose the use of the IBM type computer and COMAU type machine. Therefore, maximum indication on the resource to be used must be given by business users before a designer makes technical choices.

4.5 Define the Resource Output

A Resource Output is defined as a set of textual statements indicating information to be recorded on the usage of the resources after execution of an Enterprise Activity. In other words, Resource Output states what information needs to be collected on the usage of Resources during the execution of an Enterprise Activity.

Let us see an example. For a machining activity, one may wish to record the following information for further machine and tool maintenance as the Resource Output[9]:

```
RESOURCE OUTPUT:        - record actual machining time
                        - record tool use for each tool used
                        - record change times
```

4.6 Define the Organisational Aspects

Each template created during the model engineering process should identify the person or organisational unit responsible and authorised for creating, using and maintaining the template in engineering and operational use[10]. This information is provided in the organisation view and will be used to structure the enterprise organisation.

```
DESIGN RESPONSIBILITY: - identify organisational entity responsible
                         for creating, using and maintaining
                         the record

DESIGN AUTHORITY:        - identify organisational entity authorised
                         for creating, using and maintaining
                         the record
```

Arriving at this stage, the definition of an Enterprise Activity is completed at the Requirements Definition Modelling Level. All the Enterprise Activities must have already been documented using description template as shown below:

---

[9] Note: Since at the Requirements Definition Modelling Level, only requirements are defined, Resource Output is only defined under special conditions, namely when a business requirement on this specific information (described as text) regarding resource usage must be provided to be used elsewhere in the model, and especially for the resource management. Otherwise the Resource Output can be left undefined at the Requirements Definition Modelling Level.

[10] Note: Only engineering responsibility and authorisation are defined at the requirements modelling level.

Template: ENTERPRISE ACTIVITY

ENTERPRISE ACTIVITY: EA-005, ANALYSE SCHEDULE

TYPE:	Management/Plan/Decide
IDENTIFIER:	EA-005
NAME:	ANALYSE SCHEDULE
DESIGN AUTHORITY:	DE/BO/PG

A. Functional Description
OBJECTIVE:
CONSTRAINT:
DECLARATIVE RULE: DR-04 / Condition to Raise Event
　　　　　　　　　　 DR-05 / Condition to accept workplan
DESCRIPTION:　　　From Simulation Results, ANALYSE
　　　　　　　　　　　 SCHEDULE
　　　　　　　　　　 makes decision to generate:
　　　　　　　　　　 - either new workplan, or
　　　　　　　　　　 - request for capacity modification
　　　　　　　　　　 - or Event to PRODUCTION CONTROL
　　　　　　　　　　　　 (unable to fulfil actual Production Scenario)

　　INPUTS

FUNCTION INPUT:　　OV-103-04 / Proposed workplan
　　　　　　　　　　　 OV-110-00 / Simulation Results
CONTROL INPUT:
RESOURCE INPUT:

　　OUTPUTS

FUNCTION OUTPUT:　OV-103-03 / Released Workplan
CONTROL OUTPUT:　 EV-98, EV-10
RESOURCE OUTPUT:

ENDING STATUSES:　completion status:
　　　　　　　　　　 "good" (workplan may be issued)
　　　　　　　　　　 "impossible" (external decision required)
　　　　　　　　　　 "modification" (request for modification)

REQUIRED CAPABILITIES:
　　　　　　　　　　 - Human resource/Shop Management Class 1

B. Structure Description

WHERE USED:　　　 DP-01 / EXCEPTION MANAGEMENT
　　　　　　　　　　 DP-02 / ORDER MANAGEMENT

4.7 Describe Required Capability

The description of Capabilities (requirements in term of resource performance) required by Enterprise Activities is a major task of the Resource View at the

Requirements Definition Modelling Level. In principle, to dissociate capture of requirements (Requirements Definition Model) from system design (Design Specification Model), the Business user is assumed defining only his needs and not the solutions. Nevertheless, an Enterprise Activity called Milling DriveShaft implies obviously a milling machine.

Human Resource is a particular type of Manufacturing resources. Although business users are free to define the required human capability, classifying human resources into categories may help identifying the required human resource capability. For example in the Aerospatiale case study, Human Resources are classified into the following classes:

Management Oriented:
- Manager class 1:   define the profile of shop managers
- Manager class 2:   define the profile of assistant managers

Operator Oriented
- Operator class 1:   define the profile of high qualification operators
- Operator class 2:   define the profile of middle qualification operators
- Operator class 3:   define the profile of low qualification operators

Each class describes a coherent collection of human capabilities for a person able to perform several different tasks. For example, the Shop Management Class 1 human resource capability required for the Enterprise Activity ANALYSE SCHEDULE can be defined using description template as follow:

Template: HUMAN CAPABILITY

```
TYPE:              Management/Plan/Analyse
IDENTIFIER:        RC-01
NAME:              Shop Management Class 1

DESCRIPTION:       Shop Management Class 1 defines aptitudes
                     required to make high level decisions at shop
                     level, and to support EA such as
                   "Analyse Schedule" and
                   "Analyse Exception".

ABSTRACTION LEVEL: Required

CAPABILITY:        Understand: reported events
                   Judge: accept failure/repair as an actual
                     (un)availability
                   Decide: start of "Update Shop Capacity"
```

When defining Machine Resource Capabilities such as milling machine capabilities, it is straight forward to consult catalogues for milling machines where major characteristics can be found such as: milling volume, number of axes, surfacing, accuracy etc.. These characteristics are used here for the definition of the milling machine capabilities. In the Aerospatiale case study, the required capabilities of the milling machine for the Enterprise Activity "MILL DRIVESHAFT" are described in the template below.

Template: MACHINE CAPABILITY

TYPE:	Operational/Transform/MetalCutting/Prismatic
IDENTIFIER:	RC-95
NAME:	Milling Machine (class 1)
DESCRIPTION:	Defines aptitudes required to transform prismatic parts by metal cutting operation in defined volume and accuracy level.
CAPABILITIES:	- X-Length in [200, 500]
	- Y-Length in [100, 300]
	- Z-Length in [200, 350]
	- accuracy < .005
	- surfacing Ra < .001
	- others to be defined

5   Information Analysis

Having finished the Operational Analysis, all the Enterprise Activities employed in a Domain by the Domain Processes have been defined. During the Information Analysis, business users have to establish the link between the Function View and the Information View of the Requirements Definition Model by defining the Enterprise Objects of the Domain and the Object Views involved in the Function Input/Output and Control Input of the Enterprise Activities.

The purpose of the Information Analysis is therefore to capture the information needs of a particular enterprise and to provide sufficient detail to allow the consistent derivation of these information requirements into the Information View of the Design Specification Model. The scope of the Information Analysis should essentially be limited to the set of information required to support the execution of Enterprise Activities defined in the Function View. The objective is to provide an overall information structure. The level of detail of the Information Analysis is a priori governed by the level of detail decided in the Function View and other Views.

To perform the Information Analysis, CIMOSA provides a modelling language based on the concepts of Enterprise Objects (i.e. simple or complex entities of the enterprise), Object Views on Enterprise Objects (as perceived by users or applications), Object Relationships (connecting pairs of objects), Object Abstraction Mechanisms (as semantic object links, i.e. generalisation and aggregation), Information Elements (i.e. groups of data items). Integrity rules are also used in this phase to collect information requirements concerning the constraints on information and information conformity to real-world reality.

It is considered that at the Requirements Definition Modelling Level, it is not always necessary to define Enterprise Objects, Abstraction Mechanisms between Enterprise Objects and Object Relationships. Only Object Views, their Information Elements have to be defined. However the present CIMOSA User Guide recommends to define Enterprise Objects, Abstraction Mechanisms between the Enterprise Objects and Object Relationships in order to get more precise information requirements. Especially this makes it easier to derive the conceptual schema at the Design Specification Modelling Level.

Information Analysis is split in the following steps:

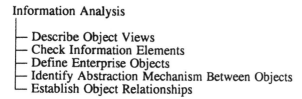

The following Generic Building Blocks are used in the Information Analysis phase:

Object View
Enterprise Object
Information Element
Integrity Rule
Abstraction Mechanism
Object Relationship

5.1   Describe Object Views

Having defined the Function Input, Function Output and Control Input of Enterprise Activities as Object Views in the Operational Analysis, the first step of the Information Analysis consists in describing these Object Views in terms of Information Elements and/or Object Views without referring to the Enterprise Objects on which these Object Views are defined.

Some Business Users may find it more logical to define Enterprise Objects first and then define the Object Views on these Enterprise Objects. In fact both methodologies are possible within CIMOSA. However, the present CIMOSA User Guide recommends to start from describing Object Views and then define Enterprise Objects. The reason is that first, when an Object View is defined it may happen that the Enterprise Object(s) on which the Object View is defined is not known; second, starting from defining Enterprise Objects might lead to the definition of some Enterprise Objects on which no Object Views are defined as the Input and Output of the Enterprise Activities in the Function View. Third, and most importantly, only information needed for the business operation is modelled.

As already mentioned, Object View is the most important construct for the Information View at the Requirements Definition Modelling Level. Generally speaking, an Object View is the description of a particular aspect of an Enterprise Object. It describes a specific set of properties owned by an Enterprise Object from a given stand-point. It is made of Information Elements and/or other Object Views. An Information Element is any item of information which is being considered as indivisible at the Requirement Definition Modelling Level. It represents the lowest level of granularity, or atomic level of the CIMOSA Information View. Its data type can be basic (integer, Boolean...) complex (array, list..) user-defined, or formatted file contents.

As mentioned above, an Object View is defined as a set of Information Elements and/or Object Views which must be in turn described in terms of Information Elements. An example shows Object View "OV-1-1" is composed of Information Elements IE-333, IE-335 and another Object View OV-11-1 which in turn is composed of IE-555 and IE-556. In the Aerospatiale case study, the Control Input of the Enterprise Activity "CREATE TOOL" is defined as an Object View OV-031-02 "FORMAL TOOL". This Object View is described in detail by its properties (Information Elements):

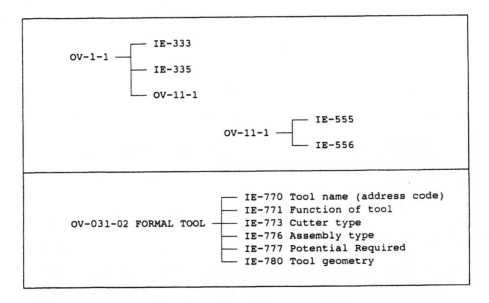

Another Object View example developed in the Aerospatiale case study is OV-06 "TOOL Status". Both examples demonstrate that an Information Element can be used in several Object Views. The Information Elements IE-770 and IE-780 are used in both Object Views.

```
                             ┌── IE-770 Tool name (address code)
                             ├── IE-774 Tool length
     OV-06 TOOL STATUS ──────┼── IE-778 Tool location
                             ├── IE-779 Tool potential
                             └── IE-780 Tool geometry
```

When describing the two Object Views, Business Users do not make reference to the Enterprise Object on which the Object Views are perceived. But it is obvious that the Enterprise Object in question is concerned with a tool-like object which will be formally defined after all the Object Views are described. One of the reasons for not performing at the same time the description of Object Views and definition of Enterprise Objects is that it allows to define some abstract Enterprise Objects later according to all the identified Information Elements in a more rational way. An Object View is formally defined by:

- its name
- the leading Enterprise Object it is defined on,
- other related Enterprise Objects it is defined on, (when it is defined on several Enterprise Objects)
- list of properties which characterise it, and
- some constraints on the definition of some of its properties as well as a selection clause constraining the set of possible occurrences allowed in the extension of the Object View.

Template: OBJECT VIEW

OBJECT VIEW: OV-031-02, FORMAL TOOL

TYPE:	to be defined
IDENTIFIER:	OV-031-02
NAME:	FORMAL TOOL
DESIGN AUTHORITY:	DD/BO/P
NATURE:	Information

DESCRIPTION: Formal description of Cutting Tool to be create for particular operation.

LEADING OBJECT:
RELATED OBJECTS:

PROPERTIES: Name (address code)
    Function
    Cutter type
    Assembly type
    Potential Required
    Nominal geometry

CONSTRAINTS: /

The leading Enterprise Object is the Enterprise Object which is the main focus of the Object View. Related Enterprise Objects are other Enterprise Objects from which Information Elements of the Object View are extracted. In the Aerospatiale case study, the Object View: "FORMAL TOOL" is defined using the description template above (except the items of LEADING OBJECT and RELATED OBJECTS which will be defined later). Whenever a business user describes an Object View, he must ensure that the Information Elements and/or Object Views he creates don't exist already. The same Information Element and/or Object View cannot have two different identifiers. Moreover, he must, as much as possible, create Objects Views using Object View types defined in the Partial Models.

5.2 Check Information Elements

Reaching this step, it is supposed that all the Object Views are described in terms of Information Elements, and a list of all the Information Elements identified is established[11]. Before Defining the Enterprise Objects from these Object Views, business users must first purify the list of Information Elements by detecting synonyms, ambiguities, redundancies etc. Normally, each time when an Information Element is identified during the Object Views description phase, that Information Element must be described in detail by a template. One should check if all the items of the template are filled in except the item "RELATED OBJECTS" which will be filled in after Enterprise Objects will have been defined. An example of the template description of Information Element is shown below.

Template: INFORMATION ELEMENT

```
INFORMATION ELEMENT

  TYPE:               Administrative data
  NAME:               Enterprise_Address
  IDENTIFIER:         IE-10

  DESCRIPTION:        Describe address of enterprise

  DATA TYPE:

      record
                      Enterprise Identification: string (20)
                      Street Name: string (30)
                      Complement: string (30)
                      Postal Code: (string (8)
                      City: string (15)
                      State: string (10)
                      Country: string (15)
      end

  BELONGS TO:         Enterprise

  RELATED OBJECTS:

  RELATED VIEWS:      OV-299 / Delivery
                      OV-342 / Supplier Order
                      OV-762 / Purchase Order,
                      OV-333 / Procurements

  SYNONYMS:           Company Address, Address
```

---

[11] Note: for any modification on the Information Elements·(delete, identifier change, etc.), the related Object Views using the modified Information Element must also be updated.

Furthermore, it is important to note that some Information Elements of some Object Views may be derived from other Information Elements of some Enterprise Objects (i.e. their values are calculated from other values), and thus do not belong to any specific Enterprise Objects. In this case, the relation linking these Information Elements is defined as an Integrity Rule on the derived Information Element. Constraints imposed on Information Elements to ensure the validity and correctness of Information Elements are therefore expressed by Integrity Rules for the following cases:

- existence constraints: for instance, unicity of Information Elements used as identifiers, no duplicate values allowed for same Information Elements etc.
- domain constraints: there are limitations on the range of values allowed for some Information Elements. For instance, a person age is an integer between 0 and 120.
- functional dependency constraints: an Information Element Y is said to be functionally dependent on Information Element X if it corresponds exactly one value of Y to each distinct value of X. In other words, it does not exist two values of Y for each value of X.
- consistency constraints: Any time that the value of an Information Element Y can be calculated from the value of n other Information Elements X1, X2, ..., Xn, this means that there is redundancy in the Information System. To control such redundancy, a mathematical relation f must exist between these values such that $Y = f(X1, X2, ..., Xn)$.

Integrity Rules must be described using description template. An example about inertia acceleration in CNC machines which provides a consistency constraint is shown below:

Template: INTEGRITY RULE

```
INTEGRITY RULE

TYPE:               Technical data
NAME·               Torque rule
IDENTIFIER:         IC-3
DESIGN AUTHORITY:   F. Ceri

DESCRIPTION:        In direct drive systems of CNC machines,
                    amount of torque required to accelerate any
                    inertia is· T = J * a      where

                          T = Torque (Nm)
                          J = Moment of inertia (kgm ")
                          a = angular acceleration (rad/s")

RELATED INFORMATION ELEMENTS:
                    IE-456 / Torque of CNC_Machine
                    IE-659 / Moment of Inertia
                    IE-660 / Angular_Acceleration
```

5.3   Define Enterprise Objects

The third step of an Information Analysis consists in deriving Enterprise Objects from the Object Views and from the list of the Information Elements. The theory of functional dependencies allows to do it in a structured way. Enterprise Objects describe generalised entities (concrete or abstract) of the Enterprise and are defined by attributes (called Properties) which can be either Information Elements or lower-level Enterprise Objects (also called Sub-Objects) or sets of Information Elements or Enterprise Objects. This recursive definition allows the construction of very high level Enterprise Objects which can be decomposed into more and more basic properties (down to Information Elements) and therefore constitute an object hierarchy.

An important issue of the Information Analysis is the differentiation between "sub-object" and Object View of a higher level Enterprise Object; if part of an Enterprise Object (set of properties) is such that none of its properties is shared by another part of the Enterprise Object, then and only in then, can this part be considered as a sub-object (Enterprise Object defined as part of the higher level one). Otherwise, this part is only a particular aspect (Object View) of the Enterprise Object[12].

For illustration purpose, considering the example given in 2.4.1, the analysis of the Information Elements composing the Object View OV-1-1 leads to the identification of the Enterprise Object EO-1 as shown below. EO-1 is an Enterprise Object which is composed of Information Elements IE-333, IE-334, IE-335, IE-336 and another Enterprise Object EO-11. The Object View 1 (there may be many Object Views on the same Object) on the Enterprise Object EO-1: OV-1-1, is composed of IE-333, IE-335 and the Object View OV-11-1 on the Enterprise Object EO-11.

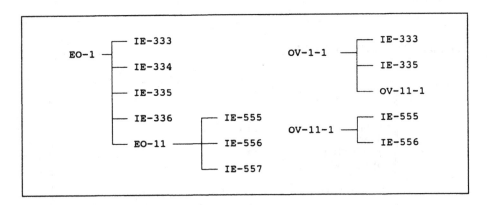

In a similar manner, the Object Views involved in the Function Input, Function Output and Control Input of the Enterprise Activities in the Aerospatiale FMS Domain, led to the identification of the set of Enterprise Objects. As an example, part of these Enterprise Objects is listed below with some of them being concrete

---

[12]   Note: An Object View is allowed to cover a complete Enterprise Object as well as being limited to an Information Element.

Although most of Object Views are strictly related to one Enterprise Object of which they give a particular perception, certain Object Views may draw their properties from several interrelated Enterprise Objects. In this case, the field RELATED OBJECTS (in the Object View template) must be filled.

objects such as Part, Pallet, Cutting Tool etc. Others are abstract ones like Machine Operation, Set-up Procedure, ...

Enterprise Objects

Part
Manufacturing Order
Process Plan
Workstation
Machine
Machine Operation
Process Phase
Operator
Part Program
Set-Up Procedure
Cutting Tool
Pallet
etc.

To further illustrate the relation between Object View and Enterprise Object, let us see the examples: Object View "FORMAL TOOL" and Object View "TOOL STATUS" presented in §2.4.1. These two Object Views allow to define the Enterprise Object "CUTTING TOOL", which is composed of the following Information Elements (incomplete). Which implies the Object Views "Tool Status" and "Formal Tool" are two Object Views on the same Enterprise Object "Cutting Tool".

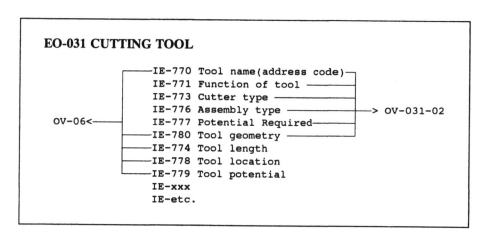

5.4   Identify the Abstraction Mechanism between Objects

To allow the connection of Enterprise Objects to form a semantic information model, CIMOSA proposes two kinds of Object Abstraction Mechanisms (as well as any kind of user-defined Relationships described in 2.4.5.):

Generalisation   (ISA link)
Aggregation   (PART OF link),

162

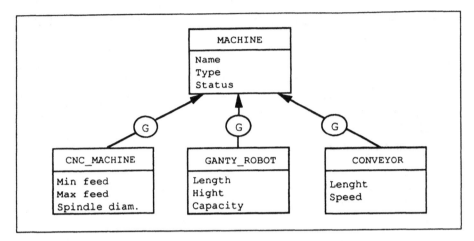

Fig. 3.7 Example of Generalisation type

Generalisation (ISA): In the description of a particular Enterprise Object it is often simpler to define it from another Enterprise Object as being a more particular (or more general) one[13]. As an illustration example for the Generalisation type Abstraction Mechanism, CNC machines, gantry robots and part conveyors are specialised types of machines. The graphic representation is shown Fig. 3.7. Some examples for the Generalisation type abstraction mechanism developed in the Aerospatiale case study are shown in Fig. 3.8. From this examples, one can see that the "MACHINE" is the generalisation of "MACHINE TYPE"; EMPLOYEE is the generalisation of "OPERATOR" and "MANAGER"; "TOOL" is the generalisation of "CUTTING TOOL".

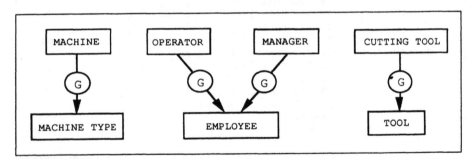

Fig. 3.8 Example of Generalisation type

Aggregation (PART OF): In addition to relationships by which a basic Enterprise Object can be considered as a Property of a broader one, it can be useful to define a Part_Of relationship from a component Object to the larger Object in order to indicate the existence-dependency between the **part** and the **whole**. Such a relationship (called a Strong Aggregation) from EOi to EOj ("EOi is Part_Of EOj")

---

13   Note: an Enterprise Object can be involved in one or more ISA links as a child of one or more higher-level Enterprise Objects. This means that it can inherit properties of two or more higher-level Enterprise Objects.

implies that any occurrence of EOi cannot exist if a related occurrence of EOj does not exist, or, when an occurrence of EOj is destroyed, the related occurrence of EOi is destroyed. For example: Enterprise Object "Part" can be defined by several sub-objects considered as a structuring of its properties. In that case (strong aggregation), the destruction of the "Part" leads to the destruction of its components. On the opposite, the Enterprise Object "Product" (comprising several Parts) can be destroyed independently of its components.

A **Weak Aggregation** (no Part_Of link is required in the definition of the Sub-Objects) means merely that an Enterprise Object can be described as a 'free association' of Enterprise Objects without implying any condition of existence-dependency. For example: Enterprise Object MACHINING OPERATION (see FMS Case Study) is described as an aggregation of sub-Objects such as MACHINE TYPE, SET-UP PROCEDURE, PART PROGRAM, TOOL LIST and OPERATOR TYPE. Deleting a MACHINING OPERATION does not lead to the destruction of MACHINE TYPE, SET-UP PROCEDURE, PART PROGRAM, TOOL LIST and OPERATOR TYPE. This aggregation is a weak aggregation and therefore the Enterprise Object MACHINE TYPE does not refer to MACHINING OPERATION by a Part_Of link.

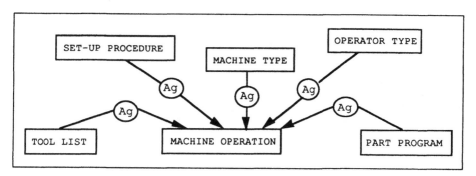

Fig. 3.9 Example of weak Aggregation

Remark: Whenever a 'List of' (or 'Set of') Enterprise Objects is involved in the description of super-objects, the relationship is necessarily a weak aggregation because it concerns occurrences of sub-objects. For instance, Toolset described as a List of Tools (and others) which occurrences can be destroyed whereas its components (cutting Tools) can be re-employed for other tasks.

5.5 Establish Object Relationships

When two Enterprise Objects can be connected neither by Generalisation type Abstraction Mechanism, nor by Aggregation type Abstraction Mechanism, an application dependant, user-defined link among Enterprise Objects is needed. It is called "Object Relationship". In other words, an Object Relationship between two Enterprise Objects is created for the purpose of the CIM system applications[14]. It does not describe natural relations between Enterprise Objects.

---

[14] Note: Object Relationships will be transformed into Entity Relationships in the Conceptual schema of the Information View of the Design Specification Model. However, there is no direct translation mechanism from an Object Relationship to an Entity Relationship.

Template: OBJECT RELATIONSHIP

```
OBJECT RELATIONSHIP

TYPE:              Product data
NAME:              End product
IDENTIFIER:        OR-01
DESIGN AUTHORITY:  S.M. Smith / Product Definition

DESCRIPTION:       Type of Object Relationship defines relation
                   between part object type and machine object
                   type

ORIGINATOR:        Machine
RELATED_TO:        Part

FUNCTIONALITY:     m:n
```

The Object Relationship is represented by a directed arc labelled by the relationship name and indicates the functionality connecting the two Enterprise Objects. An example of Object Relationship "Makes" connecting two Enterprise Objects "Machine" and "Part" is shown in Fig. 3.10. The arc is a single arc if it is a one-to-one relationship, has one end as a craws-foot if it is a one-to-many relationship and has a craws-foot on both ends if it is a many-to-many relationship. Each Object Relationship should be defined using description template. The description template of the above example is shown above. Another example developed in the Aerospatiale case study shows the Object Relationship "Perform" between the Enterprise Objects "Machine Operation" and "Workstation" (see Fig. 3.11).

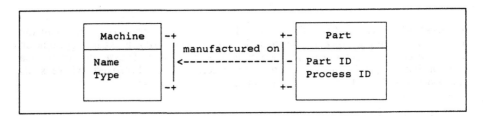

Fig. 3.10 Object Relationship Example

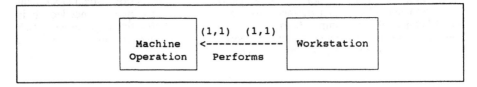

Fig. 3.11. An example of Object Relationship in the Aerospatiale case study

Template: ENTERPRISE OBJECT

ENTERPRISE OBJECT: EO-031, CUTTING TOOL

TYPE: Resource/Mobile
IDENTIFIER: EO-031
NAME: CUTTING TOOL
DESIGN AUTHORITY: DE/BO/P

DESCRIPTION: CUTTING TOOL is an object defined by its
                       operational functionality and provided with
                       elements needed to give it that functionality
                       on a defined MACHINE-Type.
                       Cutting part of the Tool is managed as a
                       consumable (limited potential).

ABSTRACTION RELATIONS:

       ISA: TOOL
       PART OF: Nil

PROPERTIES: Tool Status / OV
                       Absolute name
                       Function code
                       Life potential
                       Length
                       Radius

     Set of [1, #]   EO-051 Tool Holder
                       EO-052 Intermediate element
                       EO-053 Cutting element

During Enterprise Object identification, the Business User must avoid definition of redundant objects. Input/output elements of Enterprise Activities which seem related to two Enterprise Objects, most probably form a unique one to which tradition and manufacturing culture give generally different names. As an example, in the FMS Case Study a one-to-one link ties a "Batch" to a "Manufacturing Order", the first Enterprise Object has been discarded and considered as the Physical View of the second one. Fig. 3.12 shows an example of the semantic information model developed in the Aerospatiale case study. Arriving at this step, all the Enterprise Objects must have been already properly described using description template[15]. As an example, the Enterprise Object "CUTTING TOOL" is described above.

From the Information Analysis point of view, it is assumed that only Object Views and Information Elements are involved in the Function Input, Function Output and Control Input of Enterprise Activities. Thus Object Views are the major hook between the Function View and Information View of the CIMOSA Requirements Definition Model.

---

[15]   Note: Any Enterprise Object must have an unique identity, meaning that no two identical Enterprise Objects can exist at any time (they at least differ by their identifier).

166

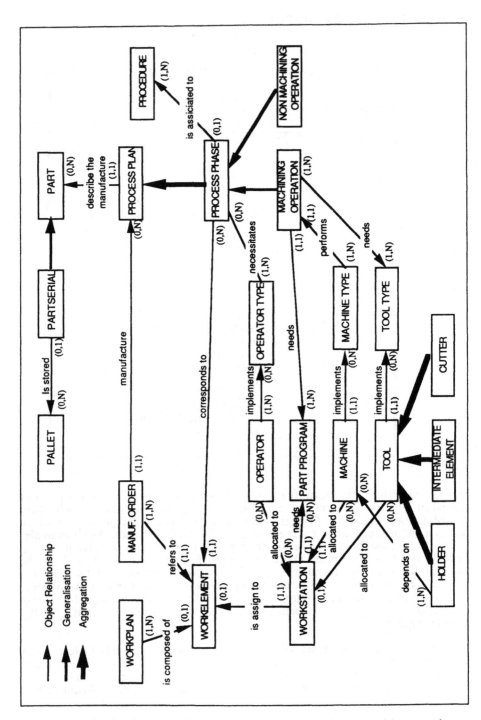

Fig. 3.12. Relationships between the Enterprise Objects identified in the Aerospatiale case study

Part 4

Technical Reports

Part 4 contains selected AMICE project reports on the Open System Architecture for CIM (CIMOSA). These reports provide additional information on enterprise integration, formal representation of modelling constructs and an IIS executable language. The reports indicate the current status of the work on CIMOSA being undertaken by the ESPRIT Consortium AMICE.

I   Enterprise Integration

1   Introduction

Enterprise Integration (EI) is a major issue for industrial enterprise operation. The enterprise internal information systems heritage and the legacy of mergers, take-overs, joint ventures, etc. make this integration very much a necessity for any enterprise to improve operation efficiency and thereby the business competitiveness in the global market.

In addition to integrating todays heritage and legacy systems, integration is a need arising from the continuous evolution of enterprises driven mainly by external changes such as business and economic opportunities, technical innovations or changes in the financial, social and political environment. In reaction to these external challenges the enterprise has to impose internal adaptations in relevant areas of the operation. With other words, the integrated systems of today will become tomorrows heritage systems waiting for being integrated again. Enterprise integration will become an engineering task and profession in its own right: Enterprise Engineering.

Enterprise integration is mainly concerned with existing systems to coexist with new technology in both the manufacturing and IT domain. Even with new system components engineered according to new paradigms in modelling and implementation, they still have to interoperate with existing parts of the enterprise operation. With an average life time of e.g. 12 years for Mainframe applications[1] there will be many years of coexistence with such applications to come.

Therefore, any new methodology and technology used in enterprise operation has to provide means for interoperating with the existing world. The most promising approach to achieve interoperability between incompatible systems seems to be the identification and common representation of information objects shared between different parts of the system. With this approach of minimum unification an agreement on common representation has to be negotiated and kept only between partners sharing the same objects. This enables identification of classes of information objects according to their degree of sharing e.g. private, common, public. This is the approach taken also by people working in artificial intelligence and expert systems on classes of ontologies.

CIMOSA provides solutions for enterprise integration both for re-engineering and coexistence with heritage and legacy systems.

2   Enterprise Integration - State of the Art

Enterprise integration has a long history. Division of Labour could only start from a view of the whole operation identifying its parts and their relations[2]. Even F. W. Taylor's approach to improve enterprise efficiency was driven by a systems view on the manufacturing operation, but taking an extreme deterministic view on operation decomposition.

More recent attempts to enterprise integration focussed on linking parts of the operation rather than decomposing and breaking them down further. Starting from

---

[1]   H. T. Goranson, paper at ICEIMT
[2]   Adam Smith, An Inquire into the Nature and Cause of the Wealth of Nations, (Modern Library, New York, 1937)

the needs of manufacturing enterprises especially in the USA work has been carried out sponsored by government agencies in Computer Integrated Manufacturing (CIM). ICAM, CAM-I, work in NBS are some of the initiatives carried out and IDEF, DPMM and AMRF[3] are results coming from this early work. In Europe ESPRIT has been the major initiate in this area with numerous ESPRIT project focussing on different aspects of enterprise integration from enterprise engineering (EP 34) to business (EP 688 & follow ones), operation (EP 955 & follow-ones, 2277) and system architectures (EP 2267).[4]

3 SWG EIRT (Supplier Working Group Enterprise Integration Reference Taxonomy) and its Relation to CIMOSA

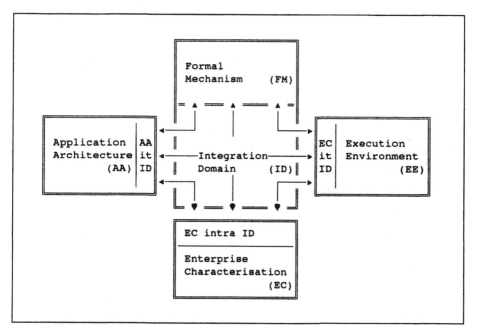

Fig. 4.1.1: Supplier Working Group - Enterprise Integration Reference Taxonomy

---

3)   ICAM: Integrated Computer Aided Manufacturing (US Air Force project 1105: Conceptual Design for Computer Integrated Manufacturing
    CAM-I: Computer Aided Manufacturing - International
    NBS: National Bureau of Standards (today NIST: National Institute of Standards & Technology)
    IDEF: ICAM DEFinition language
    DPMM: Discrete Parts Manufacturing Model of CAM-I
    AMRF: Automated Manufacturing Research Facility of NBS/NIST
4)   EP 34: Design Rules for Computer Integrated Manufacturing Systems
    EP 688&ff: European CIM Architecture (AMICE)
    EP 955&ff: Communications Network for Manufacturing Applications (CNMA)
    EP 2277: CIM for Multi-Supplier Operations (CMSO)
    EP 2267: Integrated Systems Architecture (ISA)

Work sponsored by the US Air Force and carried out by the Supplier's Working Group (SWG) has lead to an Enterprise Integration Reference Taxonomy (EIRT). Technical issues derived from this work have been summarised in a MCC Technical Report[1] which has been used for the discussions held in the ICEIMT workshops[2]. As part of the EC/US cooperation the SWG-EIRT and CIMOSA have been mapped onto each other and their particular contribution to EI has been evaluated.

3.1 SWG EIRT

The Supplier's Working Group has structured the current Information Processing environment into four subareas connected by a namespace for binding and integration. The namespace has been redefined and renamed as integration domain by the ICEIMT working groups. Fig. 4.1.1 shows the subareas and their connections via the integration domain.

Definitions for subareas of the reference taxonomy and their contents (information and services) are given by H. T. Goranson, representing the US Air Force (reprinted):

ENTERPRISE CHARACTERIZATION (EC): consists of both Information in the context of the enterprise, and information about that information used to integrate the enterprise information (perhaps in conjunction with services). Other kinds of information may be included here, for example information generated by the AA for its own use such as data dictionaries. Also included is information generated by the EE for internal use, for example security or configuration management models. All models are in the EC, together with other information not traditionally called models. Collectively, this information "characterizes" the enterprise. If all this information were formally modelled, and integrated in some way, then the EC would constitute the complete enterprise model.

APPLICATION ARCHITECTURE (AA): consists of both the Application Services and architectural services used to support them. Examples of application services may be application programs. Other application services may be processes which are modelled in the EC but which themselves are non-automated. Other types of Application Services may be tools to create and support application programs and tools to create and support EC models. The term "Architecture" is employed here because the details of how the Application Services are inter-related internally is important to how the enterprise is integrated. So the AA contains Application Services, meta-application services (for example repositories) if the architecture specifies them, and the architecture itself.

EXECUTION ENVIRONMENT (EE): consists of the Execution Services, both hardware and software. Certain support services, for example distributed computing resources management, are included in the EE. It is understood that the EE is always implemented as an architecture, usually layered. Here, the term "Environment" is deliberately used in contrast to the term "Architecture" because most of the architectural details of the computing infrastructure should be invisible to the EI problem. Key characteristics of the architectures are captured in the definitions of different EE computing paradigms (the ID Computing Paradigms) in an architecture and vendor-independent manner.

INTEGRATION DOMAIN (ID): is a basic entity discrete from the AA, EE, and EC, in that it consists of neither Services or Information. Rather it is the domain (formerly called the "space") where the EI interactions occur. By definition, the EI problem is the ID problem. Interactions in the ID will be supported by services in the AA and/or EE and information in the EC.

InterID: is the ID which integrates the AA, EE via service linkages, and the EC to the services by conceptual and representational mechanisms. The InterID was formerly termed the NameSpace, but the term was modified to a more neutral meaning based on the workshops. Mechanisms in the InterID include at least naming, binding and state management conventions. Probably others are involved as identified in the workshops.

IntraID's: are the ID's which integrate internally within the AA, EE, and EC[5].

- The EC IntraID is the collection of methods and techniques used to integrate information (primarily models) in the EC. Since model integration and EI are widely acknowledged as tightly related, the EI InterID and the EC IntraID are likely to use the same formal mechanisms (defined below as the Federation Mechanism, FM). As with the InterID services, EC IntraID activity is performed by services in the AA and EE.

- The AA IntraID is by definition the Application Architecture. Examples are Repositories and Frameworks. Another common, rudimentary architecture is conformance of Application Services to a single data structure.

- The EE IntraID is that subset of the layered "platform" architectures cogent to the discourse of EI. Rather than deal with the full diversity of solutions in specific architectures, only certain key architectural characteristics are captured as major Computing Paradigms.

  ID COMPUTING PARADIGMS: are the major approaches to dividing services between the AA and the EE. This concept recognizes that certain services, for example data management services, could reasonably be considered either AA or EE services. It leverages the fact that vendors and users currently have only a few basic approaches to the ID, and these approaches have rigid boundaries between the AA and EE. These boundaries are useful, and in any case must be accommodated.

FORMAL MECHANISM (FM)[6]: is the collection of technologies and philosophies which enable both the EI InterID and the EC IntraID. EI conventions will include both ID conventions and FM technologies. Probably the former will be shared, possibly in standards, and the latter shared, probably in pre-competitive technologies. This term was previously termed "Federation Mechanism", but was changed because the term was too reflective of a specific philosophy of FM's.

SERVICES: the collection of all of the computing services found in an enterprise. Services consist of those supported both by hardware and software, and are arranged in complex architectures, typically layered. All services are included in this category, whether available throughout the enterprise or not. Services can be purchased by the enterprise, or especially built for a specific application or function. Since services are either bought or built, enterprises have a good idea of their costs, if not their efficacy. Most of these costs appear in the technology marketplace. In the Reference Taxonomy, services are exactly the sum of the AA and EE, and have been termed by some the "sea of services". Services are differentiated into "Application Services" and "Execution Services", defined below.

APPLICATION SERVICES: those services used directly to perform the work of the enterprise. Other ways to say this are: to support all of the functions of the enterprise, or to execute its processes. In both cases, the work, functions and processes are those visible to the information infrastructure, but not necessarily automated themselves. Application Services are differentiated from Execution Services in that enterprise modelers need to "understand" the internal activities of Application Services, since they are reflective of the actual business. Only limited visibility into Execution Services is required by enterprise modelers. In the Reference Taxonomy, Application Services are wholly in the Application Architecture (AA).

EXECUTION SERVICES: those services required to support the Application Services of the enterprise. These are "secondary" services, typically deeper in a layered architecture, and include activity directly on the hardware. Execution Services differ from Application Services in that complete, specific details of the Execution Services are not required by enterprise modelers.

An example of such a detail is knowledge about the "state" of a service. Some services may be Application Services in one enterprise and Execution Services in another. The differences are captured in the definitions of different Integration Domain (ID) Computing Paradigms, defined below. In the Reference Taxonomy, Execution Services are wholly in the Execution Environment (EE).

INFORMATION: the collection of all of the information found in an enterprise. As with services, information is of differing types. Included are formal models of the enterprise functions, similar models of the enterprise infrastructure, and data used by applications. Information is differentiated from services: the information can be a model OF a service, contain information ABOUT a service, or be information USED BY a service. Some is well structured, some not; some is explicitly acknowledged, some not. Both product data and models and both process data and models are information. All information is included in this category, whether available throughout the enterprise or not.

The specific collection of information in an enterprise is unique to that enterprise; that is, it is largely created by the enterprise: it does not appear in the technology marketplace. For this and other reasons, businesses do not know how much they spend on information, apart from services. Recognizing this need, the SWG performed a survey of businesses worldwide and determined the cost to be of an order of magnitude equal to all services combined. In the Reference Taxonomy, Information is contained wholly in the Enterprise Characterization (EC).

3.2 SWG EIRT Relation to CIMOSA

The SWG-EIRT is concerned with todays heritage and legacy systems and tries to cope with heterogeneity through formal mechanisms accommodating late registration and binding of system components. CIMOSA provides an engineering solution for unification of re-engineered systems. CIMOSA also provides a solution for integration of heterogeneous systems for the early binding case; the case in which shared objects are identified and registered for the sharing entities at build time. The Integrating Infrastructure provides common execution support - no further binding information is required at run time.

CIMOSA can be seen as a special case of the SWG-EIRT in which enterprise characterisation (EC) and application architecture (AA) are unified and linked during the enterprise engineering phase using the CIMOSA Reference Architecture. The run time integration domain (ID) is provided by the services of the Integrating Infrastructure. All of the CIMOSA IIS service entities themselves are linked via protocols and interfaces.

In addition, four of these service entities provide the EE intra integration domain through their integrating platform characteristics aimed at integrating heterogeneous IT environments. The AA intra integration domain is provided by the business service entity which executes CIMOSA and non-CIMOSA processes provided the shared objects are identified at build time. The formal mechanism (FM) applied in CIMOSA is the concept of shared objects which are identified together with their sharing entities during model engineering.

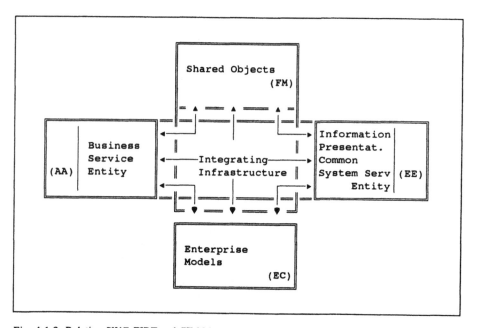

Fig. 4.1.2: Relation SWG-EIRT and CIMOSA

Fig. 4.1.2 shows the relations between the SWG-EIRT and CIMOSA according to the current understanding. A more detailed description of the mapping is provided in a paper of the ICEIMT[3].

4 CIMOSA concepts on Enterprise Integration

Any new methodology and technology to be used in enterprise integration has to provide means for interoperating with the existing world. CIMOSA enables integration of heritage and legacy systems through two different concepts: Domain Processes and Functional Entities. Enterprise operations are to be structured according to CIMOSA in two distinct levels linked to each other by events:

Upper Level Structure:

an event driven network of cooperating Domain Processes.

Lower Level Structure:

an explicit description of functionality and behaviour of the individual Domain Process presented as a network of Enterprise Activities/Functional Operation initiated by events and driven by an explicit set of Procedural Rules.

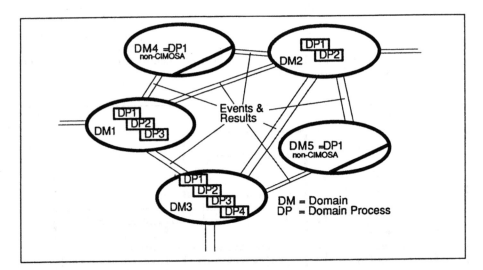

Fig. 4.1.3: Network of Domain Processes

Applying the upper level structuring concept (Domain Process network) leads to a model of the enterprise operation structured into cooperating entities (IT applications) which cooperate via exchange of objects or messages (requests and results). Cooperating processes may be both CIMOSA domain processes and non-CIMOSA processes. Which implies the internal structure of these entities may either be known (modelled according to CIMOSA) or not. The resulting model will be a network of cooperating entities which cooperate via exchanging objects as shown in Fig. 4.1.3.

Using the approach of shared objects the CIMOSA domain process concept will provide a very convenient solution for integration of heritage and legacy systems. Shared objects would be the information which may be either results produced by one process and used by another one or requests (events) for producing results. Identification of both the sharing processes and the shared information objects allows to establish the integration base. An object representation common to all sharing processes provides the base for information interchange. The CIMOSA information representation would be sufficient for unification of the exchanged information. In addition, indentifying the entities sharing the same objects enables the definition of groups of entities which need to be notified if modifications of object representations are required.

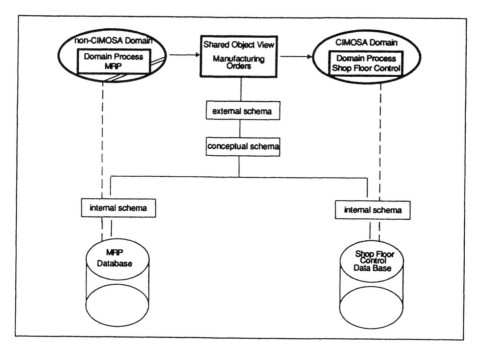

Fig. 4.1.4: Cooperation via Shared Objects

An example could be a non-CIMOSA MRP application cooperating with a shop floor control application modelled according to CIMOSA as shown in Fig. 4.1.4. The shared objects are the manufacturing orders issued by the MRP application and received by the shop floor application. These objects have to be modelled for the shop floor application as Object Views expressed as part of an Enterprise Object and containing Information Elements. These Object Views are expressed for the IT representation and subsequent processing as external schemas. External schemas which are part of the conceptual schema and are implemented on the relevant data base according to their internal schemas. Therefore, the manufacturing orders represented according to the MRP application are transformed into a representation according to CIMOSA for the shop floor application. The transformation is achieved through schema conversions described and included in the services of the IIS Information entity.

Integration through the use of the functional entity concept would enable the use of non-CIMOSA applications inside CIMOSA domain processes. Decomposition of the Domain Process would lead to Enterprise Activities and Functional Operations. The latter would be executed via non-CIMOSA applications which would be used as encapsulated resources providing sufficient capabilities for executing the specific functional operations.

176

One of the processes shown in Fig. 4.1.3 is further detailed in Fig. 4.1.5 into a network of Enterprise Activities. Fig. 4.1.6 which represents the further decomposition an Enterprise Activities shown in Fig. 4.1.5 into Functional Operations and their relations with Functional Entities. Functional Entities are supposed to provide the capabilities required to execute the Functional Operation. Therefore, the non-CIMOSA application has to fit the needs of the Functional Operation or the other way around, the Functional Operation has to use the capability provided by the Functional Entity to fulfil the required functionality. In this way non-CIMOSA applications would be accommodated inside a CIMOSA domain process.

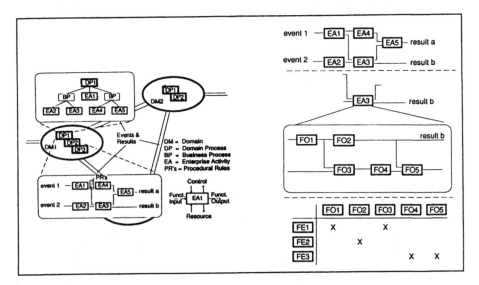

Fig. 4.1.5: Internal Structure
of Domain Process

Fig. 4.1.6: Relation between Functional
Operation and Functional Entities

Using the same example of MRP and Shop Floor applications to illustrate enterprise integration via the Functional Entity approach would require a somewhat different CIMOSA model. In order to encapsulate the MRP application the Domain Process Production Control has to be part of the model. In this case the model would again consist of two Domain Processes but Production Control as the owner of the MRP application would have to be modelled as a CIMOSA Domain Process. Fig. 4.1.7 indicates the relevant Functional Operation which produces the manufacturing orders according to customer orders received and processed through order entry.

Receiving a customer order would start the Domain Process Production Control and at some point the Functional Operation 'create manufacturing order' would be executed through the use of the Functional Entity MRP. The resulting manufacturing orders would again be received as the required object view for the start of the Shop Floor Domain Process. Parameters transferred between the Functional Operation and the MRP Functional Entity for the creation of the manufacturing orders have to be again modelled according to CIMOSA. Transformation into the different internal schemas will be as shown in Fig. 4.1.4.

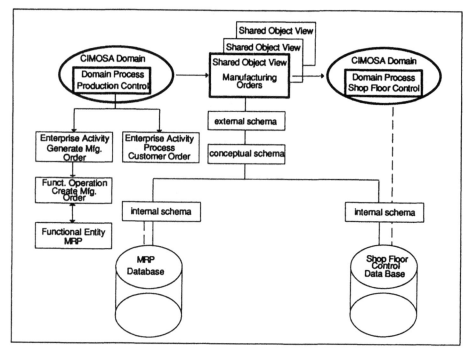

Fig. 4.1.7: Cooperation through Functional Entities

5 Conclusions

The mapping of CIMOSA onto the SWG-EIRT has indicated the capabilities of CIMOSA to cope with heritage and legacy systems. Employing the CIMOSA concepts two ways of integrating with non-CIMOSA applications are possible. On a high level of enterprise integration all entities (applications or CIMOSA processes) are seen as cooperating processes. Integration is via events and information exchanged between any two or more processes which will be described according to CIMOSA in a unifying way.

The more detailed level of CIMOSA modelling; the explicit description of CIMOSA Domain Processes in terms of internal control flow and functionality allows to integrate non-CIMOSA applications through the Functional Entity concept. This view on CIMOSA's capability for migration into the heritage and legacy environment is a result from the EC/US collaboration and especially from the International Conference on Enterprise Integration and Modelling Technology (ICEIMT) and the many discussions with the EI experts in the preceding workshops.

We would like to take this opportunity to thank all participants in this discussions as well as the CEC which together with US government agencies sponsor the EC/US initiative.

More work is still required to transfer these concepts into reality. But the continuation of the AMICE project will investigate especially these capabilities of

CIMOSA. The pre-pilot work is intended to demonstrate the feasibility of engineering (build time) unification for run time cooperation. Hopefully the results are sufficiently convincing to continue evaluation and promotion on an industrial pilot level.

6 References

[1] MCC Technical Report CAD-349-91; Technical Issues of Enterprise Integration

[2] ICEIMT Proceedings, MIT Press 1992 (Intern. Conference on Enterprise Integration Modelling Technology, Hilton Head/SC, USA, June 1992)

[3] H. H. T. Goranson 'The CIMOSA Approach as an Enterprise Integration Strategy', ICEIMT Proceedings, MIT Press 1992

II   CIMOSA - FBS Modelling Paradigm
- Formal Representation

1   Purpose and Scope

The CIMOSA Function-Behaviour-Structure modelling paradigm provides a consistent modelling approach across all the modelling levels (requirements, design, implementation) of the CIMOSA Function View. The FBS paradigm provides a functional decomposition principle and defines concepts of functionality, behaviour and functional structure in the description of enterprise tasks and operations.

2   Formal Definitions

The **Function-Behaviour-Structure (FBS) Paradigm** provides:

- a functional decomposition principle;
- three building blocks to formally model functionality, behaviour and structure of the function part of a particular Enterprise;
- an event-driven, process-based, modelling approach, called the process/activity/operation approach, to model tasks and sub-tasks of the Enterprise; and
- a set of methodological rules to apply these constructs during the function decomposition process of a particular Enterprise

Enterprise Functionality is concerned with the objectives, constraints, function inputs and outputs, control inputs and outputs, resource inputs and outputs and transfer function of well-defined enterprise tasks to be realised in terms of basic operations (or actions) using enterprise means.

Enterprise Behaviour is concerned with the flow of control or the way processes and activities are employed over time in reaction to enterprise events and according to enterprise state to fulfil the business objectives under imposed constraints (financial, administrative or technical constraints or management declarative rules). This can be described by means of procedural rules defining control structures such as precedence relationships, parallelism, branching conditions and iterative processing.

Functional Structure of an enterprise is concerned with the functional decomposition of the enterprise into processes and sub-processes and activities, and then activities into operations.

Abbreviations and Acronyms used throughout this document:

BP: Business Process
DP: Domain Process
EA: Enterprise Activity
FBS: Function-Behaviour-Structure Paradigm

3   Process/Activity/Operation Approach

AMICE has defined a Function-Behaviour-Structure (FBS) Paradigm to support the Function View Modelling Paradigms. This paradigm is based on an event-driven, process-based approach, called the Process/Activity/Operation approach.

Within an enterprise tasks are usually organised into sub-tasks (which are generically called enterprise functions). They need to be realised to achieve the business objectives. In the Process/Activity/Operation approach an enterprise is seen as a collection of inter-related but non-overlapping Domains, which are subsets of the enterprise. These Domains exchange objects between themselves and with other Domains external to the enterprise. Each Domain will be impacted by (unsolicited) real-world happenings and requests to do something. Such happenings and requests originate within some other Domain (modelled according to CIMOSA or not) and are described as Events of the enterprise. In reaction to these stimuli some enterprise functions are performed which can themselves be made of sub-functions interconnected by sets of rules defining the 'flow of control' between the sub-functions. To represent tasks and actions performed within an enterprise CIMOSA forces users to think in terms of "processes", "activities" and "operations", where operations define the lowest level of granularity to represent tasks performed within an enterprise, activities are made of operations, and processes group activities (and may be sub-processes) to form logical chains of activities interconnected by rules. Thus the enterprise is modelled as an event driven network of rule based processes.

Operations are ignored at the Requirements Definition Modelling Level (to prevent considering excessive details) and are specified and described at the Design Specification and Implementation Description Modelling Levels of CIMOSA. Concepts of the Process/Activity/Operation approach are further detailed in the following sections.

4 Basic Notation

An enterprise is a dynamic system subject to deterministic and non-deterministic perturbations having inputs and outputs and made of a certain number of passive and/or interacting elements, also called objects. These elements concern functions, resources, humans, applications, information entities and so on.

Let us consider an enterprise E. It is assumed that E is made of a non-empty set D of Domains D_1, D_2, ..., D_n,

where each Domain D_i is a functional area of the enterprise.

Each Domain contains a finite number of enterprise functions ef_1, ef_2, ..., ef_m (i.e. tasks) which can be hierarchically organised or not.

We denote:

Ev_E: the set of all Events (i.e. unsolicited requests or real-world happenings) relative to enterprise E (endogenous or exogenous Events of the enterprise).
Ev_D: the sub-set of Ev_E of Events relative to Domain D of enterprise E only.
Ev_{ef}: the sub-set of Ev_D of Events relative to the enterprise function ef only (i.e. involved in the triggering of ef), provided that ef is at the top of a functional decomposition hierarchy.

OV_E: the set of all Object Views (i.e. physical or information appearances) of real-world objects used, processed or produced within enterprise E. Object Views are made of information elements (lowest level of information granularity) and/or other Object Views (recursive definition). Object Views which are information entities are defined as external schemata on some data schema expressed in terms of some data model (e.g. the relational or object-oriented model).

OV_D: the set of all Object Views used, processed or produced within Domain D.

R_E: the set of all Resources (including the Functional Entities) used in the enterprise E.

R_D: the set of all Resources used in Domain D only.

Then we define:

$Name_{ef}$: the name or identifier of enterprise function ef;

Def_{ef}: a textual description of the enterprise function ef;

Obj_{ef}: a set of business objectives of the enterprise applicable to ef;

Cst_{ef}: a set of business constraints of the enterprise (i.e. administrative, managerial, financial, strategic, technical or other constraints) applicable to ef;

DR_{ef}: a set of so-called Declarative Rules representing imposed business rules (i.e. combinations of objectives and constraints linked by the logical operators AND, OR, NOT and IMPLY) which may impact the way ef is executed;

ES_{ef}: a set of possible ending values called Ending Statuses returned at the end of the execution of ef and characterising its execution status. Each Ending Status can be defined as a predicate expressed in first-order predicate logic;

FI_{ef}: Function Input of ef defined as a (possibly empty) sub-set of OV_D indicating objects received by ef to be processed;

FO_{ef}: Function Output of ef defined as a sub-set of OV_D indicating objects produced or returned by ef;

CI_{ef}: Control Input of ef defined as a (possibly empty) sub-set of OV_D indicating objects providing run-time data or control data to ef;

CO_{ef}: Control Output of ef defined as a (possibly empty) sub-set of the power set of Ev_D. In other words the Control Output of ef gives the list of Events generated by ef, if any;

RI_{ef}: Resource Input of ef defined as a non-empty subset of R_D (can be left undefined at requirements level);

RO_{ef}: Resource Output of ef indicating Resource usage or status after the execution of ef;

$Algo_{ef}$: a deterministic algorithm for enterprise function ef employing so-called Functional Operations, i.e. basic units of work which can be performed by at least one of the Functional Entities (elements of R_D if ef is an element of D) of the enterprise (lowest level of granularity of functionality).

PRS_{ef}: a finite set of so-called Procedural Rules, i.e. control structures (sequential, iterative, conditional, branching, rendezvous) defining the logical sequence of execution of lower level enterprise functions within enterprise function ef according to the enterprise state, i.e. values of Ending Statuses of lower level enterprise functions used by ef. PRS stands for Procedural Rule Set.

Where-Used$_{ef}$: a list of enterprise function identifiers of all enterprise functions employing enterprise function ef;

Employs$_{ef}$: a list of enterprise function identifiers of all enterprise functions employed by enterprise function ef;

5   Function-Behaviour-Structure Paradigm

The Function-Behaviour-Structure (FBS) modelling approach of CIMOSA (see Fig. 4.2.1) is made of three basic concepts to model the functions of enterprises as its name suggests. They can be formalised as follows using the previous notations:

Definition 1: **Enterprise functionality** describes what is being done (i.e. operational tasks) using the resources of the enterprise over time, consuming inputs and producing outputs. The functionality of an enterprise function ef can be formally defined as a 12-tuple

$$F_{ef} = (Def_{ef}, Obj_{ef}, Cst_{ef}, DR_{ef}, FI_{ef}, FO_{ef}, CI_{ef}, CO_{ef}, RI_{ef}, RO_{ef}, ES_{ef}, Algo_{ef})$$

where Obj_{ef} is a non-empty set, the union of FI_{ef} with FO_{ef} is a non-empty set, RI_{ef} defines resources to be used and ES_{ef} is a non-empty set. The algorithm $Algo_{ef}$ (which can be left undefined at the requirements level) is such that:

$$(FO_{ef}, CO_{ef}, RO_{ef}) = Algo_{ef} (FI_{ef}, CI_{ef}, RI_{ef})$$

Definition 2: **Enterprise behaviour** defines the evolution of the enterprise state over the time in reaction to enterprise Event generation or conditions external or internal to the enterprise. It is defined by means of a set of rules (so-called Procedural Rules) which govern the sequence of execution of enterprise functionalities according to the system state (event-driven control flow). The behaviour of an enterprise function ef can be formally defined as a 2-tuple

$$B_{ef} = (Ev_{ef}, PRS_{ef})$$

where PRS_{ef} is a non-empty set of Procedural Rules and Ev_{ef} is a set of Events involved in the triggering conditions of the rules.

Procedural Rules define control structures typical of manufacturing environments such as precedence relationships, parallelism, branching conditions, rendezvous and iterative processing, depending on enterprise Events and conditions internal or external to the enterprise. They can be defined by the following general syntax:

ON < triggering condition >   DO < action >

where < action > indicates one or more enterprise functions to activate next and < triggering condition > defines the conditions which must be met to activate these enterprise functions using values of events and ending statuses.

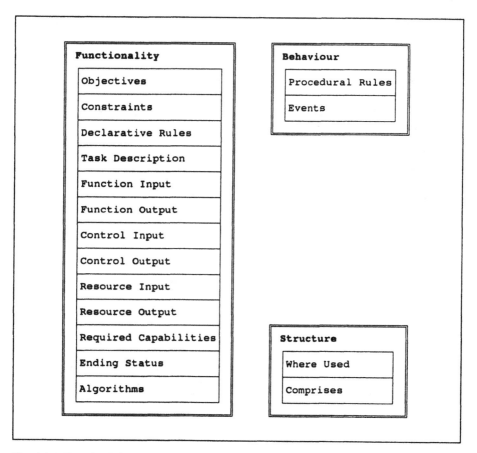

Fig. 4.2.1: Function-Behaviour-Structure Model

Definition 3: Enterprise functional structure describes the functional decomposition of the enterprise functions of enterprise E. This can be achieved by means of a pair of pointers attached to each enterprise function ef

$$S_{ef} = (\text{Where-Used}_{ef}, \text{Employs}_{ef}{}^{7}).$$

Definition 4: The full functionality F of an enterprise E is defined by the functionality F_{ef} of all its enterprise functions ef.

Definition 5: The full behaviour B of an enterprise E (respectively, of Domain D) is defined by the behaviour B_{ef} of all its enterprise functions ef.

Definition 6: The state of an enterprise E at time t is defined by the state of its enterprise functions, of its resources and of its information system at time t.

Using the previous notations and the three blocks (Functionality, Behaviour, Structure), one can provide a formal definition for generic concepts of processes (for behaviour) and activities (for functionality) as follows:

Definition 7: A process P is a structure which governs the sequence of a finite set of tasks (processes or activities) and which can be defined as a 9-tuple

$$P = (\text{Name}_{ef}, \text{Def}_{ef}, \text{Obj}_{ef}, \text{Cst}_{ef}, \text{DR}_{ef}, \text{Ev}_{ef}, \text{PRS}_{ef}, \text{ES}_{ef}, \text{Employs}_{ef})$$

where Obj_{ef} is non-empty, PRS_{ef} is non-empty and Employs_{ef} is non-empty.

Definition 8: An activity A is a structure which performs a task (Algo_{ef}) and which can be defined as a 13-tuple

$$(\text{Name}_{ef}, \text{Def}_{ef}, \text{Obj}_{ef}, \text{Cst}_{ef}, \text{DR}_{ef}, \text{FI}_{ef}, \text{FO}_{ef}, \text{CI}_{ef}, \text{CO}_{ef}, \text{RI}_{ef}, \text{RO}_{ef}, \text{ES}_{ef}, \text{Algo}_{ef})$$

where Obj_{ef} is non-empty, the union of FI_{ef} and FO_{ef} is non-empty and ES_{ef} is non-empty.

It is assumed that (1) processes are triggered when their triggering conditions are verified (i.e. their sets of Procedural Rules can be activated), and (2) each activity produces a unique Ending Status value (i.e. a termination state) upon its completion.

From these definitions it is obvious that

- processes can be made of processes (i.e. sub-processes) and/or activities
- activities have no behaviour as defined previously
- activities are low level enterprise functions which are employed by processes (no Employs list)

The three blocks of the FBS model can be used to define the functional structure of a part of the enterprise in the form of a hierarchy (functional decomposition) as illustrated by Fig. 4.2.3.

---

7   Note: One pointer would obviously be enough (for instance, Employs_{ef}). For convenience reasons we make use of both.

Definition 9: The functional structure of an enterprise E is a non-empty forest of trees, the nodes of which are enterprise functions such that leaves of the trees are activities only and all other nodes are processes.

Important Remark: The main purpose of the FBS approach is to provide a clear separation between enterprise functionality and enterprise behaviour, so that one can be updated with limited impact on the other. This is one of the most important basic principles of CIMOSA.

To capture more of the semantics of CIM applications CIMOSA defines two types of processes, namely Domain Processes (sitting at the top of a functional decomposition) and Business Processes (intermediate levels), and one type of activities, called Enterprise Activities (leaves of functional decompositions). These constructs are discussed in detail in subsequent sections of this report.

Definition 10: A **Domain** D is an encapsulation of a non-empty finite set DP_D of Domain Processes DP_1, DP_2, ..., DP_r, each one contributing to the realisation of some objectives (Domain Objectives) under some constraints (Domain Constraints) applicable to the Domain, together with the relevant set Ev_D of Events (Ev_D is the union set of sets of Events for all Domain Processes belonging to D), a non-empty set OV_D of Object Views, and a non-empty set $DRel_D$ of Domain Relationships. More formally,

$$D = (Name_D, Obj_D, Cst_D, DP_D, Ev_D, OV_D, DRel_D)$$

where $Name_D$ is the name of the Domain.

Definition 11: A **Domain Process** is an enterprise function DP formally defined as a 15-tuple

$$DP = (Name_{DP}, Def_{DP}, Obj_{DP}, Cst_{DP}, DR_{DP}, FI_{DP}, CI_{DP}, RI_{DP}, FO_{DP}, CO_{DP}, RO_{DP}, PRS_{DP}, Ev_{DP}, Employs_{DP}, Where\text{-}Used_{DP}) \text{ where}$$

$Name_{DP}$ is the name of the Domain Process;

Def_{DP} is the process description (i.e. narrative text explaining what the Domain Process DP is about and how to attain the objectives);

Obj_{DP} is a non-empty set of business objectives relatively to its functionality and behaviour. These are objectives or sub-objectives of the Domain to which this Domain Process belongs;

Cst_{DP} is a (possibly empty) set of business constraints relatively to its functionality and behaviour (i.e. what constrains achievement of the objectives);

DR_{DP} is a (possibly empty) set of Declarative Rules of the Domain Process representing imposed business rules;

FI_{DP} is the Function Input made of a (possibly empty) set of Object Views defining what the Domain Process needs as inputs to be transformed when it starts;

CI_{DP} is the Control Input made of a (possibly empty) set of Object Views indicating information objects used but not modified by or objects constraining the execution of the Domain Process or object providing run-time data;

RI_{DP} is the Resource Input. It is left undefined at the requirements level;

FO_{DP} is the Function Output made of a (possibly empty) set of Object Views defining what the Domain Process produces as outputs (i.e. end results);

CO_{DP} is the Control Output made of a (possibly empty) set of Events, occurrences of which can be generated in the course of the process. It can be left undefined at the requirements level;

RO_{DP} is the Resource Output made of a textual statement defining requirements on resource usage, if any;

PRS_{DP} is the non-empty set of Procedural Rules describing the flow of control of the Domain Process;

Ev_{DP} is a non-empty set of Events, occurrences of which are directly used to trigger the set of Procedural Rules of the Domain Process occurrences;

Where-Used$_{DP}$ is the reference to the Domain employing Domain Process DP;

Employs$_{DP}$ is a non-empty set of references to next lower level structures (Business Processes and/or Enterprise Activities) employed by this Domain Process.

FI_{DP} and FO_{DP} define the global functionality of the Domain Process DP, if required. They respectively define the objects used at the beginning of the process (Function Input) and the objects produced as the end result of the process (Function Output). Function Input and Function Output have been provided to ease the top-down design process of Domain Processes (therefore making possible the traceability of inputs and outputs), and for the purpose of connecting inputs and outputs of a Domain to inputs and outputs of the Domain Processes. They are by no means mandatory. The same applies to all other inputs and outputs. It is not necessary to define the values of the Ending Status of Domain Processes because (1) they are not used anywhere in the model, and (2) they can always be derived from the values of Ending Statuses of employed enterprise functions.

Definition 12: A **Business Process** is an enterprise function BP formally defined as a 15-tuple

$$BP = (Name_{BP}, Def_{BP}, Obj_{BP}, Cst_{BP}, DR_{BP}, FI_{BP}, CI_{BP}, RI_{BP}, FO_{BP}, CO_{BP}, RO_{BP}, PRS_{BP}, ES_{BP}, Employs_{BP}, Where-Used_{BP}) \text{ where}$$

$Name_{BP}$ is the name of the Business Process;

Def_{BP} is the process description (i.e. narrative text explaining what the Business Process BP is about and how to attain the objectives);

Obj$_{BP}$ is a non-empty set of business objectives relatively to functionality and behaviour of BP;

Cst$_{BP}$ is a (possibly empty) set of business constraints relatively to functionality and behaviour of BP (i.e. what constrains achievement of the objectives);

DR$_{BP}$ is a (possibly empty) set of Declarative Rules of the Business Process representing imposed business rules;

FI$_{BP}$ is the Function Input made of a (possibly empty) set of Object Views defining what the Business Process needs as inputs to be transformed when it starts;

CI$_{BP}$ is the Control Input made of a (possibly empty) set of Object Views indicating information objects used but not modified by or objects constraining the execution of the Business Process or objects providing run-time data;

RI$_{BP}$ is the Resource Input. It is left undefined at the requirements level;

FO$_{BP}$ is the Function Output made of a (possibly empty) set of Object Views defining what the Business Process produces as outputs (i.e. results);

CO$_{BP}$ is the Control Output made of a (possibly empty) set of Events, occurrences of which can be generated in the course of an occurrence of the process. It can be left undefined at the requirements level;

RO$_{BP}$ is the Resource Output made of a textual statement defining requirements on resource usage, if any;

ES$_{BP}$ is the non-empty set of Ending Status values defining all possible termination states of the Business Process (must be consistent with the Ending Statuses of the employed enterprise functions);

PRS$_{BP}$ is the non-empty set of Procedural Rules describing the flow of control of the Business Process;

Where-Used$_{BP}$ is the reference to next upper level structures (Domain Processes or Business Processes) employing Business Process BP;

Employs$_{BP}$ is a non-empty set of references to next lower level structures (Business Processes and/or Enterprise Activities) employed by Business Process BP.

Definition 13: An **Enterprise Activity** is an enterprise function EA formally defined as a 14-tuple

$$EA = (Name_{EA}, Def_{EA}, Obj_{EA}, Cst_{EA}, DR_{EA}, FI_{EA}, FO_{EA}, CI_{EA}, CO_{EA}, RI_{EA}, RO_{EA}, RC_{EA}, ES_{EA}, Algo_{EA}, Parent_{EA}) \text{ where}$$

Name$_{EA}$ is the name or identifier of the Enterprise Activity;

Def_{EA} is the task description, i.e. narrative text explaining what the Enterprise Activity is supposed to do;
Obj_{EA} is a non-empty set of objectives relatively to this functionality. These are sub-objectives of the objectives of the parent structures;
Cst_{EA} is a (possibly empty) set of constraints relatively to this functionality (i.e. what constrains achievement of the objectives);
DR_{EA} is a (possibly empty) set of Declarative Rules representing imposed business rules for this Enterprise Activity. They may be inherited from the parent structures;
FI_{EA} is the Function Input defining the (possibly empty) set of Object Views to be processed and transformed;
FO_{EA} is the Function Output defining the non-empty set of Object Views produced or returned by the activity;
CI_{EA} is the Control Input defining the (possibly empty) set of Object Views providing run-time information or information constraining the execution of the activity but not modified by the activity;
CO_{EA} is the Control Output providing the (possibly empty) set of Events, occurrences of which can be raised by occurrences of this Enterprise Activity;
RI_{EA} is the Resource Input. It is left undefined at the requirements level;
RO_{EA} is the Resource Output (defined as a pure text) describing the resource status after the execution of the Enterprise Activity;
RC_{EA} is the (possibly empty) set of Capabilities required by the Enterprise Activity (and defined in the Resource View);
ES_{EA} is the non-empty set of Ending Status descriptions defining under which conditions the Ending Statuses can be obtained;
Algo_{EA} specifies the functionality to be performed. It is left undefined at the requirements level;
Parent_{EA} is a non-empty set of next upper level structures (i.e. Domain Processes or Business Processes) using this activity.

FI_{EA}, FO_{EA}, CI_{EA}, CO_{EA}, RI_{EA}, RO_{EA}, RC_{EA} and Algo_{EA} define the full functionality of the Enterprise Activity. They are linked by the following relationship:

$$(\text{FO}_{EA}, \text{CO}_{EA}, \text{RO}_{EA}) = \text{Algo}_{EA} (\text{FI}_{EA}, \text{CI}_{EA}, \text{RI}_{EA})$$

subject to RC_{EA} and DR_{EA}
and with union (FI_{EA}, FO_{EA}) must be non-empty

6 Comparison between Domain Process, Business Process and Enterprise Activity

A Domain is made of a non-empty set of Domain Processes and Resources (including Functional Entities) processing real-world objects. Each Domain Process is a stand-alone process made of a hierarchy of Business Processes (sub-processes) and Enterprise Activities. It contains at least one Enterprise Activity. The Business Processes just provide a convenient way for users to structure the model as easy manageable, re-usable, blocks to deal with complexity of their model. In fact once completely designed a Domain Process equates to a <u>network</u> of Enterprise Activities which can be entered at several entry points under well-defined conditions (starting triggering conditions).

Thus the most important constructs in this approach are Domain Processes and Enterprise Activities. Indeed one could very well design a correct model using only these two constructs.

Basic concepts	DP	BP	EA	
Objectives	x	x	x	
Constraints	x	x	x	
Declarative Rules	x	x	x	
Function Input	o	o	x	
Function Output	o	o	x	Functionality
Control Input	o	o	x	
Control Output	o	o	x	
Resource Input	o	o	x	
Resource Output	o	o	x	
Required Capabilities			x	
Ending Statuses		x	x	
Procedural Rules	x	x		Behaviour
Events	x			
Where-Used		x	x	Structure
Employs	x	x		

x: mandatory   o: optional
DP: Domain Process, BP: Business Process,
EA: Enterprise Activity

Fig. 4.2.2: Construct Composition

The main differences between a Domain Process and a Business Process are that (1) a Domain Process has no parent structure (except the Domain to which it belongs), and (2) a Business Process is never triggered by Events only while Domain Processes are triggered by nothing than Events. Fig. 4.2.2 summarises these definitions.

Remark 1: In this paradigm, it becomes obvious that (1) Enterprise Activities essentially model pieces of enterprise functionality, (2) Business Processes essentially model (re-usable) blocks of enterprise behaviour, and (3) Domain Processes encapsulate enterprise functionality and behaviour contributing to the realisation of global business objectives.

Remark 2: The enterprise structure is directly represented within the constructs (Employs and Where-Used entries).

Remark 3: The paradigm allows for easy mutation of an Enterprise Activity into a Business Process and vice-versa.

Property 1: Separation of functionality and behaviour (one of the CIMOSA basic principles), making it possible to revise behaviour in order to meet changing circumstances without altering the installed functionality and vice-versa, is easily achieved.

Property 2: Traceability of objectives, constraints, Declarative Rules as well as of Function Inputs and Function Outputs is ensured from top to bottom of a functional decomposition.

Property 3: It is possible to assign a resource requirements to a set of Enterprise Activities, i.e. to a Business Process.

Property 4: For the sake of consistency the Ending Status of an enterprise function is a logical function of the Ending Statuses of its employed enterprise functions, except if it has no descendants.

Important Remark: Finally, it must be pointed out that the Function Input (respectively, Function Output) of a process (Domain Process or Business Process) **does not equate** to the sum of the Function Inputs (respectively, Function Outputs) of its subservient Enterprise Activities. The proof is that a Function Output of one Enterprise Activity can be the Function Input of another Enterprise Activity in the same process and therefore, does not belong to either the Function Input or the Function Output of that process.

7 Example

The following example describes a functional decomposition in enterprise modelling as shown in Fig. 4.2.3. The process starts with the definition of an enterprise Domain or functional area, its contents and its relation to the outside world (definition of its boundaries). Its global functionality is then defined as a set of Domain Processes. For each Domain Process its functionality part [F1] (identifying Function Input and Function Output if required) is described, as well as its behaviour part [B1] in terms of the lower level functionalities [F1x] which appear in the breakdown of the functionality of the Domain Process.

The lower level functionalities [F1x] again will be defined as Enterprise Activities (EA) with the level of detail identified. If the described functionality has to be further detailed, the behaviour [B1x] will be described as Business Processes (BP) in terms of the lower level functionalities. This process can continue to any level of detail as desired by the business user.

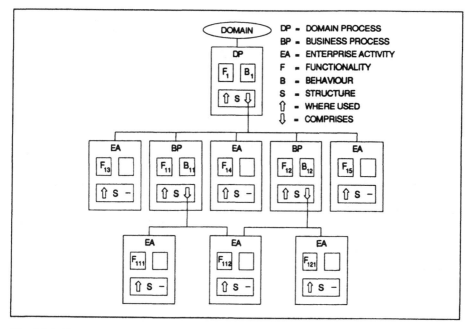

Fig. 4.2.3: Example of Function Decomposition

Principle of use

Hierarchical definition does not mean that any given enterprise function is assigned to only one parent enterprise function. Any enterprise function (except Domain Processes) can be employed by any other enterprise function regardless of their relative positions in a design hierarchy. Thus specific enterprise functions (Business Processes or Enterprise Activities) can be re-used throughout a Particular Architecture leading to economy of design.

III CIMOSA Implementation Description Language

- IDL -

its Definition and Use

1   Introduction

This report presents the status of the development by AMICE of a formal language to be used for enterprise description: at the end of the modelling phase of CIMOSA, the enterprise model obtained will be written in IDL (Implementation Description Language) and the corresponding model of the enterprise will be the IDM (Implementation Description Model). This model will be executable by the CIMOSA Integrating Infrastructure. Globally, the aim is to show which technical choices have been taken and what are the main features of this first version of IDL. For that purpose, it has been found useful to have some additional sections about formal languages, to place correctly IDL. We will also emphasize in this report the relation between the Modelling Framework (MFW) and the IIS Integrating Infrastructure). There are three main issues involved here.

---

* Analogy between the MFW and Programming Languages

There is a strong analogy between programming languages on the one hand and the generic part of each Modelling Level of the MFW on the other. The Generic Building Blocks can be considered as language constructs that together define a language. Partial Models can be compared with standard libraries, and Particular Models are a kind of program. Therefore we will refer to the Generic Implementation Building Blocks as IDL (Implementation Description Language) and the Particular Implementation Description Model as IDM (Implementation Description Model).

---

* IDM-s are Executable by the IEOE

Second, an IDM "released for operation" will be executable in the IEOE (Integrated Enterprise Operation Environment) by the Integrating Infrastructure, without any compilation or transformation into an ordinary programming language. This is what sets CIMOSA apart from other modelling techniques and software development methods used in the CIM area today. Normally one uses a standard software development method like SADT or Yourdon to specify the requirements for a software system to be built. Next, the software itself is written in a programming language like C or FORTRAN. Finally, this software is executed by a (real-time) operating system.

In the CIMOSA project, there is no such discontinuity, but between the model obtained from the MFW and written in IDL and a form appropriate for execution by the IIS services at run time, there is still a need for some transformation (compiler/interpreter), which will allow the constructs in the IDM to be executed by means of the service functions of the IIS. This link of the IIS via an interpreter to the MFW also defines an important set of requirements for the IIS, since the task of the IIS is to support the execution of IDM-s.

* IDM-s are Portable

Third, if one creates an IDM by means of the IEEE (Integrated Enterprise Engineering Environment), this model can be executed on any implementation of the IEOE. This requires implementation of both the IEEE and the IEOE have to be independent of each other in order to guarantee that the IDM will be executable. Much the same as for high level programming languages like Pascal, the AMICE project intends to define a syntax and a semantics for IDL that is independent from any particular implementation of the IEEE and the IEOE. As for all standards there is a distance both in time and space between the people that write the standard and those who implement it. Therefore, the CIMOSA standard needs to be unambiguous, consistent, complete, and concise, in order to exclude misinterpretations and incompatible products. Experience with standardization efforts of programming languages and communication protocols have shown, that without the use of formal methods, this cannot be achieved.

Chapter 2 concentrates on the first main issue, namely the **execution of IDL by means of the IIS**. After the interpreter has been defined, a prototype implementation is described. It is outlined how this prototype can be used as an input to the AMICE pre-pilot implementation of CIMOSA. Chapter 3 of this report gives an overview of the most important formal semantics specification methods. For IDL we have selected a method called structural operational semantics. This part can be skipped by readers already familiar with the subject.

Chapter 4 lists some issues in language design. One of the main open issues is to what extend the user should be given control over things like the physical distribution of the execution of an IDM. Another open issue is to what extend the user is responsible for error handling and what is the role of the IIS and the supporting operating systems in this. In order to have a stable language that can resist changes in information technology and production techniques, only mathematically well defined constructs, like integers, sets, functions and data types should be incorporated in the language as a language construct, whereas concepts like manager, resource, machine, and cell that describe knowledge of the world should be dealt with by means of standard libraries. Finally chapter 5 gives an overview of some of the **main features of IDL** currently (as they could be implemented in the IDL prototype for example).

2 Execution of IDL

2.1 Introduction

There is a link from IDL to the IIS, because an IDM will be executed by means of the service functions of the services of the IIS (see Fig. 4.3.1). However, IDL is much more abstract than the service functions that are identified for the IIS. E.g. the internal subdivision of the IIS into the Business, Information, Presentation, and Common Services should remain hidden in IDL. Also the physical distribution of the IIS over several nodes should be invisible to the user. What is needed to connect the MFW to the service functions of the IIS, is an interpreter that translates the 'high level' IDL constructs into these 'low level' service functions of the IIS. This interpreter can be located outside or inside the IEOE.

If the interpreter is outside the IEOE, then there are two formats to be specified, namely IDL as the interchange format between the MFW and the interpreter and the interface that specifies which IIS service functions are visible to the outside of

194

the IIS. A lot of IIS service functions are specified to enable the interaction between the IIS services and should be invisible to the user of the IIS. In this case the vendor of the interpreter would decide how IDL will be executed by means of the IIS service functions. In this case, the AMICE project would need to put constraints to guarantee that this is possible.

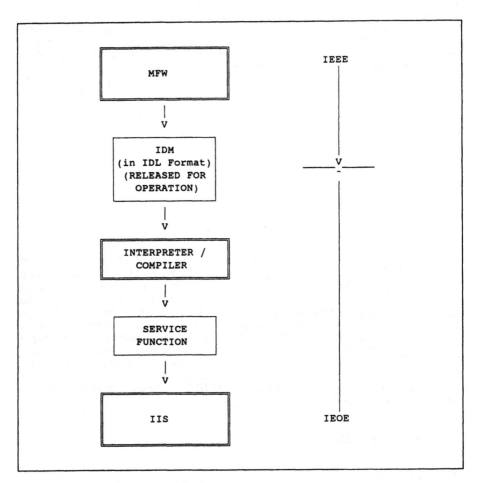

Fig. 4.3.1: Interpreter/compiler and the IIS

If the interpreter is part of the IEOE, the interaction between the interpreter and the IIS services remains hidden as an implementation issue. As before, the IDL interface, as the exchange format between the MFW and the IIS, needs to be standardized (and this time it is the only one). In this case the functionality of the interpreter will be specified by CIMOSA, which will guarantee that IDL can be executed by means of the IIS services. Therefore we prefer this solution.

In parallel with the work on IDL, a scenario is defined for the CIMOSA pre-pilot. This scenario specifies for one particular IDM what will happen in the IIS. The mapping of the IDM onto the IIS services will be done by hand. In case of the interpreter this mapping is formally defined and will be done automatically. The scenario will serve as a test whether all main issues have been dealt with, either in IDL, the interpreter, or in the IIS. It helps to raise questions and requirements for IDL and the IIS. Also it directs the mapping between IDL and the IIS.

2.2 Development Life Cycle for IDL

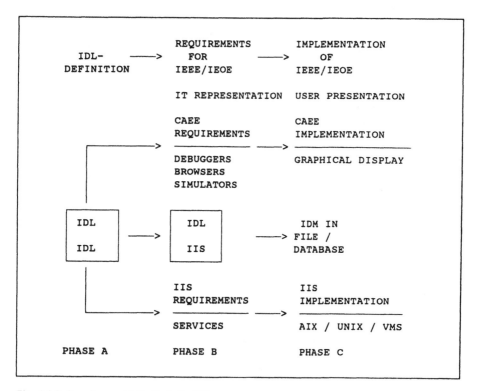

Fig. 4.3.2: Development Life Cycle for IDL

Phase A: Definition of IDL

As was already stated in the introduction, IDL should have an (abstract) syntax and semantics which are independent of any particular implementation of the IEEE and the IEOE. In Fig. 4.3.2 it is assumed that IDL is powerful enough to express its own abstract syntax and semantics.

Phase B: Requirements for IEEE and IEOE

This definition of IDL will serve as an input for the requirements for the IEEE and the IEOE. In this step the IT representation for the MFW languages will be chosen. For the IEEE the definition of IDL determines the language that will have to be supported. The IEEE consists of debuggers, browsers, and simulators for this language.

The main objective of the IEOE is to support the execution of IDL. In the IEOE it must be decided which issues will be handled by the interpreter and what will be the responsibilities of the IIS services. If the responsibilities of the IIS services have been identified, this will give a coherent and complete set of requirements for the IIS.

Phase C: Implementation of IEEE and IEOE

The user representation such as the concrete syntax for the language constructs, will be determined in this step. The implementation technology for the exchange of models between the IEEE and the IEOE will be selected. This could be done by means of a file exchange, by means of a common database, or by means of a communication protocol between the IEEE and the IEOE. Currently too many implementation details are predefined in the FRB, such as the graphical representation of procedural rule sets, the concrete syntax of language constructs, SQL as the database language at the implementation level, and the fact that models will have to be stored in the SD services in order to be accessible by the other services for their execution.

The next section defines a number of steps that need to be fulfilled for each of the phases A, B, and C.

2.3   Prototype Implementation of IDL

This section describes the two life cycles for phase A and B. The first life cycle aims at the porting of IDL onto any execution platform such as the IIS or a standard operating system (Fig. 4.3.3). The second life cycle ports both IDL and the IIS onto an operating system (Fig. 4.3.4). This is the most likely life cycle for the pre-pilot. The '*' in Fig. 4.3.3 and 4 indicates the new in each step of the life cycles.

Step I: Prototype Implementation of IDL

Since IDL is an extension of ML, first the core part of ML has to be implemented based on the formal specification of ML [Mil90]. The main difference between IDL and ML is the absence of exception handlers, since exceptions in IDL will be dealt with by special events in the concurrency part of IDL. Next, the extension with concurrent processes has to be implemented. Some further extensions are needed, like PROLOG-like declarative rules, data types like set and bags, modules with import and export, and subtyping and inheritance. The PROLOG-like declarative rules are necessary to facilitate the formal semantics specification of IDL in IDL itself by means of structural operational semantics. The other extensions are needed to make IDL upwards compatible with EXPRESS.

Step II: Formal Specification of IDL in IDL

If one wants to port IDL onto an execution platform, a formal language specification of IDL in IDL itself will have to be created by means of reverse engineering. Since IDL is an executable language, the formal specification of IDL is executable also. Thus a program F in IDL can be executed by a specification of IDL in IDL, which can be executed by the prototype implementation of IDL. This guarantees that the formal specification of IDL in IDL is compliant with the prototype, since both step I and Step II must have the same results for the same program F. The output of the prototype will be a set of test programs and a formal specification of IDL in IDL. Because a formal language specification is not enough to give a user a sound intuitive grasp of the language, this formal specification will have to be accompanied by a user manual, that gives examples of how to use the language properly. The formal language definition is mainly aimed at language implementors. However, it also serves as the ultimate language reference manual for users in case of ambiguities. This situation is quite similar to the present use of BNF syntax definitions for programming languages. A user types in programs based on his intuitive knowledge of the syntax of the language. He will reference the formal syntax definition only when he encounters problems.

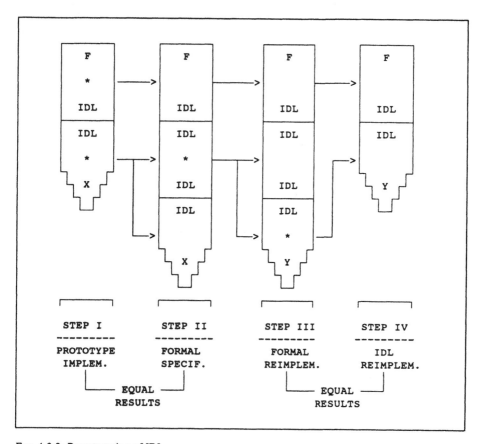

Fig. 4.3.3: Bootstrapping of IDL

Step III: Bootstrapping of IDL

Based on the formal specification of IDL, IDL can be reimplemented by means of bootstrapping on another platform.

198

Step IV: Reimplementation of IDL

After this formal reimplementation of IDL the formal language definition can be dismissed. The language can be executed on the new platform directly. Implementation issues like performance can be dealt with now. Currently IDL can be implemented using the formal specification of ML and some additional specifications for the concurrency part. For the porting of IDL and the IIS onto an execution environment the first step of the life cycle is the same.

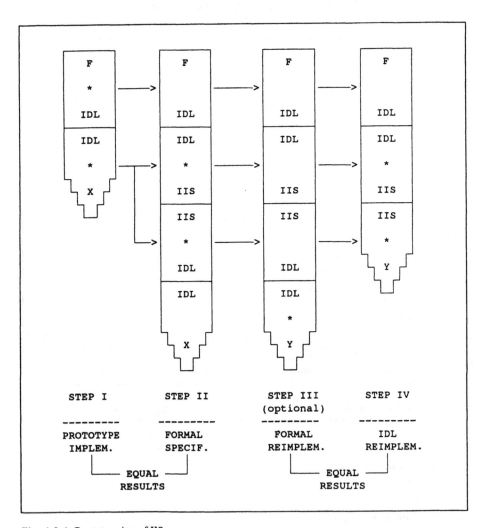

Fig. 4.3.4: Bootstrapping of IIS

Step I: Prototype Implementation of IDL

This step is identical for both life cycles.

Step II: Formal Specification of IDL in IIS and of IIS in IDL

Instead of creating a formal semantics specification of IDL in terms of IDL, two formal specifications need to be created. The first one is a formal specification of the interpreter that executes IDL by means the services of the IIS. This specification can be written in IDL. The second one is a formal specification of the services of the IIS. Until now LOTOS is selected for this purpose. However, if IDL would be selected for this specification, one has a unified approach for the language IDL, its formal specification, and its interpretation and execution by means of the IEOE. This would also close the loop between the MFW and the IIS. On the one hand IDL is executed by means of the IIS, and on the other hand CIMOSA would use its own specification method to specify the IIS.

Step III (Optional): Bootstrapping of IDL

After this second step there is an optional step to reimplement IDL itself by means of the first life cycle in order to be able to simulate the formal specifications created in the previous step on the target platform.

Step IV: Bootstrapping of IIS

Indifferent from whether one implements step III, based on the formal specification of the IIS in IDL, the IIS can be reimplemented on another execution environment by means of bootstrapping. The interpreter that executes IDL by means of the services of the IIS will have to be reimplemented in a language that is supported by the target platform.

2.4 Distribution of the IIS

IDL is executed by a physically distributed runtime environment (IEOE) that consists of a set of nodes (Fig. 4.3.5). A physically distributed system consists of multiple autonomous processors that do not share primary memory but cooperate by sending messages over a communication network. Each processor in such a system executes its own instruction stream and uses its local data, both stored in its local memory. Occasionally, processors may need to exchange data by sending messages to each other over a network.

Some people are dissatisfied with message passing as the basic communication primitive and have developed communication models that do not directly reflect the hardware communication model. One step in this direction is to have processors communicating through a (generalized form of) procedure call, like rendezvous or RPC (Remote Procedure Call). A more fundamental break with message passing is achieved through communication models based on shared data. Although implemented on a physically distributed system, such shared data systems are logically non-distributed. A logically distributed system consists of multiple software processes that communicate by explicit message passing. This concerns the logical distribution of data used by the software, rather than the physical distribution of the memories. In a logical non-distributed system processes communicate through shared data.

There are four combinations of physical and logical distribution, each of which is viable:

a. logically distributed software running on physically distributed hardware:
A typical example is a collection of processes, each running on a separate processor and communicating by sending messages over a network.

b. logically distributed software running on physically non-distributed hardware:
This class has the same logical multiprocess structure as the previous one, only now the physical message sending is simulated by implementing message passing using shared memory.

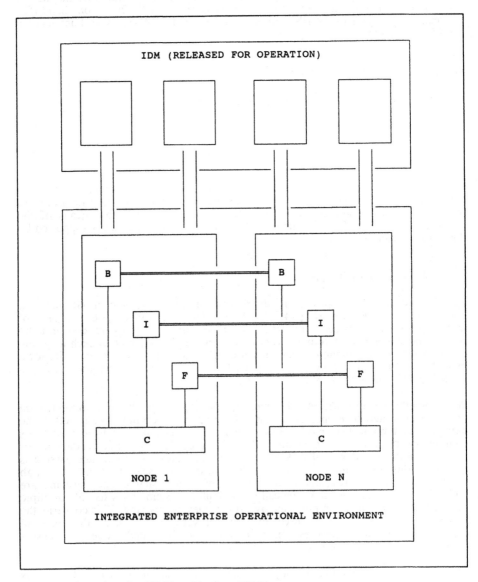

Fig. 4.3.5: Execution of an IDM by a Distributed IEOE

c. logically non-distributed software running on physically distributed hardware: This class tries to hide the physical distribution by making the system look like it has shared memory. In such cases the implementation rather than the programmer deals with the physical distribution of data over several processors.

An intuitive example of such a system is a telephone system. A user just dials a telephone number in order to be connected with the selected telephone set. He doesn't have to know the physical distribution of the telephone network and how his messages are routed over this network to the other end of the line.

d. logically non-distributed software running on physically non-distributed hardware: This class also communicates through shared data, only the existence of physical shared memory makes the implementation much easier.

Distributed programming implements distributed applications on distributed architectures. The main issue that distinguishes distributed programming from sequential programming is mapping. Mapping is the ability to assign different parts of a program to be run in parallel on different processors, either to make optimum use of the available processors or to increase the reliability or availability of the program. Some languages give the programmer control over mapping. If not, mapping is done transparently by the compiler and the run-time system, possibly assisted by the operating system. There are three approaches for assigning parallel units to processors, whether the assignment is done by the programmer or the system: the processor can either be fixed at compile time, fixed at run time when the unit is created, or not fixed at all allowing the process to be executed on different processors during its lifetime.

---

* Open Issue: logically non-distributed or logically distributed IIS

In case of the IIS we have a physically distributed hardware, but as can be seen above, this does not imply that the IDM will have to be logically distributed. Basically the decision whether the IIS will be logically non-distributed or logically distributed boils down to the choice whether the mapping of processes onto nodes in the IIS will be done automatically or will be specified by the user in his IDM.

2.5 Aggregation Levels within the IEOE

In the IEOE it is possible to discern a number of aggregation levels, each having its own level of detail (see Fig. 4.3.6). Each aggregation level provides an interface with more abstract processes that serve as resources to the next upper layer, and is implemented on top of the processes (and thus resources) provided by the layer underneath. Going from top to bottom in Fig. 4.3.6 the following aggregation levels can be discriminated:

* Computer Hardware

At the lowest aggregation level the micro programming of the computer hardware provides the computer instruction set as an abstract interface. It shields intricate issues like multiple instruction and data prefetching, multiple instruction decoding, memory interleaving, caching, direct memory access, and bus allocation.

* Operating System

Most operating systems support multiuser, multitasking, multiprocessing, and networking. The operating system should hide for the user how data processing resources like CPU's, core memory, and disk space are distributed among the users and active processes.

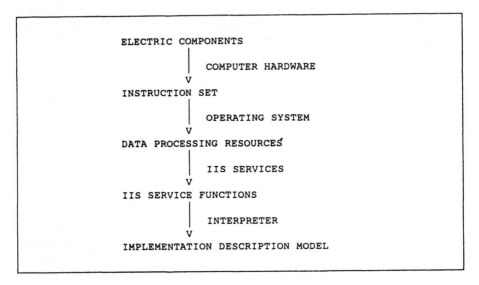

Fig. 4.3.6: Levels of aggregation within the IEOE

* IIS

On top of such a "standard" operating system the IIS is implemented according to the CIMOSA specifications.

* Interpreter

The IEOE contains an interpreter that executes the released IDM by means of the IIS service functions. In this IDM it is specified how the company operates. Although the IIS is implemented on top of an existing operating system, there is no specification, which functions are implemented by the operating system, which by the IIS, and which functions will be programmed by the user in the IDM.

Since the IIS is implemented on top of existing operating systems and because user programs specified in IDL are executed on top of the IIS, it is important to have a clear specification, which part is responsible for which functions. An important issue is failure detection and recovery. The ability to detect and recover from partial failure of a system may be used to write programs that can tolerate hardware failures. The basic method for dealing with such failures is to provide a mechanism for failure detection. With this approach, the programmer is responsible for cleaning up the mess that results after a process crash. The major problem is to bring the system back into a consistent state. This usually can only be done if process crashes are anticipated and precautions are taken during normal computation. To release the programmer from all these details, models have been suggested to make recovery from failures easier. Ideally, the system should hide all failures from the programmer. Alternatively, the programmer can be given high-level mechanisms for expressing which processes and data are important and how they should be recovered after a crash. If, for example, an error occurs, because a file cannot be found, this error could be handled by the:

* Operating System

The fact that the file couldn't be found is considered to be a fatal error and the execution of the IDM is stopped.

* IIS

An error message is send by the SD service to the B service, and the B service can take appropriate actions, like calling a standard exception handler. This relieves the user of having to specify control constructs like "if file cannot be found then ... , else ..." which obfuscates the program.

* Implementation Description Model

In this case the procedural rule set will have to contain a rule that states "if file cannot be found, then ...".

---

* Open Issue: user control versus automatic implementation

It is still to be decided what will be given under the control of the user via IDL and what will be implemented automatically. If an issue is implemented automatically, it will have to be implemented by the interpreter, the IIS, or the supporting operating system.

3   Overview of Formal Semantics Specification Methods

3.1   Introduction

In the field of formal language semantics specifications it is common practice not to define the semantics of a programming language based on its concrete syntax, but to map this concrete syntax, which was mainly designed for human readability, onto an abstract syntax, that only preserves the characteristic features. As can be seen from Fig. 4.3.7, the fact that operation A and B are performed in parallel before operation C, can be expressed in many different ways. However, the semantics of each of these representations is independent from arbitrary characteristics such as the use of brackets, colons, boxes, or arrows. How this abstract syntax can be specified will be described in the section on the algebraic specification methods.

Independent of what formal semantics specification method is used, a compiler or interpreter can be subdivided into a parser and an evaluation module (Fig. 4.3.8). The parser of an interpreter/compiler reads a program in a concrete syntax representation, verifies that it has the proper syntax, and converts it into the corresponding abstract syntax tree. There are standard techniques, like attribute grammars, to specify the behaviour of this part. Therefore we will not deal with this part any further.

The second part, the evaluation module, evaluates the abstract syntax tree into its corresponding output in case of an interpreter, or transforms it into an equivalent program in a target language in case of a compiler. In doing so, the evaluation module defines the semantics of the program. The behaviour of the evaluation module can be specified by means of formal semantics specification methods as classified in Fig. 4.3.9. The first major classification is the subdivision in property-oriented methods and model-oriented methods.

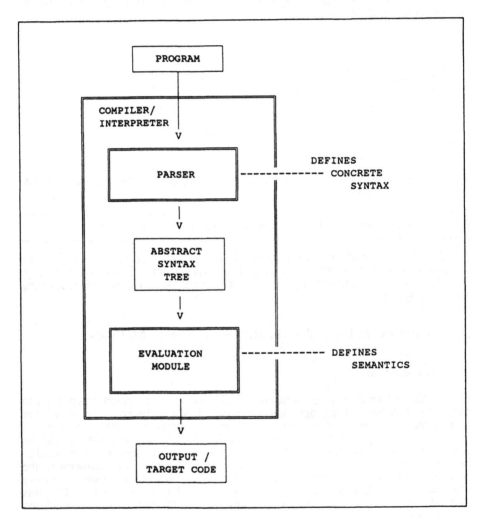

Fig. 4.3.8: Generic Structure of an Interpreter/Compiler, or Language Definition

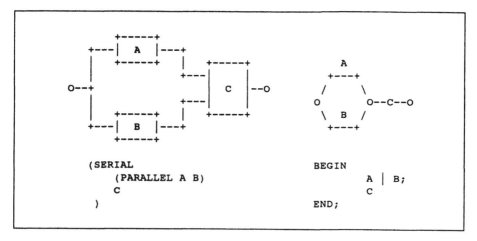

Fig. 4.3.7: Different Textual and Graphical Representations with the same Abstract Syntax Tree

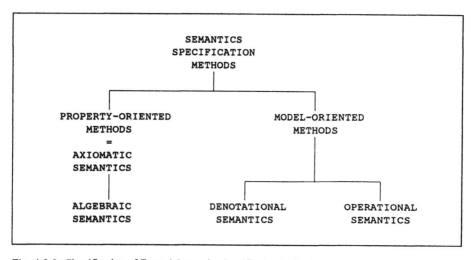

Fig. 4.3.9: Classification of Formal Semantics Specification Methods

3.2 Property-Oriented Specification Methods

A property-oriented specification method describes a specification in terms of clauses about the external behaviour of a realization. One way is to write down all the consistent properties of the systems behaviour that one has in mind. Next, one minimizes the basic collection of properties by throwing out properties that are the consequences of the remainder. Such a collection of basic properties is known as an axiomatization of the specification. This is why these methods are also referred to as axiomatic semantics. The properties for a specification of an exclusive-or gate are listed in Fig. 4.3.10. Advantages are that the specifications are minimal, and fit with verification methods very well. A disadvantage is that for bigger realizations it is very difficult to specify a complete and consistent set of axioms. In general this kind of specifications is much harder to comprehend. A subclass of property-oriented specification methods are the algebraic specification methods.

3.3 Model-Oriented Specification Methods

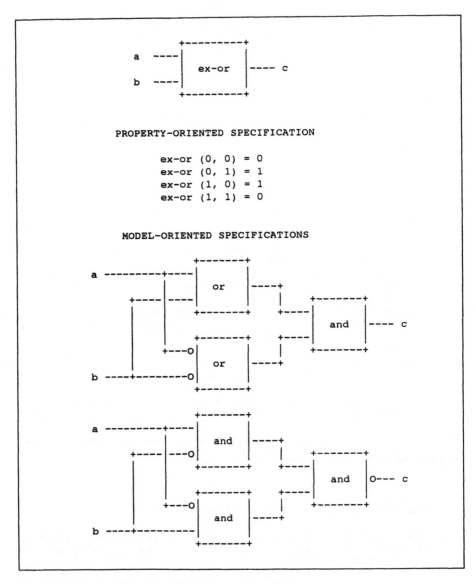

Fig. 4.3.10: Property-Oriented and Model-Oriented Specifications

In a model-oriented specification, the required realization is described by means of a model that is constructed as a compound structure, using a set of more fundamental objects as base material, the existence of which may be taken for granted. The properties of the compound object are derived from how the basic components are put together and from the underlying properties of the constituent components. Two examples of a model-oriented specification for an exclusive-or gate are given in Fig. 4.3.10. These kind of specifications are much easier to read than property-oriented specifications, because they suggest one of the possible solutions that fit the requirements. This is also one of the weaknesses: they suffer from overspecification, since if one of the two model-oriented specifications for the exclusive-or gate is given, the implementor may overlook the other possible realization of the same functional behaviour. Model-oriented specification methods can be subdivided into operational semantics specification methods and denotational semantics specification methods.

3.4 Operational Semantics

Operational semantics methods define an interpreter that maps the abstract syntax tree onto a state-oriented model that describes the dynamic behaviour of a program. The state defines the value of each variable and which values have been pushed on the parameter passing stack. One of the disadvantages of an operational definition is that the language can be understood only in terms of the interpreter. No implementation-independent definition exists. Another problem is the interpreter itself: it is represented as an algorithm. If the algorithm is written in an elegant notation, then the interpreter can give insight into the language. Unfortunately, interpreters for nontrivial languages are large and complex, and the language used to write them is often as complex as the language being defined. Therefore, operational semantics is not very suitable for standardization efforts like that for IDL.

3.5 Denotational Semantics

In a denotational semantics specification an elaboration function or valuation function maps each node of the abstract syntax tree onto its model (Fig. 4.3.11). Although we try to stay away from the mathematical intricacies of this method, a number of characteristics can be outlined here.

* semantics follows syntax:

Each node of the abstract syntax tree is mapped onto exactly one construct that is used to define its semantics (see Fig. 4.3.11). This construct is not an elementary gate as in the case of the exclusive-or gate specification, nor is it a transistor or resistor as would be the case in an electrical schema for a television set, but an element of a so-called Scott Domain. If a < DECL > and a < STMT > occur inside a < PROGRAM >, this implies that the meaning that is used to model the behaviour of < PROGRAM >, must take the meanings of < DECL > and < STMT > as sub-building blocks.

* context freeness = abstract from where used:

If the same syntactic construct can occur in different places (as is the case for < EXPR > in Fig. 4.3.11), then it must be modelled by means of exactly the same construct in each of these cases. Thus the same syntactic construct must be mapped on the same meaning by the valuation function, independent of where this construct occurs.

208

* composability = abstract from how implemented:

If the same syntactic construct can be implemented in different ways (egg. if the <STMT> in Fig. 4.3.11 could be an if statement or an assignment statement), then the meanings of this syntactic construct must be interchangeable. This implies that from the outside each of them must have exactly the same interface.

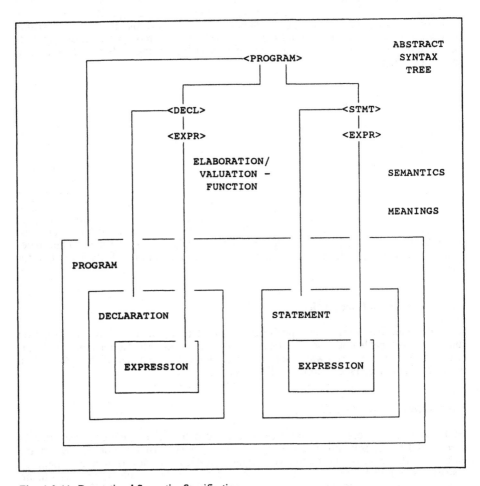

Fig. 4.3.11: Denotational Semantics Specification

One of the advantages of denotational semantics is its rigourous mathematical founding, since everything is modelled by means of Scott Domains. No other method has been used to specify such a broad range of language constructs as denotational semantics, which makes it very attractive for application to IDL. Most existing programming languages, such as PL/1, ALGOL, Pascal, ADA, and LISP, have been given a denotational semantics, and a vast amount of literature is available on denotational semantics.

The use of BNF-like syntax specification languages as input for parser generators led to the obvious idea to use denotational semantics specifications as input for evaluation module generators. However, a drawback of this approach is that generated evaluation modules are too slow for most practical applications. One of the areas that is still under research is the modelling of concurrency. Since Scott Domains have function-like properties, the modelling of concurrency has always been problematic. Denotational semantics achieves its mathematical rigour by using a single mathematical concept to model all the language constructs. Therefore, if a denotational semantics is provided, it is very difficult to discover the basic motivations and assumptions that underlie its structure and chosen style. An additional problem is that certain choices that underlie the semantics specification are very difficult to change, because such choices affect large parts of the semantics specification.

3.6 Structural Operational Semantics

Although the name "structural operational semantics" suggests that this formal semantics specification method is a special kind of operational semantics, it is a method that is closer to denotational semantics than to operational semantics. In case of an operational semantics it is the meaning that is state-oriented, whereas for structural operational semantics it is the semantics, ie. the mapping of the abstract syntax tree onto the meaning that has a dynamic behaviour or state. In case of denotational semantics this mapping is a function without a state.

The advantage of structural operational semantics is that a number of issues like non-determinacy and concurrency can be modelled easier than in a denotational semantics. If non-determinacy or concurrency is to be modelled by means of a denotational semantics, this requires very complicated meanings, so-called power domains, which lack a clear intuitive meaning and are complex mathematical constructs. However, in case of a structural operational semantics one can no longer derive overall mathematical properties of language constructs or programs, as is possible in case of a denotational semantics.

3.7 Algebraic Semantics

This section describes how abstract syntax and semantics can be described by means of algebraic specifications. Suppose, that we want to specify the abstract syntax for integer expressions which consist of constants (0, Succ (0), Succ (Succ (0)), ...) and the add operation +, then this can be done by means of the algebra Int:

```
type Int
operations
        0    : ()  -> Int;
        Succ : Int -> Int;
        _+_  : Int x Int -> Int;
axioms
        /* no axioms */
end
```

The signature part, listed under 'operations', defines all well formed integer expressions. Therefore, it is sometimes referred to as the syntactic part of the algebraic specification. Egg. 'Succ (Succ (Succ (0))) + Succ (0)' is a well formed integer expression. One of the basic assumptions in initial algebra semantics is that each value that can be constructed by means of the operations, represents a different value, unless equality can be proven by means of the axioms provided in the 'axioms' part. Since this part is empty, this algebra is a so-called free algebra or term algebra, and each expression represents a different value. The semantics for integer expressions can be specified by adding equations in the 'axioms' part, which define the equality of certain expressions, as in the following algebra:

```
type Int
operations
        0         : () -> Int;
        Succ      : Int -> Int;
        _+_       : Int x Int -> Int;
axioms
    forall
        INT1, INT2: Int;
    ofsort Int

                    0 + INT2 =              INT2;
            Succ (INT1) + INT2 = Succ (INT1 + INT2);
end
```

The equation '0 + INT2 = INT2' implies, that '0 + Succ (Succ (0))' and 'Succ (Succ (0))' are two expressions that refer to the same value (0 + SS0 and SS0 in Fig. 4.3.12). 'forall INT1, INT2: Int' describes variables that are used in the equations, and 'ofsort Int' specifies the type of the left-hand side and right-hand side values of the axioms. Because the behaviour of operations can be changed by changing the equations, the 'axioms' part of an algebraic specification is sometimes referred to as the semantics part. Sets of expressions that refer to the same value, are equivalence classes (see Fig. 4.3.12). In each class one value is chosen to be the canonical term, ie. it is considered to be the elementary representation for the value that is referred to by all the expressions in the equivalence class (0, S0, SS0, SSS0, ... in Fig. 4.3.12). These elementary representations can be generated by means of a canonical initial algebra:

```
type Int'
operations
        0      : () -> Int;
        Succ   : Int -> Int;
axioms
        /* no axioms */
end
```

This is also an initial term algebra, because it has an empty set of axioms. If we compare this algebra with algebra Int, we discover that the signature part of algebra Int contains two types of operations: constructors, like 0 and Succ, that belong to both the initial algebra and its corresponding canonical intial algebra, and selectors like +. In a constructor-oriented algebraic specification the operations part indicates which operations are constructors and which operations are selectors, as can be seen in the next specification for algebra Int.

```
type Int
operations
    constructors
        0          : () -> Int;
        Succ       : Int -> Int;
    selectors
        _+_        : Int x Int -> Int;
axioms
    forall
        INT1, INT2: Int;
    ofsort Int

                0 + INT2 =                  INT2;
        Succ (INT1) + INT2 = Succ (INT1 + INT2);
end
```

The axioms part only contains equations that describe the properties of selectors. Another rule is, that for each selector there is one equation for each constructor.

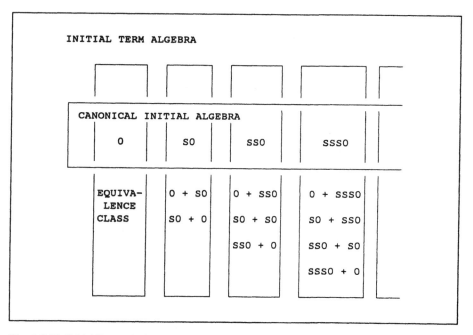

Fig. 4.3.12: Initial Term Algebra, Canonical Initial Algebra, and Equivalence Classes for Integer

3.8 Semantics Specification Method for IDL

All the described formal specification methods have their strengths and weaknesses. Since we are aiming for a standardization effort for IDL, an operational semantics is too much implementation oriented. A denotational semantics would certainly be the most preferable choice. However, the specification of parallelism by means of denotational semantics is quite complicated. Since we only want an unambiguous semantics for IDL, we propose to use structural operational semantics for the definition of the IDL. Also the fact that IDL is an extension of ML, and the formal semantics specification of ML uses structural operational semantics [Mil90], is a reasons for its application to IDL. For the definition of the abstract syntax of IDL we propose to the algebraic semantics approach.

3.9   Models, Languages, and Meta-languages

MODEL	PRODUCT DATA		
	STRUCTURED PROGRAMMING OBJECT ORIENTATION DATA DRIVEN PROGRAMMING		
LANGUAGE	PASCAL	IDL	EXPRESS
	DENOTATIONAL SEMANTICS	STRUCTURAL OPERATIONAL SEMANTICS	?
METALANGUAGE	DOMAIN THEORY	STRUCTURALLY DEFINED SETS	TARSKIAN SEMANTICS FOR FOPL

Fig. 4.3.13: A Number of Languages with their Meta-languages

Now, that we have described a number of formal semantics specification methods, it is important to note that there is an analogy between the level where a model is described in a language and the meta-level where the language itself is described by means of a metalanguage. In Fig. 4.3.13 one model (in this case a product description) is described in several languages, which themselves are defined by means of different meta-languages. Meta-languages are to languages, what languages are to models. Techniques like structured programming, object orientation, and data driven programming, are guide-lines how to structure a model in a language, such that issues like separation of concerns, limitation of propagation of changes, and separation of behaviour and implementation, are implemented best. For the meta-level similar techniques have been defined.

It is important to make a distinction between our definition of metalanguage and what we would call a representation model. A representation model, which is called a meta-model by some people, is a definition of an abstract syntax for all the language constructs. This mainly specifies what are the data elements of each construct. Our metalanguage is used to specify the semantics of the language constructs.

We can compare our approach for the formal semantics definition of IDL with a number of other language formalization efforts. In this example Pascal is defined by means of denotational semantics. Denotational semantics describes how language constructs like procedures, parameters, local variables, types, etc. can be defined by means of elements in so-called Scott Domains. The semantics of these domains is defined by means of the domain theory of Dana Scott.

Structural operational semantics is used for the semantics definition of IDL. It is founded on a mathematical technique called structural induction [Hen90] [Plo83]. An important development in the CIM area is STEP. STEP uses EXPRESS as its language [EXP91]. The SUMM (Semantic Unification Meta-Model) [Ful91] will be used to define the semantics of EXPRESS. SUMM is founded on the Tarskian Semantics for First Order Predicate Logic. Currently it is unclear how all the language constructs in EXPRESS can be modelled by means of First Order Predicate Logic. Even if FOPL is extended by means of modal operators as in dynamic logic or temporal logic, the specification of most language constructs remains an open issue.

4   Some Issues in Language Design

4.1   Limitations of Formal Systems

At the beginning of this century logicians, especially Alfred Tarski, made it clear that one has to be very careful with what can be spoken about in a formal language in order to avoid paradoxes or semantic antinomies, like the liar paradox. This paradox could be paraphrased like: "This sentence is not true". Self reference and recursion are the most complicated issues in semantics.

A lot of knowledge cannot be formalized. In most cases only the functional behaviour of a system can be described formally, leaving issues like ergonomics and aesthetics to the human subjective judgement. Even the Peano axioms for natural numbers do not fully capture our knowledge of numbers, since it does not formalize the notion of lucky number.

On the other hand, people have a natural tendency to read too much into the behaviour of a formal system, as revealed by the well known program ELIZA that is able to have a sensible conversation. The fact that an automated formal system (egg. in PROLOG) could execute the following famous syllogism: "Socrates is human. All humans are mortal, thus Socrates is mortal", does not give the system any knowledge about human beings and mortality.

4.2   Expressive Power

In most cases a high level programming language relieves the programmer from a lot of detailed bookkeeping problems like register allocation, parameter stack manipulation, and symbolic naming of variables and Goto addresses. Some people think that because of this, high level programming languages are more expressive than machine language. However the opposite is the case. Each PASCAL program corresponds to an equivalent translated machine language program, but there are machine language programs that are not the compiled version of a PASCAL program. Thus PASCAL is less expressive then machine language.

Another tendency, is to put as many constructs as possible into a language. This leads to very complicated languages, thick reference manuals, and expensive implementations, that will be used only partially. Thus a language should be dedicated to its purpose as much as possible instead of trying to construct the all encompassing language (like ADA or PL/I). Egg. in a lot of CIM applications it is questionable whether a real-time language is needed. Time stamping may be sufficient. In that case, time becomes a property of an event, just like any other property, such as colour, name, or size, making the language semantics much easier.

4.3 Language Constructs versus Standard Libraries

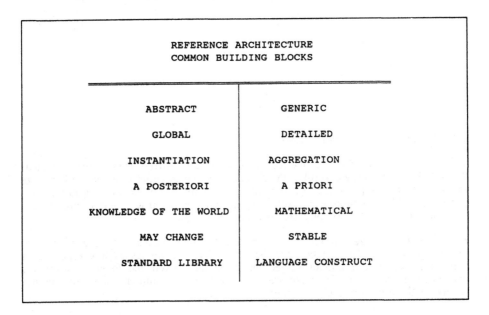

Fig. 4.3.14: Language Constructs versus Standard Libraries

From a user point of view, all the constructs defined by CIMOSA such as object, enterprise function, resource unit, and cell, belong to the generic level of the MFW. However, some of these constructs, partially instanciated, should be available as standard libraries since they capture "knowledge of the world" (see Fig. 4.3.14). Although it may be agreed what constitutes a robot today, technological developments may make the notion ambiguous or obsolete within a few years. In order to protect IDL against technological changes, only mathematical concepts like sets, functions, integers, strings, and variables should be implemented as language constructs, since their semantics is most stable. The world has changed substantionally, but old languages like FORTRAN and COBOL can still be used.

An interpretation of "generic" is "what is common to all enterprises". Not only concrete, atomic concepts like integers, sets, and processes are common to all enterprises, but also abstract, global concepts like financial administration, managing director and responsibility. If one uses atomic concepts, larger models are created out of smaller ones by means of aggregation going from the generic towards the particular side of the MFW. E.g. the generic level contains concepts like integer and string. A partial model of an employee may state that an employee has a name of type string and an age of type integer. In a particular enterprise an employee may have a name of type string, an age of type integer, a employee number of type integer, and a home address of type string.

In case of global concepts specific details that apply to a branch of industry or a particular enterprise are added when going along the instantiation axes of the MFW. Egg. a company has an integer amount of employees. A small enterprise has between 1 and 50 employees, whereas one particular small company may have 27 employees. A problem is, that the abstract, global concepts that apply to all companies, do not always have a mathematically well defined meaning. If these constructs are included in the generic part of the MFW, IDL may have constructs that are ambiguous and non executable.

Therefore the generic level of the MFW should be made of a set of atomic, mathematical concepts that are implemented as language constructs and a set of global concepts, that are provided as standard libraries and which may change in time to adopt to technological changes. The partial models in the MFW are other libraries addressing the needs for a specific branch of industry. Thus the distinction "generic", "partial" and "particular" is mainly determined by who constructs the model, namely CIMOSA, a branch of industry, or a particular company. For the execution of models only the execution of the language constructs is relevant. If these can be executed so can the standard libraries, whether they belong to the generic level or to the partial level of the MFW.

5   Main Features of IDL[8]

5.1   Overview

Although IDL has not been defined in the FRB yet, some of its characteristics can be inferred from the other Modelling Levels of the MFW. There is a continuity between RDL (Requirements Definition Language), DSL (Design Specification Language), and IDL. It is even suggested to use the same kind of constructs at all three Modelling Levels of the MFW. Thus IDL will be quite similar to the other languages of the MFW.

Since ML offers most of the language constructs that are needed for IDL and sets new standards for programming languages, like FORTRAN, COBOL, and ALGOL did, ML was chosen as the basis for IDL. Fig. 4.3.15 gives an overview of the most important features of IDL. At a gross level IDL is the unification of ML [Wik87], process algebra (like CCS [Mil80], TCSP [Bro84], or LOTOS [OSI87] [Ehr91]), and PROLOG [Clo84]. IDL inherits from ML functional programming, procedural programming by means of the usual control structures (if-then-else- and while-do-statements), user defined types, abstract data types, and constructor oriented algebraic specifications.

IDL includes concurrency implemented by means of parallel processes which affect shared variables, and concurrency implemented by means of distribution and

---

8   Note that this report, in the next sections, only summarizes some of the main characteristics of IDL. A first version of the syntax definition of IDL has already been drawn however, but it would have been too large to be included it in this report.

216

communication where parallel processes can only exchange information via communication channels.

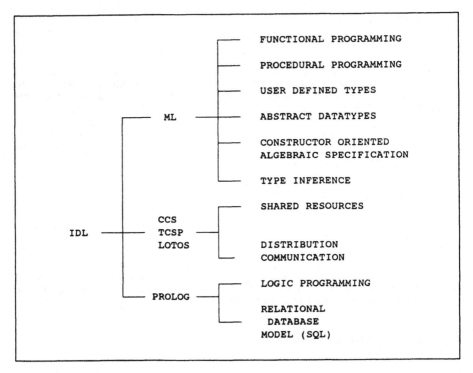

Fig. 4.3.15: Most Important Features of IDL

Finally, the expressive power of PROLOG should be included in IDL, because this would enable us to use IDL as its own metalanguage and it would define the relation between SQL and the rest of the Implementation Description Level of the MFW. At this moment SQL is still the only database paradigm supported by CIMOSA at the Implementation Description Level. The integration of PROLOG (and SQL) with the other parts of IDL is quite problematical, since languages like PROLOG, LISP, and SQL have a value oriented semantics, whereas procedural languages like ML, C, PASCAL, and FORTRAN have a variable oriented semantics. In a value oriented semantics identifiers can only refer to a value like in "let x == 5 in <exp> end", where 'x' is equal to 5 during the execution of the expression <exp>. No updating or assignment is allowed, thus an assignment statement like "x := x + 5" is absent in these languages. In a variable oriented semantics identifiers do not refer to values but to variables (ie. memory locations) which can change their values during the execution of the program.

5.2 Four Level Semantics for IDL

Most procedural languages like FORTRAN, C, Pascal, and ALGOL 60, have a two level semantics [Bac78]. An expression level and a statement level separated by the assignment statement. For IDL two additional levels have been defined on top of these two.

The first layer comprises the right hand side of the assignment statements. This is the orderly world of expressions, a world that has useful algebraic properties that can be described by an algebra of functions. It is the layer in which most computations take place. It implements atomic state transitions from state value to state value. The functions in this layer are composed of primitive functions, like add, subtract, transpose, not, append, and length, and functional forms. Functional forms are operations that take functions as operands and return compound functions as a result.

On top of this first layer a second layer is defined, that contains the state and the sequential statements in the language. The primary statement in this layer is the assignment statement. All the other statements of the language exist in order to make it possible to perform a computation that must be based on this primitive construct. Structured programming can be seen as a modest effort to introduce some order into this chaotic world.

In the third layer parallel dynamic behaviour can be specified. By means of procedural rule sets each process can be decomposed into a number of subprocesses and finally into sequential processes. In the fourth layer the structure of a system can be specified. At the root of the IDM we have the enterprise and its environment that are both modelled as a system. By means of structural decomposition each system can be subdivided into subsystems and eventually into elementary systems. Each elementary system contains a number of parallel processes, which form the root for the previous level of decomposition. Fig. 4.3.16 is a proposed mapping of IDL constructs onto their corresponding CIMOSA constructs.

IDL	CIMOSA
SYSTEM	DOMAIN
PARALLEL PROCESS	BP
SEQUENTIAL STATEMENT	EA
EXPRESSION	FO

Fig. 4.3.16: Four Semantic Layers of IDL and their Mapping onto CIMOSA

5.3 Type Inference in IDL

Polymorphism in programming languages refers to data or programs which have many types, or which operate on many types. Parametric polymorphism is a property of programs which are parametric with respect to the type of some of their parameters. Parametric polymorphism is called explicit when parameterization is obtained by explicit type parameters in procedure headings, and corresponding explicit applications of type arguments when procedures are called. In this case, parametric polymorphism reduces to the notion of having parameters of type 'type'. Here is a definition of a polymorphic identity with explicit type parameters and its application to a Boolean and an integer:

```
        val iden = fun (a : t, t : type) => a end;
        iden (true, bool);
        iden (3 + 4, int);
```

Parametric polymorphism is called implicit when the above type parameter and type applications are not admitted, but types can contain type variables which are unknown, yet to be determined, types. If a procedure parameter has a type variable or a term containing type variables as its type, then that procedure can be applied to arguments of many different types. Here is an implicit version of the polymorphic identity (where 't is a type variable), and its application to an integer and a Boolean:

```
        val iden = fun (a : 't) => a end;
        iden (3 + 4);
        iden (true);
```

Implicit polymorphism can be considered as an abbreviated form of explicit polymorphism, where the type parameters and applications have been omitted and must be recovered by the language processor. Omitting type parameters leaves some type-denoting identifiers unbound, and these are precisely the type variables. Omitting type arguments requires type inference to recover the lost information. In implicit polymorphism one can totally omit type information by interpreting the resulting programs as having type variables associated to parameters and identifiers. The programs then appear to be type-free, but rigourous type checking can still be performed. IDL combines the flexibility of typeless language like LISP with the robustness of a strongly typed language like PASCAL.

Polymorphic types were already known as type schemas in combinatory logic. Extending Curry's work, and collaborating with him, Hindley introduced the idea of principle type schema, which is the most general polymorphic type of an expression, The unification algorithm devised by Robinson (which is also the core of PROLOG) can be used to calculate the principle type schema of an expression. Milner rediscovered many of these ideas while implementing the first version of ML and showed that the type system is sound and decidable.

Parametric polymorphic type systems support compile-time type checking, static typing, and treatment of higher-order functions. Static typing is the ability to determine the absence of certain classes of run-time faults by static inspection of a program. Thus the execution of an IDL program consists of two phases. In the first phase, after the program has been parsed and found syntactically correct, the program is inspected for typing errors by means of an elaboration function. In the second phase the program is executed by means of an evaluation function (Fig. 4.3.17). Thus a single abstract syntax tree has two meanings: a type meaning determined by the elaboration function and a value meaning determined by the evaluation function. Both meanings can be specified by means of the formal semantics specification methods listed in chapter 2.

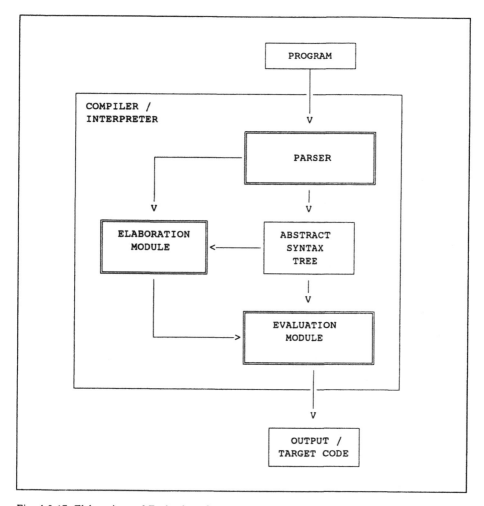

Fig. 4.3.17: Elaboration and Evaluation of an Abstract Syntax Tree

A type expression can be a type variable like 'a, 'b, 'c, ... standing for an arbitrary type, a type constant like int, bool, real, ... , or a type function like 'a X 'b (Carthesian Product Type), 'a -> 'b (Function Type), list ['a], ... , that take one or more types as arguments. In the most general form of the type functions given above the type parameters 'a and 'b can be replaced by arbitrary type expressions to give more specialized pair, function, or list types. Type expressions containing type variables are polymorphic. Expressions containing several occurrences of a type variable, like in 'a -> 'a, express contextual dependencies, in this case between the domain and the co-domain of a function type. The type-checking process consists in matching type operators and instantiating type variables. Whenever an occurrence of a type variable is instantiated all the other occurrences of the same variable must be instantiated to the same value: legal instantiations of 'a -> 'a are int -> int, bool -> bool, ('b X 'c) -> ('b X 'c), etc. The contextual instantiation process is performed by unification. Unification fails when trying to match two different type operators (like int and bool) or when trying to instantiate a variable to a term containing that variable (like 'a and 'a -> 'b, where a circular structure would be built). In general, the type of an expression is determined by a set of type combination rules for the language constructs, and by the types of the primitive operators. The following expression calculates the length of a list:

```
val len = fun (l) => if nil(l) then 0
                             else 1 + len (tl (l)) end;
```

The type of len is list ['a] -> int. This is a polymorphic type as len can work on lists with any kind of elements (as long as the elements within one list are of the same type).

Type-checking can be viewed in two ways:

* System of Type Equations

Type-checking is done by setting up a system of type constraints. Type-checking consists of verifying that the system of constraints is consistent (i.e. it does not imply int = bool), and then to solve it with respect to the type variables.

* Type Inference System

A type-checking algorithm implements a formal system by providing a procedure for proving theorems in that system. Not all formal systems admit type-checking algorithms. If a formal system is too powerful (i.e. we can prove many things in it), then it is likely to be undecidable, and no decision procedure can be found for it. Type-checking is usually restricted to decidable type systems, for which type checking algorithms can be found.

A type inference rule for conditional expressions is:

```
A |- B : bool    A |- C1 : 't1    A |- C2 : 't1
---------------------------------------------------
         A |- if B then C1 else C2 : 't1
```

The horizontal bar reads 'implies'. An assumption x : 't is the association of a variable x with a type 't. The notation A |- e : 't means that given the set of assumptions A, we can deduce that the expression e has type 't. A type checking algorithm can be extracted from this inference system. In this view a type checking algorithm is a proof heuristic.

5.4 Pattern Matching in IDL

In IDL arguments to functions can be matched against different forms of patterns in order to be analysed, and the computation can then proceed accordingly. Pattern matching is the opposite process of constructing a data object. For each way of constructing a data object, there is a corresponding type of pattern. The result of matching against a pattern is an environment, that is, a set of bindings. There are several types of patterns.

* Variable Pattern

A pattern which consists of only a variable (a name) matches anything. The result of the match is an environment in which the name is bound to the matched data object. Pattern matching against a variable therefore results in the naming of a data object or a part of it.

```
val f1 = fun a => a + 10 end;
f1 (10);
```

When applying f1 to 10, for instance, 10 is matched against the pattern a, and the environment { a = 10 } is returned. In matching against a variable, no analysis takes place. Matching against a variable therefore always succeeds.

* Tuple Pattern

IDL functions always have one parameter. If in another programming language a list of parameters would be used, in IDL this has to be stated explicitly by creating a tuple of parameters, like the tuple pattern < a, b > in:

```
val add = fun < a, b > => a + b end;
add (< 100, 200 >);
```

If add is applied to tuple < 100, 200 > this will result in an environment { a = 100 , b = 200 }, thus the tuple argument is decomposed into its constituent parts 100 and 200.

* Wild Cards Pattern

In the definition of the function first, that returns the first element of a tuple, a wild card can be used as second pattern, because the value of the second element is irrelevant:

```
val first = fun < a, _ > => a end;
```

* Alternative Patterns

A tuple can be constructed in only one way, but for most data types there are several ways of constructing their objects. There are two Boolean constructors, true and false, and when writing a function taking a bool as argument, one may want to split the computation into two cases. This is done by the use of alternative patterns:

```
        val not = fun
                   true => false  |
                   false => true
        end;
```

When matching against alternative patterns, the patterns are tried one after the other until one that matches is found. If the alternative patterns are overlapping, the order of matching against patterns is essential.

5.5   Processes in IDL

* Processes and Events

We will use the following syntax for behavioural expressions or processes:

```
<BExpr> ::=
'let' <Decl  > 'in' <BExpr> 'end'   (local declarations)
  | <BExpr> '  []' <BExpr>           (choice)
  | <BExpr> '  ||' <BExpr>           (parallel)
  | <BExpr> '  >>' <BExpr>           (enable)
  | <BExpr> '  [>' <BExpr>           (disable)
  | 'case' <pattern> '=>' <BExpr>{'|' <pattern> '=>' <BExpr>}
                                                            'end'
                                     (case statement)
  | <action prefix>


<action prefix> ::=
<event> ; <  action prefix>          (sequence)
  | 'stop'                           (deadlock)
  | 'exit' '(  ' <expr> ')'          (ending status)


<event> ::=
'i'                                  (internal event)
  | <identifier>                     (synchronization event)
  | <identifier> '''                 (complementary synchronization
                                                            event)
  | <identifier> '!' <expr>          (send communication event)
  | <identifier> '?' <identifier>    (receive communication event)
```

Most of these constructs will be explained below.

The ultimate unit in the behaviour of a process is an event. Events are regarded as instantaneous. They have no duration. Also the length of the time interval that separates events has no relevance, but only the relative order in which events occur is of interest.

Take a pair S, T of processes over the alphabet { a, b, c, d } depicted by their state transition graphs:

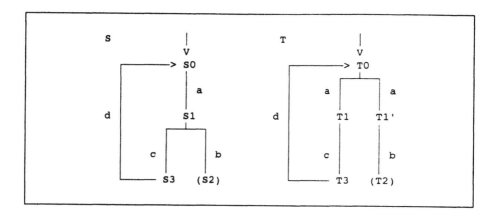

The initial states are S0 and T0 and the accepting states are S2 and T2 respectively. A process over the alphabet { a, b, c, d } can also be thought of as a black box, whose behaviour can be investigated by asking it to accept events one at a time. So each box has four gates, one for each event:

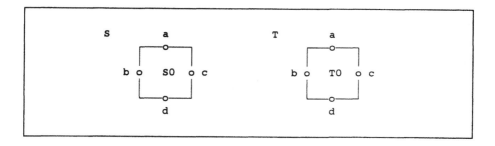

There are four events we can do. Doing an a-event on S (secretly in state S0, but the observer doesn't know that) consists in probing the a-gate, with two possible outcomes in general:

1. failure - the gate is locked.

2. success - the gate is unlocked (and secretly a state transition occurs).

In fact we cannot distinguish between S and T in their initial states, by a single event. The a-event succeeds in each case, and the other three fail. After a successful a-event on each process, which may yield

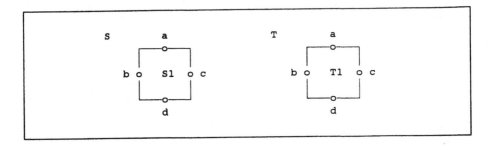

we may try another event in our aim to see if the processes are equivalent or not. Clearly a b-event now succeeds for S and fails for T, though the other three events fail to distinguish them. After trying the b-event, then, can we conclude that S and T are not equivalent ?

No, because T's response to the a-event could have been different and unlocked the b-gate. Following this argument further, we may feel forced to admit that no finite amount of events could prove us that S and T are, or are not, equivalent. But suppose that we can control the condition which determines the choice of transition in case of ambiguity (for example T at T0 under an a-event). Now by conducting an a-event under all possible conditions, we can find that S's b-gate is always unlocked, but that T's b-gate is sometimes locked, and we can conclude that the acceptors are not equivalent.

* Unobservable events

We may have transitions labelled by the unobservable event ı. Consider **R** a modification of S:

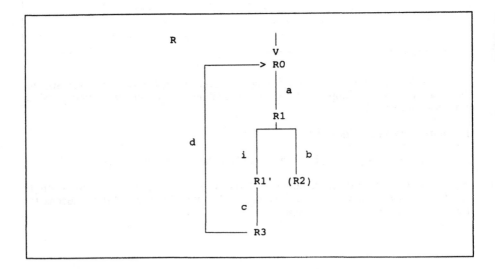

In the conventional sense, R and S are equivalent. However, the i-transition means that R in state R1 (that is, after an event at the a-gate) may at any time move silently to state R1', and that if a b-event is never attempted, it will do so. Thus, if we attempt a b-event on R, after the successful a-event, there are some conditions in which we will find the b-gate permanently locked. If on the other hand we attempt a c-event (after a a-event), we shall in all conditions find the c-gate eventually unlocked. (Eventually, because although R may take a little time to decide on its i-transition, it will do so, since no b-event is attempted). This is the reason why no pair of R, S, and T are equivalent.

* Composition

The execution of a system can be divided into two phases. In the first phase the structure of the system (compound process) is established. Its nodes are the (elementary) processes and their connections are the gates. In the second phase the processes denoted by the nodes communicate via these gates, while the system remains fixed. We are not interested in all systems, but only those which may be built from the nodes (processes) by the operations of composition, and restriction. If P1 and P2 are processes, then the parallel composition P1 || P2 is formed by joining every outer gate in P1 to every outer gate of P2 whose event label complements that of P1. If a is an event label then a' is its complement event label and vice versa. Let us look at a particular case in which P1 and P2 each have just two capabilities, and where [] is the choice operation:

```
P1 = a .P1' [] b .P1"
P2 = a'.P2' [] b'.P2"
```

Then P1 || P2 will have, first, four capabilities of communication directly with its environment, at ports labelled a, b, a', and b' respectively. One of these is a, since P1 would transform itself into P1', which we call a renewal of P1. The corresponding renewal of the composite is a new composite P1' || P2 indicating that the second component is unchanged. Similarly, the first capability of P2 gives a capability a' of the composite. But since P1 and P2 may communicate between their ports labelled a and a', their composite will also contain all members of P1' || P2', and both components are renewed. Thus the total capability of P1 || P2 consists of the capabilities of both P1 and P2 isolated enriched by the possibility of an unobservable dialogue between P1 and P2.

* Restriction

```
begin
    a1 ; stop
||
    let
        val a1 = gate (<>)
    in
        begin
            a1' ; stop
        end
    end
end;
```

Just like local variables in a programming language can only be read and changed by a restricted sets of statements, we would like to restrict the number of processes that can take part in a event by means of declaration of local gates. In the example above the local declaration "val al = gate (< >)" prevents the synchronization between event al and event al'.

* Formal Semantics for Processes

The definition of a state transition system can be extended to that of a labelled state transition system in order to be able to restrict the number of possible transitions to model the events between processes. A resumption is a final state S or a tuple S |- C consisting of a process C and the state S before its execution.

Consider how to execute an output command a!v from a state S where the value of expression v is 2. Intuitively the execution takes one step and consists of outputting 2 to gate a. At the beginning we have resumption S |- a!v and at the end the resumption S, since the act of outputting 2 to gate a does not change S. Thus "outputting 2 to a" is to do with the transition itself and not with the resumptions involved and we write this as

$$S \ |- \ a!v \ -a!2-> \ S$$

thereby labelling the transition with the description of the event of a!2 with its environment.

Equally for an input command S |- a?x we will have a transition

$$S \ |- \ a?x \ -a?2-> \ S+[x=2]$$

where a?2 means that a?x inputs 2 from gate a resulting in $S+[x=2]$ (which is S changed so that x has the value 2).

Now a!v and a?x can be considered as complementary send and receive events which "fuse together" into a single unobservable event i of handshake communication, similar to what we have just described for pure synchronization between complementary events a and a'. For a parallel command a!v || a?x we have the transition

$$S \ |- \ a!v \ || \ a?x \ -i-> \ S+[x=v]$$

where we label the transition with the unobservable event i, meaning that no event occurs with the environment of the parallel command. The transition relations satisfy the following rules:

```
* Sequence

                        true
            ---------------------------------
            s |- a?x;C -a?v-> S+[x=v]  |- C

                    true
            ----------------------------
            s |- a!v;C -a!v-> s  |- C

                    true
            ------------------------
            s |- i;C -i-> s  |- C
```

```
* Choice

                s |- C1 -a-> s'|- C1'
            ----------------------------------
            s |- C1 [] C2 -a-> s' |- C1'

                s |- C2 -a-> s' |- C2'
            ----------------------------------
            s |- C1 [] C2 -a-> s' |- C2'
```

```
* Parallel

                s |- C1 -a-> s' |- C1'
            -------------------------------------
            s |- C1 || C2 -a-> s' |- C1' || C2

                s |- C2 -a-> s' |- C2'
            -------------------------------------
            s |- C1 || C2 -a-> s' |- C1 || C2'

                s |- C1 -a!v-> s  |- C1'
                s |- C2 -a?v-> s' |- C2'
            -------------------------------------
            s |- C1 || C2  -i-> s' |- C1' || C2'
```

In many cases we will omit the exchange of values during communication and the state from the transition relations.

* Process Types

Types for processes (behavioural expressions) can be defined similar to types for expressions in ML. The type of a process is determined by its last event. If this event is 'stop', then the process type is 'void' (like for assignment statements). If the last event of a process is 'exit (<expr>)', then the process type is equal to the type of expression <expr>.

5.6 Semantic Unification and Orthogonalization

IDL is the unification of a set of languages, like ML, CCS, and PROLOG. This unification not only requires a syntactic integration, but also a semantic unification. E.g. the notion of integer in ML, PROLOG, and CCS, needs to be the same. In this case this may not be very complicated. Other issues, like local variables and parameter passing, are much harder to unify. PROLOG does not have the notion of local variable declarations, since it creates a new binding automatically whenever a new variable is needed. CCS and PROLOG do not have types, which requires that the type theory of ML is extended for CCS and PROLOG.

The language constructs should also be orthogonal, which implies that they should be semantically independent. If a successful semantic orthogonalization has been achieved, the defined constructs can be combined in any possible way. Egg. at each point in a parallel process a sequential expression <expr> can be embedded (including local declarations) by means of an internal event, like

```
    <BExpr> ; i (<expr>) ; <BExpr>
```

On the other hand at each point in a sequential expression a parallel process can be embedded by means of

```
    <expr> ; begin <BExpr> end ; <expr>
```

Similarly, function declarations, procedure declarations, and process declarations are almost similar both in syntax and semantics. Variables and gates have the same scoping rules and type inference rules. All this would not have been possible without a clear formal semantics analysis of all the language constructs.

5.7 One Meta-language

In this report inference rules were applied to type inference for expressions.

E.g. for the conditional statement we had:

```
    A |- B : bool    A |- C1 : 't1    A |- C2 : 't1
    ------------------------------------------------
            A |- if B then C1 else C2 : 't1
```

Similarly the evaluation of expressions can be expressed by means of inference rules. For the conditional statement this becomes:

```
        S |- B = true      S |- C1 = v1
        --------------------------------
        S |- if B then C1 else C2 = v1

        S |- B = false     S |- C2 = v2
        --------------------------------
        S |- if B then C1 else C2 = v2
```

In this case the evaluation function of a denotational semantics is defined by means of a set of inference rules. We also had evaluation rules for parallel processes, like the following rule for choice:

```
              S |- C1 -a-> S' |- C1'
        --------------------------------
        S |- C1 [] C2 -a-> S' |- C1'

              S |- C2 -a-> S' |- C2'
        --------------------------------
        S |- C1 [] C2 -a-> S' |- C2'
```

It is exactly this kind of rules that constitutes the structural operational semantics approach. The fact that these rules can be applied easily to such a broad range of language constructs was one of the main reasons for the choice of structural operational semantics for IDL.

6 Conclusions

One of the main benefits of CIMOSA in a CIM environment compared to existing software development methods and computer languages is, that an IDM can be executed by the IEOE without any compilation or transformation into an ordinary programming language. IDL plays a key role as the exchange format between the IEEE and the IEOE, and its syntax and semantics needs to be standardized. This standard needs to be unambiguous, consistent, complete, and concise, in order to exclude misinterpretation and incompatible products. Experience in other standardization efforts has shown, that without the use of formal methods this cannot be achieved. Formal semantics specification methods can be subdivided in property oriented methods, such as algebraic semantics, and model oriented specification methods such as operational semantics and denotational semantics. Each of these methods has its own strengths and weaknesses. Structural operational semantics was chosen as the formal semantics specification method for IDL, because it can be applied easily to a broad range of language constructs, and because the formal semantics specification of ML also uses structural operational semantics.

IDL is the unification of ML, process algebra (like CCS, TCSP, or LOTOS) and PROLOG. It supports functional programming, procedural programming, user defined types, abstract data types, constructor oriented algebraic specification, type inference, concurrency with parallel processes with shared resources, distribution and communication, logical inference, and relational database theory.

A prototype of IDL should be implemented to evaluate issues such as intuitive clearness, user-friendliness and the correctness of the formal language specification. This prototype can be developed by means of the references [Car87], [Dam82], [Mil78], [Mil90], [Tof90], and [Wik87]. The output of this prototype will be a set of test programs, a formal specification of IDL in IDL, or two formal specifications, namely a formal specification of the interpreter that executes IDL by means the services of the IIS and a formal specification of the services of the IIS. In addition to these formal specifications a user manual will be needed for IDL.

7   Abbreviations

B   = Business Services
BNF   = Backus Naur Form, Backus Normal Form
C   = Common Services
DSL   = Design Specification Language
DSM   = Design Specification Model
EA   = Enterprise Activity
F   = Front End Services
FOPL = First Order Predicate Logic
FRB   = Formal Reference Base
HLL   = High Level Language
I   = Information Services
IDL   = Implementation Description Language
IDM   = Implementation Description Model
IEOE = Integrated Enterprise Operation Environment
IEEE = Integrated Enterprise Engineering Environment
IIS   = Integrating Infrastructure
MFW   = Modelling Framework
RDL   = Requirements Definition Language
RDM   = Requirements Definition Model
SD   = System Wide Data

8 References

[Bac78] Backus J., Can Programming be Liberated from the von Neumann Style? - A Functional Style and its Algebra of Programs, Communications of the ACM, vol. 21 / no. 8 / pp. 613-641 / August 1978

[Bro84] Brookes S.D. / C.A.R. Hoare / A.W. Roscoe, A theory of Communicating Sequential Processes, Journal of the ACM, vol. 31 / no. 3 / pp. 560-599 / July 1984

[Car87] Cardelli L., Basic Polymorphic Typechecking, Science of Computer Programming, vol. 8 / pp. 147-172 / 1987

[Clo84] Clocksin W.F. / C.S. Mellish, Programming in Prolog, Springer-Verlag, 3rd ed. 1987

[Dam82] Damas L. / R. Milner, Principal Type-Schemes for Functional Programs, POPL 82 (Proc. of the 9th Annual ACM Symposium on Principles of Programming Languages), pp. 207-212 / January 1982

[Ehr89] Ehrig H. / J. Buntok / P. Boelm / K.-P. Hasler / F. Nuernberg / C. Rieckhoff / J. de Meer, Towards an Algebraic Semantics of the ISO Specification Language LOTOS, P.J. van Eijk / C.A. Vissers / M.Diaz editors, The Formal Description Technique LOTOS, pp. 249-268 / North-Holland / 1989

[EXP91] EXPRESS Language Reference Manual, ISO TC184 / SC4 / WG5, March 8, 1991

[Ful91] Fulton J.A., The Semantic Unification Meta-Model - Technical Approach, ISO TC184 / SC4 / WG3, October 15, 1991

[Hen90] Hennessy M., The Semantics of Programming Languages - An Elementary Introduction using Structural Operational Semantics, John Wiley & Sons Ltd. / 1990

[Mil78] Milner R., A Theory of Type Polymorphism on Programming, Journal of Computer and System Sciences, vol. 17 / pp. 348-375 / 1978

[Mil80] Milner R., A Calculus for Communicating Systems, LNCS 92 / Springer-Verlag / 1979

[Mil90] Milner R. / M. Tofte / R. Harper, The Definition of Standard ML, MIT Press / 1990

[Neu91] Neuhold E.J. / Paul M., Eds., Formal Description of Programming Concepts. IFIP State-of-the-Art Reports, Springer-Verlag 1991

[Plo83] Plotkin G.D., An Operational Semantics for CSP, in: Bjorner D. (ed.), Formal Description of Programming Concepts II, pp. 199-223 / North-Holland / IFIP / 1983

[Tof90] Tofte M., Compiler Generators - What They Can Do, What They Might Do, and What They Probably Never Do, Springer-Verlag / 1990

[Wik87] Wikstrom A., Functional Programming Using Standard ML, Prentice-Hall Inc. / 1987

Table of Figures

Part 1: Management Overview

Part 2: CIMOSA Technical Description

234

Table of Templates

Part 3: User Guide on Requirements Definition Model

Springer-Verlag
and the Environment

We at Springer-Verlag firmly believe that an international science publisher has a special obligation to the environment, and our corporate policies consistently reflect this conviction.

We also expect our business partners – paper mills, printers, packaging manufacturers, etc. – to commit themselves to using environmentally friendly materials and production processes.

The paper in this book is made from low- or no-chlorine pulp and is acid free, in conformance with international standards for paper permanency.